Youth Justice

Local and Global

Dedications

Nicola: For Amal Treacher Kabesh, who is much missed.

Roger: For Maggie, again – with many thanks for your endless patience.

Youth Justice

Local and Global

NICOLA CARR and ROGER SMITH

SAGE

Los Angeles | London | New Delhi
Singapore | Washington DC | Melbourne

SAGE

Los Angeles | London | New Delhi
Singapore | Washington DC | Melbourne

SAGE Publications Ltd
1 Oliver's Yard
55 City Road
London EC1Y 1SP

SAGE Publications Inc.
2455 Teller Road
Thousand Oaks, California 91320
SAGE Publications India Pvt Ltd

SAGE Publications India Pvt Ltd
Unit No 323-333, Third Floor, F-Block
International Trade Tower Nehru Place
New Delhi 110 019

SAGE Publications Asia-Pacific Pte Ltd
3 Church Street
#10-04 Samsung Hub
Singapore 049483

Editor: Natalie Aguilera
Assistant Editor: Rhoda OlaSaid
Production Editor: Neelu Sahu
Copyeditor: Rosemary Campbell
Proofreader: Elaine Leek
Indexer: Melanie Gee
Marketing Manager: Ruslana Khatagova
Cover Design: Francis Kenney
Typeset by KnowledgeWorks Global Ltd
Printed in the UK

Library of Congress Control Number: 2022946460

British Library Cataloguing in Publication data

A catalogue record for this book is available from the British Library

ISBN 978-1-5297-3260-3
ISBN 978-1-5297-3259-7 (pbk)

At SAGE we take sustainability seriously. Most of our products are printed in the UK using responsibly sourced papers and boards. When we print overseas we ensure sustainable papers are used as measured by the PREPS grading system. We undertake an annual audit to monitor our sustainability.

Contents

About the Authors vii

List of Abbreviations ix

1. **Youth Offending and the Subject of Youth Justice** 1
2. **Explaining Youth Crime** 13
3. **Responses to Youth Offending** 43
4. **Comparative Youth Justice** 67
5. **Children's Rights and Youth Justice** 89
6. **Comparative Youth Justice in the United Kingdom** 111
7. **Trends in Youth Justice** 135
8. **Youth Justice Subjects** 157
9. **Youth Justice and Intersecting Systems** 177
10. **Taking Account of the Views of Children and Young People** 197

References 221

Glossary 247

Index 251

About the Authors

Nicola Carr is a Professor of Criminology at the University of Nottingham. Prior to becoming an academic she worked as a probation officer in a Youth Offending Team in London. She has carried out a broad range of research with children and young people. This has included research exploring young people's experiences of justice in their community as well as young people's experiences of different sanctions.

Roger Smith is a Professor of Social Work at the University of Durham. He has been involved in youth justice work since the early 1980s, as a probation officer, head of social policy, researcher and educator. His social work background has meant that he has approached this work with the aim of ensuring that the best interests of children are met, whilst addressing any concerns associated with their behaviour. His research into youth diversion and into youth justice systems and their effects have informed his view that young people and society are best served by practices and policies which tackle injustice in its widest sense and always put children first.

List of Abbreviations

AA	Appropriate Adult
ACE	Adverse Childhood Experience
ACM	Age of Criminal Majority
ADHD	Attention Deficit Hyperactivity Disorder
ASBO	Anti-Social Behaviour Order
ASD	Autism Spectrum Disorder
AWYOS	All Wales Youth Offending Strategy
CCE	Child Criminal Exploitation
CHS	Children's Hearing System
CPP	Child Protection Plan
CPT	Committee for the Prevention of Torture
CR	Community Resolution
CSE	Child Sexual Exploitation
DMC	Disproportionate Minority Contact
DUP	Democratic Unionist Party
ECHR	European Convention on Human Rights
ECtHR	European Court of Human Rights
ECM	Enhanced Case Management
FASD	Foetal Alcohol Spectrum Disorder
FTE	First Time Entrant
GIRFEC	Getting it Right for Every Child
GSP	Gender-Specific Programming
JJC	Juvenile Justice Centre
LAC	Looked After Child/Children
MACR	Minimum Age of Criminal Responsibility
MoJ	Ministry of Justice
NEET	Not in Education, Employment or Training
NGO	Non-Governmental Organisation
OBTJ	Offences Brought to Justice
OJJDP	Office of Juvenile Justice and Delinquency Prevention
PCE	Positive Childhood Experiences
PACE	Police and Criminal Evidence (Act)

PEN	Psychoticism, Extraversion and Neuroticism (Model)
PNC	Police National Computer
PPS	Public Prosecution Service
PSNI	Police Service for Northern Ireland
PTSD	Post-traumatic Stress Disorder
PYP	Participatory Youth Practice
RFPP	Risk Factor Prevention Paradigm
RUC	Royal Ulster Constabulary
SDLP	Social and Democratic Labour Party
SCH	Secure Children's Home
SEN	Special Educational Needs
SNP	Scottish Nationalist Party
STC	Secure Training Centre
TIC	Trauma Informed Care
TRM	Trauma Recovery Model
UNCRC	United Nations Convention on the Rights of the Child
UUP	Ulster Unionist Party
WSA	Whole System Approach
YEC	Youth Engagement Clinic
YJA	Youth Justice Agency
YJB	Youth Justice Board
YOT	Youth Offending Team
YRO	Youth Rehabilitation Order

1
Youth Offending and the Subject of Youth Justice

Objectives

- This chapter will explore some of the definitions regarding youth offending and youth justice.
- Readers will be introduced to key orientating concepts.
- The chapter will help the reader to identify the historical development of youth justice.
- The chapter will also provide readers with an overview of the overall structure and themes covered in the book.

Introduction

This chapter begins with a consideration of some key definitions. This includes categorisations of children and childhood, and the remit of youth justice systems. We then proceed to discuss some historical perspectives, including the 'emergence' of the category of juvenile or youthful offenders within specific geographical and historical contexts. After that we then provide an outline of the structure of the book and some of its key themes.

Definitions, Assumptions and Unresolved Questions

Starting with definitions might seem somewhat tedious or even bland. However, these are so important to our core understandings of the subject of young people and crime, that it is impossible to avoid the question. In fact, as we will quickly discover, the search for clear and consistent definitions itself lays bare many of the underlying challenges involved in investigating and understanding youth offending and youth justice. We could perhaps start by considering those agreed international standards which do seem to offer a degree of certainty, and this will undoubtedly be helpful. But, following this, we must also acknowledge the many key questions which these standards, and the apparent consensus they represent, leave unresolved.

The UN Convention on the Rights of the Child (UNCRC), adopted in 1989 and subsequently ratified by 196 nations, has come to be seen as a landmark statement, setting out a commonly agreed position amongst nations for the establishment of an equitable and positive framework for the care, well-being and development of children. Importantly, this has established a definition of childhood, and its recognition of a distinctive life stage, spanning the years 0–18. In the modern era, certainly, childhood has come to be seen as distinguished by certain common characteristics, which encourage us to see and treat children differently from adults.

Childhood itself can be further divided into distinct phases, which are conventionally understood as stages on a journey towards adulthood and full citizenship, with all the rights and responsibilities that entails. These stages are demarcated in a number of different ways, such as: biological changes (puberty, for example); educational settings (such as junior or senior school); post-school transitions; and legal rights, obligations or protections (film classifications, right to drive, age of sexual consent). Here, we can see that there are a bundle of expectations, provisions and requirements which together constitute the protections, settings and special provisions which are believed to be necessary both to sustain and structure childhood.

In parallel with the recognition of childhood as a specific life stage, we have also seen a substantial growth in fields of study which have sought to account for its distinctive features, and inform the development of services and interventions to improve children's lives and maximise their potential, notably in the social sciences, but also, increasingly, in the field of neuroscience. Specific aspects of children's development have been investigated, and the identification of their changing capacities and behaviours has been linked to ideas about their ability to think about other people, their understanding of the consequences of their actions, the extent to which they can 'defer gratification', and their ability to control impulsive tendencies. Although the ideas emerging from the study and analysis of changing patterns of children's lives and behaviours have been and remain contested, they all tend to share the common feature of treating childhood as a distinctive field of inquiry.

From the extensive body of knowledge and the implicit assumptions we have acknowledged, has emerged an approach to framing and delivering services for children which is based on the belief that they are not yet capable of exercising the full range of responsibilities associated with adulthood. In the youth justice context, this underlying assumption has been incorporated not just in the United Nations Convention on the Rights of the Child (UNCRC), but in an extensive series of specific laws, rules and guidelines, both national and international, which establish the basis for special provisions for children who break the law. International instruments of this kind include the Beijing Rules (1985), the Havana Rules (1990) and the Riyadh Guidelines (1990), which between them established a comprehensive framework for the treatment of alleged and convicted young offenders. In relation to specific countries, legislation sets out the framework for the administration of youth justice at the national level and/or regional levels. It is reported that most countries have established or are developing fully-fledged systems for dealing with young offenders (under 18) separately from adults (Zimring et al., 2017).

In essence, this emerging pattern is supported by the core presumption that children cannot be expected to act with the same level of personal responsibility (and thus accountability) as adults. Put simply, the same behaviour would be evaluated and dealt with differently if committed by a child as opposed to an adult. Interventions would also be informed by the continuing developmental needs of a child, and recognition of the importance of promoting the child's current and future well-being. Whilst this does effectively reflect the common elements of a widely held international consensus, we must also recognise the influence of the unresolved issues identified. Disagreement, debate and continuing uncertainty about core features of childhood, youth crime and young offenders are widespread, as will become clear. Thus, for instance, the relatively straightforward principle of 'minimum intervention', that is, that formal intervention should be based on the least intrusive and harmful options available, is open to wide and conflicting interpretation.

Similarly, the age at which children are deemed to acquire criminal responsibility varies substantially by country and jurisdiction, as well as being liable to change over time, as seen in recent years in both Ireland and Scotland, for instance. At the same time, though, the age at which children are determined as acquiring full responsibility for any crimes they commit is less than 18 years in nearly all jurisdictions. Here, then, we immediately encounter one of the core underlying tensions running through youth justice and the treatment of young people who come into conflict with the law. In essence, this is a question of whether their 'needs' as children should take precedence over their 'responsibilities', as offenders. For those of us with an interest in youth justice, this contradiction lies at the heart of many of the enduring questions we face in making sense of the crimes of the young, on the one hand, and the way in which youth justice is delivered, on the other.

From one perspective, there is no question that we should adopt the fundamental principle of 'children first', which should take precedence over calls to hold young people to account for their crimes, and impose punishments or other forms of behaviour control. From another, some argue that this principle should be at the very least subject to modification, depending on what we know about the nature of any offence, the level of intent and culpability, and the underlying expectation that children, especially as the get older, should be expected to accept responsibility for their actions.

Historical Perspectives

Not only are we able to observe variations in approaches to the treatment of young people who come into conflict with the law in the present day, but we also need to understand how contemporary practices have developed. In the same way as perceptions of childhood have changed over time, so have our assumptions about youth crime. It is also the case, however, that some attitudes and assumptions are less likely to shift in the course of history. Indeed, young people and their behaviour have been a persistent source of comment and concern. This is perhaps typified by a well-known quotation from Shakespeare's *A Winter's Tale*:

> I would there were no age between ten and three-and-twenty, or that youth would sleep out the rest; for there is nothing in the between but getting wenches with child, wronging the ancientry, stealing, fighting ... (Act 3, Scene 3)

Cox and Shore (2002) refer to a number of similar complaints dating from the 17th century; and a number of earlier quotations from Greek philosophers express similar sentiments about youthful disrespect for their elders.

Nonetheless, historic fears and disapproval of young people are not altogether dissimilar to contemporary anxieties about their anti-social behaviour of one kind or another. Contemporary fears are nothing new, and as Pearson (1983) has observed, there appears to be a cyclical character to popular concerns about youthful deviance. We may be tempted to infer from this that nothing changes, and there is an endemic quality to the perceived threat to social order posed by the younger generation.

Despite this, others would argue that we should not overemphasise the sense of continuity associated with the view that youth has always been a problem. Instead, we should recognise that social change and the reordering of established relationships within communities and between sectors of the population are bound to have an effect on young people, and that this will be historically specific. Major social trends, such as industrialisation, originating in the

19th century, and globalisation, emerging in the later 20th century, are believed to have fundamentally changed the nature of social relations. Included within this, of course, is the reconstruction of childhood and youth.

For some, indeed, these distinct life stages have only really become established in their own right as a consequence of industrialisation and the associated social realignments. Ariès (1962), for example, has suggested that childhood as a distinctive phase of the life cycle only took shape in the late medieval era, as societies began to adapt to the economic forces and demands which led to industrialisation. His view is that the relative absence of children from most forms of artistic and cultural representation before modern times suggests that children were not understood as having a distinctive identity or place in the social order.

This, similarly, was reflected in the family-based distribution of labour which tended to mean that there was no clear division of roles and tasks according to age. Others, however, have criticised Ariès for overlooking contrary evidence which does suggest that generational differences did exist before the onset of industrialisation (Pollock, 1983). Although this issue has been hotly debated, a case has also been made for the middle ground: 'one might say that the medieval world probably had a concept of childhood but conceptions of it that were very different from our own' (Heywood, 2001: 15).

Despite these apparent differences amongst historians of childhood, there is much less debate over the effects of changes in society associated with emerging market economies and the coming industrial age. Substantial upheavals in the forms of social organisation could be linked to the emergence of mechanisation and market economies. The restructuring of the workforce, new shift patterns, changing skills requirements, urban development and changing patterns of consumption could all be seen as factors having an effect on the organisation of family life, and the nature of childhood itself. The consequences of change on such a scale were unpredictable, but the disruption of established ways of life was almost certain to have destabilising effects. One such was the increasing visibility of children whose lives appeared to be disorganised and uncontrolled. By 1816, for example, the situation had become so troublesome that the Committee for Investigating the Causes of the Alarming Increase of Juvenile Delinquency in the Metropolis had published a report, which claimed (p. 13) that 'Dreadful is the situation of the young offender: he becomes the victim of circumstances over which he has no control', blaming this on 'The want of employment – the prevalence of improvident marriages – the degrading tendencies of the poor laws – and the increased facilities for the consumption of spirituous liquors ...'.

A number of 19th-century accounts seem to highlight the 'metropolis' as a particular cause for concern (Shore, 1999). The growth of towns and cities changed the nature of communities and transformed family life, whilst at the same time, rendering those who did not conform to respectable norms much more visible, and, by extension, threatening.

Further impetus was given to emerging fears about the crimes of the young with the increasing formalisation of the justice system. The *Vagrancy Act of 1824*, for example, extended the definition of the offence, making young people more liable to summary conviction simply for being out on 'the streets' (Shore, 1999: 33). The subsequent establishment of the modern police force in 1829 probably also contributed to the prevailing mood regarding the threat posed by child offenders.

The associated formalisation of criminal justice processes and records certainly lent itself to a sense of a growing problem, which was reflected in the official response to youth crime. The first juvenile penal institution in the United Kingdom was opened at Parkhurst in 1838 (Hendrick, 2006: 6), by virtue of legislation in the form of '*An Act for Establishing a Prison for Young Offenders*'; and the number of under-17s sent to prison had increased from 9,500 in 1838 to 14,000 ten years later (Muncie, 2009: 54).

Whilst these developments were certainly indicative of a climate of fear of the young, they were associated with a parallel concern about the factors contributing to their delinquencies. They were increasingly viewed as vulnerable to harmful influences and inadequate upbringing. The Victorian era witnessed a substantial growth in philanthropic concern for children and young people, associated with a range of initiatives to improve the living conditions of those experiencing various forms of deprivation, which themselves were seen as significant causes of crime.

Reformers such as Mary Carpenter began to make the case for differential treatment of juvenile offenders, on the basis that some, at least, were capable of being reformed. In 1847, the *Juvenile Offenders Act* was the first legislation in the United Kingdom to make special provision for some children (minor offenders under the age of 14) to be dealt with distinctively by the courts. In addition, building on the earlier model offered by the Mettray reformatory in France, the case was made for a state-run programme of similar institutions, whose aim would be to compensate for young offenders' exposure to neglect and lack of parental discipline. A structured regime of skills training, moral guidance and the removal of temptation should provide the right framework for the rescue of young delinquents and their preparation for productive adult life, according to a British parliamentary select committee of 1853 (Muncie, 2009: 57).

Immediately following this committee's report, the *Youthful Offenders Act 1854* was passed, establishing reformatories for convicted juvenile offenders; whilst shortly afterwards the *Industrial Schools Act 1857* prescribed a similar institutional model for non-offending children at risk of neglect (Hendrick, 2006: 6). Similar institutional initiatives have been noted across Europe at roughly the same time, in Germany, Belgium and the Netherlands. Importantly, even at this early stage in the development of modern youth justice systems, two significant distinctions had begun to emerge. One of these was the demarcation clearly being drawn between those children who were 'perishing' and those who were judged to be 'dangerous' (Shore, 1999: 7). Those who were experiencing adverse circumstances, such as poverty or neglect, but had not yet become offenders should be viewed and treated differently to those who were already criminals, and who were already committed to this path. The legislative distinction between these two types of institution (industrial and reformatory schools) helped to cement such underlying assumptions in place. At the same time, gender differences also became apparent in the ways in which male and female offenders were viewed. Offences typically associated with boys were those of theft and violence, whilst girls were viewed as more prone to 'crimes' linked to sexual transgressions: 'it is clear that in many cases girls were sent to reformatories for different reasons to the boys' (Shore, 2003: 116).

Towards the latter stages of the 19th century, the separate pathway for the treatment of juvenile delinquency became more clearly marked out. As Hendrick (1997) has suggested, this trend mirrored wider developments, as childhood in general became more clearly identified as deserving of scientific interest and state intervention. Alongside the issue of delinquency, interest was growing in children's education and general well-being, as it became more apparent that new forms of preparation and discipline would be necessary to meet the needs of a rapidly changing society. Hendrick (1997: 47) suggests that the 1880s, in particular, 'was an important decade in the history of children's welfare' since it saw the beginnings of an extensive public debate about children's physical and mental condition.

To some extent, the issue of juvenile crime was subsumed under the wider question of how best to promote children's well-being. This was a time when poverty was being 'rediscovered', whilst school-based education was coming to be viewed as an essential means by which children could be prepared to play a proper part in 'a healthy, co-operative society ... with a cohesive social and moral fabric', and 'to replace the chaos and immorality that appeared to be widespread ...' (Hendrick, 1997: 45). Delinquency, and its solutions, thus began to become incorporated in the wider project of understanding childhood problems, and developing 'universal' services to promote a healthy upbringing and produce the next generation of productive citizens.

What is Youth Justice?

We have used the term 'youth justice' in this book as it is a term that is generally used when describing the system which deals with children and young people who come into conflict with the law. However, we recognise the limits of this term. For one, not all of the countries that we discuss have specifically delineated youth justice systems. Secondly, the definition of what constitutes 'youth' varies across time and place. Children's rights standards, most notably the United Nation Conventions on the Rights of the Child (UNCRC), define anyone under 18 as a 'child', and, as we will explore throughout this text, these standards have been important in setting benchmarks for how the criminal justice system should operate in relation to children.

In the jurisdictions of the United Kingdom (England and Wales, Scotland and Northern Ireland), the youth justice system deals with children, and for the most part the provisions or accommodations of the youth justice system do not extend to young people aged over 18. However, in some countries the remit of youth justice systems extends into youth and early adulthood (e.g., in Germany), in recognition of the more protracted nature of youth transitions and the process of 'emerging adulthood', a topic that we cover in Chapter 5. In a recent commentary, the United Nations Committee on the Rights of the Child has advocated the use of the term 'child justice' instead of 'youth justice' or 'juvenile justice' (UN Committee on the Rights of the Child, 2019), and while we recognise the merit of this approach, the focus of this book is on how specific fields, problematic subjects and proposed remedies come to be defined across time and space. 'Youth justice' is such a field, in which the subjects, that is the young people who come into contact with the system and are processed through it, can come to be defined by it. As we will see, it is also a field in which, a variety of 'remedies' to deal with the 'problem' of youth crime are proposed. As we will illustrate, these concerns shift across time and space. For this reason, we do not limit our analysis to a specific age range, we do, however, explore many of the age-based delineations (such as the minimum age of criminal responsibility [MACR]), through which the contours of the system are defined.

Structure and Themes of the Book

The next chapter of the book explores some of the diverse theoretical explanations that have been put forward to explain youthful offending. The discussion in Chapter 2 notes that some of these explanations are historically and culturally specific, and there are many competing (and sometimes contradictory) perspectives. At various times these perspectives have informed different policies and practices in youth justice, an issue discussed in further depth in Chapter 3, where some of the responses to youthful offending are considered.

Comparative youth justice

In recent years increasing attention has been focused on the comparative dimensions of criminal justice systems and practices. This has included comparative analyses of different youth justice systems and differential responses to children and young people who come into conflict with the law. Some of the most influential comparative work has linked the differences in criminal justice systems in different countries to political and economic institutions and structures. For example, Cavadino and Dignan's (2006a, b) work on political economies and criminal justice puts forward an argument that differential responses to crime and punishment are linked to the extent to which countries have 'inclusive' or 'exclusive' political economies. Their analysis has also been extended to the field of youth justice (and discussed in Chapter 4).

Further comparative work in youth justice has taken place within the frame of children's rights standards, with analysis exploring the extent to which international standards such as the United Nations Convention on the Rights of the Child (UNCRC) and associated instruments are applied in different contexts globally. Work in this vein has included global comparative analyses of the different minimum ages of criminal responsibility (MACR) in various countries (Cipriani, 2009/2016), as well as analyses of compliance with rights standards in settings such as youth detention (Goldson and Kilkelly, 2013), where conditions across the world vary markedly.

Some of the challenges of comparative research are explored in Chapter 4, including some of the pitfalls identified by Nelken (2009, 2015, 2017), who has written extensively on the topic. He cautions against some methodological challenges, including *ethnocentrism, relativism* and *foil comparisons* (see Chapter 4 for a full explanation and discussion). In this chapter and throughout the book we also highlight the fact that much of the scholarship on youth justice has tended to focus on the 'Global North'. This is partly related to patterns of knowledge production, including the dominance of the English language in academic publishing (Connell, 2007). Inevitably, this book replicates some of these problems, through the fact that because of our own linguistic limitations we have only been able to access materials in the English language. However, we do try throughout the text to note the gaps in scholarship and to draw on international examples throughout.

Another problematic highlighted in relation to comparative criminological (and youth justice) research, is that the nation state is the most common unit of analysis, meaning that in comparative research of this nature the system and practice in one country tends to be compared with another. However, as we illustrate throughout the book, there are also examples of significant variations in the application of policy and practice *within jurisdictions*. This theme is particularly evident when we begin to delve into the differences evident both *between and within* the jurisdictions of the United Kingdom.

Children's rights and youth justice

International rights standards relating to children, including those with specific relevance to children and young people who come into conflict with the law, and the youth justice system are discussed in Chapter 5 of the book. These include universalist standards such as the United Nations Convention on the Rights of the Child (UNCRC) as well as guidelines which have been specifically developed to address aspects of youth justice, including guidelines which promote the diversion of children from the justice system and those aimed at safeguarding the rights of children in detention. The Council of Europe's *Guidelines on Child-Friendly Justice* (2015) are also considered, as well as some examples of the jurisprudence of the European Court of Human Rights (ECtHR) in relation to the treatment of children in the criminal justice system.

While there has been much rhetorical emphasis on the importance of upholding the rights of children involved in the justice system, there are many examples of disjuncture between rhetoric and reality. In Chapter 5 we also consider some of the examples of divergence between rights in principle and the reality on the ground, including in relation to the MACR and the treatment of children in detention. Here some of the reports of the United Nations Committee on the Rights of the Child, who carry out periodic inspections of the rights compliance of different countries, are considered.

United Kingdom – Different systems, divergent approaches?

Many books on youth justice emanating from the United Kingdom tend to overwhelmingly focus on England and Wales, where there have been lots of notable changes and policy developments over recent decades, and a significant amount of research and scholarship. In this book we have attempted to broaden the focus by including more coverage of the different jurisdictions of the United Kingdom, and the distinct contours of youth justice policy and practice therein. We therefore draw on work which has explored the youth justice systems in Scotland, Northern Ireland and Wales as well as in England. Some previous comparative analyses have suggested that despite the claims regarding the 'distinctiveness' of the different systems in the United Kingdom, what we see are merely 'illusions of difference' (Muncie, 2011). In other words, many of the underlying trends (for example an increased emphasis on risk and **responsibilisation**) in how we respond to young people who come into conflict with the law are similar. In Chapter 6 as well as describing the current systems, we explore how these claims regarding 'distinctiveness' are interesting in and of themselves, as they reflect particular ideas about children, justice and the role of the state.

Moreover, Muncie's (2011) observations about 'illusions of difference' are by now made over a decade ago. At the time Muncie wrote this article, the referendum on Scottish independence had not yet taken place, and justice and policing powers had not yet been devolved to the Northern Ireland Assembly. The Brexit referendum in 2016 which has led to the United Kingdom's departure from the European Union has since led to more calls for more fundamental constitutional changes, including a further Scottish independence referendum, while the question of whether legislative responsibility for criminal justice should be transferred from the Westminster parliament to the Welsh Senedd remains a live issue (Commission on Justice in Wales, 2019; Evans et al., 2022). It seems likely therefore that, as time progresses, we will see increased divergences between the different systems of youth justice in the United Kingdom.

As well as noting the differences in the policy and practice governing youth justice in the United Kingdom, we also explore a body of research that illustrates significant intra-jurisdictional differences in how youth justice operates within countries. Here we see differences in the rates at which children are drawn into the criminal justice system, as well as differences in what happens to them when they are there. Some of these differences are explained by different practice cultures, approaches and attitudes towards children who come into conflict with the law (Goldson and Briggs, 2021). Other differentials are evident when we look at the characteristics of young people. Here we see issues regarding the over-representation of children and young people from racial and ethnic minorities across different youth justice systems (both in the UK and elsewhere), as well as the fact that youth justice systems across the world overwhelmingly deal with children who experience socio-economic disadvantage (Phoenix, 2016; Cox, 2021; Goldson et al., 2021).

Concentration and complexity

A notable feature of youth justice in recent years across a number of countries is the fact that the numbers of young people being dealt with by these systems has been declining. There is no definitive explanation for this, but in Chapters 7 and 8 we consider these overall trends in the light of some of the theories that have been put forward. These include explanations which focus on the changing nature of young people's behaviour, as well as explanations which focus more on system effects (such as a reduction in policing numbers or changes to policing priorities). Although, as we will see these trends are not universal, and in fact have served to highlight in particular the disproportionate representation of young people from racial and ethnic minorities in criminal justice systems in different contexts.

One of the effects of the overall reduction in numbers of children and young people in the youth justice system has been a greater focus on the 'complexity' of those who remain in the system. This has led to an increased focus on the early childhood experiences of children and young people, which are sometimes framed through the perspective of 'childhood adversity'. In Chapter 8 we therefore consider some of the key insights from this literature, as well as critiques of framings of childhood adversity from individualistic perspectives.

Intersecting systems

Children and young people who come into contact with youth justice systems do not live their lives in isolation. Most, if not all children and young people, will engage with schools and some young people will have contact with systems of support such as child protection and welfare services. In Chapter 9 we explore some of the literature exploring the intersections between systems. This includes research which has documented the links between school disciplinary practices (such as school exclusions) and subsequent contact with the criminal justice system. This chapter also explores the context in which children involved in child protection and welfare services and/or placed in the care of the state, are frequently over-represented in youth justice systems. Research which explores this topic, including the potential 'criminogenic' nature of care placements, is critically considered.

The perspectives of children and young people

The perspectives of children and young people who come into contact with the youth justice system are considered throughout the book, but in the final chapter of the book (Chapter 10) we focus specifically on what some of this rich literature tells us about the lives of children and young people and the complex range of reasons and circumstances that leads to involvement with offending and contact with the system. The recent focus on participatory approaches in youth justice, including in practice and research, is also considered in this final chapter.

Conclusion

This chapter has set out some of the key orienting themes of the book. This includes a focus on definitional issues, which include conceptualisations of childhood and the remit of the youth justice system. We see that the purpose and function of youth justice systems vary across time and place, and that there are some key debates in this field. Some of the main themes of the book have been outlined, including the focus on comparative contexts, emerging issues of 'concentration' and 'complexity' and the way in which different systems intersect in children and young people's lives. The following chapters consider all of these issues in further depth.

2
Explaining Youth Crime

Objectives

- This chapter will show why theory is important in criminology.
- Readers will be made familiar with key approaches to explaining the behaviour of young people and why they may break the law.
- The chapter will help the reader to identify the origins of continuing theoretical debates in criminology and evaluate alternative explanations.
- The chapter will also enable readers to develop their own theoretical perspectives and explanations of youth crime.

Introduction – Defining Our Terms

One of the central problems we face in trying to understand youth crime is that both 'youth' and 'crime' are terms heavily loaded with assumptions and stereotypes. When we think of young people, it is likely that we associate certain qualities and characteristics in particular with them. In one Scottish survey including adults of all ages more than a third of respondents thought that young people did not take responsibility for their own actions (Scottish Government, 2017). Such beliefs seem to be linked to a wider sense of anxiety about young people being somehow different from older members of society, and more likely to be out of control. An earlier study (Roberts, 2004) provided evidence of a consistent pattern of distrust and fear of youth amongst the wider public. The sense of threat associated with young people appears to be pervasive and persistent; a 2016 study in Kenya reported on public perceptions of a rising threat of increasingly serious crime by young people (Martin and Mbugua, 2016). Schissel (2016) reported a similar growth in 'antipathy' amongst the Canadian public towards young people, associated with fears about an increasing lack of respect shown by young people. Even historical and current terms which are not 'age specific', such as 'hooligans' (Pearson, 1983), 'yobs', 'chavs' (Jones, 2012) or 'hoodies' become associated predominantly with the young in the public mind. Whilst these essentially negative perceptions are at odds with actual patterns of behaviour amongst children and young people observed over time (Davis and Dossetor, 2010), their prevalence is striking.

Similarly, popular conceptions of what counts as 'crime', which we probably all hold to some extent, may tend to overemphasise certain types of behaviour and apparent threats, often associated with young people (see Jennings et al., 2020, for example). Media reporting may be partly responsible for this emphasis on young people as offenders (Chadee, 2001; Hertsmere Young Researchers, 2011). As a result, undue attention may be drawn to the wrongdoing and misdemeanours of young people, whilst the crimes of other members of society are given relatively less attention (Baier et al., 2016). In light of this, we need to try to adjust our thinking, and frame our attempts to explain youth crime in terms of the characteristics and behaviour of young people, perhaps, rather than specifically their 'criminality'. The challenge for us is to distinguish between perceptions and evidence if we are to achieve plausible accounts which might help to explain what young people do, which might be rather different to what we think they do.

Where Do We Get Our Ideas About Young People?

Maybe you could draw up two columns, identifying the qualities and attributes of young people you know on one side; and frequently expressed views found in the media or reports of public opinion on the other.

The aim of this chapter, then, will be to try to develop and apply a framework for understanding young people's characteristics and behaviour, and to view that which comes to be formally defined as criminal as being a subset of this. Behaviour which attracts this label may be problematic or harmful, but it may not be dramatically different in nature or origin to much other behaviour which is not criminalised. Bullying in schools, for instance, is almost certainly widespread, and can be extremely harmful, but it is not typically described or treated as a criminal matter. There are good reasons for attempting to understand and prevent this kind of social harm, of course; and it may well be that the approach set out here will help us to take a broader view of young people and crime.

The chapter is organised into three main sections: firstly, we will consider widely used explanatory frameworks which frame our understanding of young people's characteristics and behaviour; then we will look at alternative and sometimes competing explanations for young people's involvement in crime and antisocial behaviour; and finally, we will try to look at the same questions from the perspective of young people themselves, and in their own words.

Explanatory Frameworks: Childhood and Youth Offending

Partly because, as discussed above, young people have frequently been the focus of concern, children and young people have become the subjects of extensive study and academic interest, drawing on a range of disciplinary perspectives, including history and anthropology, as well as sociology, psychology, criminology and neuroscience. This range of disciplinary interest has also meant that the methods of inquiry adopted by researchers have been diverse, and drawn on different traditions of inquiry, evidence-gathering and analysis. Indeed, many of these traditions take very different and conflicting approaches to the question of what counts as knowledge, and how to go about obtaining it. These differences, as we shall see, lead to intense and recurrent debates, which are certainly unresolved at present, and perhaps unlikely to be settled in the near future. For present purposes, the aim will be to outline some of the explanatory frameworks typically applied, and to consider the implications for our understanding of young people, their development and their changing behaviour. In particular, we will focus on biological, psychological and social perspectives.

Biological accounts

There is considerable debate amongst those who study adolescence (defined as the life stage between childhood and adulthood – see Chapter 1) as to the extent to which character traits and behavioural tendencies might have biological origins, and in turn whether these are genetic (inherited) or associated with the physiological and neurological changes of human growth and development.

Genetic influences and the delinquent brain?

Recent developments in neuroscience, for example, have opened up a new range of possibilities for understanding how the human brain works, and the relationship between different aspects of its functioning and our behaviours.

This has certainly brought with it a sharp contemporary focus on our capacity to measure thoughts, attitudes and predispositions, but the underlying interest in the relationship between biology and crime is not new. Famously, Cesare Lombroso, who is often referred to as the 'father' of modern criminology, is widely credited with the introduction of the idea of the 'born criminal' in the late 19th century:

> Lombroso's hypothesis of the 'delinquente nato,' the 'born criminal,' affirms that all true criminals have a number of causal connected characteristics; physical characteristics that can be shown anthropologically, and psychic characteristics that can be shown psycho-physiologically, which mark them as an individual type of mankind. From this type are recruited, quite independently of social and individual conditions, the discovered and the undiscovered criminal. (Albrecht, 1910: 72)

While Lombroso's ideas are clearly problematic, some of the underlying ideas about genetic influences and the supposed physiological origins of criminality are not too dissimilar from some current strands of criminological thought (Gibson and Rafter, 2006). Rocque et al. (2012), for example, argue that there has been a renewed interest in seeking out biological explanations of crime in recent years, following a period of time when they were discredited, not so much for their scientific limitations, but because of their associations with politically questionable tendencies, such as the eugenics movement of the late 19th and early 20th centuries, and later associations with racial stereotyping. Rocque et al. argue, however, that present day interest in the biological origins of crime is driven by a much more benevolent set of motivations, to do with 'improving the environment to promote healthy biological development early in life' (Rocque et al., 2012: 306). As they put it, 'crime prevention' in the late 19th and early 20th centuries 'involved calls to prevent so-called inferior peoples from reproducing', and this kind of morally unacceptable argument became entirely discredited with the later emergence of Nazism. They contrast this highly problematic history with the emergence of a strand of criminological research in the 1970s, which was concerned with the factors affecting child and later life-course development, some of which, at least, are associated with biological influences. Rocque et al. (2012: 307) suggest that there is a demonstrable relationship between 'neuropsychological or cognitive deficits' and 'later criminal behaviour'. Such deficits are often described in terms of lack of self-control, or inability to anticipate the consequences of one's actions, and these in turn can be linked to specific parts of the brain, which may be susceptible to 'events' such as alcohol use during pregnancy.

Rafter et al. (2016) have expanded on these ideas to provide a comprehensive account of the emergence and development of criminological theories of the brain, arguing that perhaps the earlier rejection of such theories, albeit on perfectly justifiable moral grounds, might have led to something of an imbalance. Criminology had perhaps come to overlook the body of scientific evidence which seemed to show that differences in the make-up of the brain might, in fact, lie behind differences in behaviour. Rafter and colleagues argue that the new discoveries of the biosciences were linked to an appreciation on behalf of the scientific community that there was a relationship between biological and environmental causes of crime. Hence we should be looking for explanations which are 'biosocial', and integrate the two dimensions of criminological inquiry, rather than seeing them as irreconcilable. In this way, for example, the 'nature–nurture' divide could be bridged, and we need not be forced to conclude that all behaviour stems from either inherent characteristics, on the one hand, or social influences, on the other.

Nature and Nurture

- Nature is what we think of as pre-wiring and is influenced by genetic inheritance and other biological factors.
- Nurture is generally taken as the influence of external factors after conception, e.g., the product of exposure, life experiences and learning on an individual.

www.simplypsychology.org/naturevsnurture.html#:~:text=Nature%20

Raine (2002) has also taken a 'biosocial' approach, outlining several different ways in which biological factors could interact with the young person's environment to increase the risk of violent or anti-social behaviour. This is based on emerging evidence, including: '*empirical* examples of interaction effects within the areas of genetics, psychophysiology, obstetrics, brain imaging, neuropsychology and neurology, hormones, neurotransmitters, and environmental toxins' (Raine, 2002: 311). Raine notes, in passing, that the distinction between social and biological variables is also less clear cut than might be expected: 'There is much that is social about biological variables (e.g., head injuries leading to brain dysfunction are caused by the environment) and much that is biological about social variables (e.g., genetic factors, and their biological predispositions, contribute to bad parenting)' (Raine, 2002: 312). Nonetheless, he goes on to itemise some of the potential biological factors associated with anti-social or aggressive behaviour, along with sources of supporting evidence.

Twin Studies: What Do They Tell Us About Delinquency?

Twin studies, for example, are believed to offer persuasive evidence of genetic factors in predisposing individuals to offend. In these studies, typically, the likelihood of twins who are genetically identical (monozygotic) becoming offenders is compared to those who are not (dizygotic) with the aim of identifying the proportionate influence of genetic factors on their behaviour. One large early study provided evidence of a greater tendency for criminality to be inherited amongst children whose rural or relatively affluent social environment was not identified as **criminogenic** (Christiansen, 1977). Kendler et al. (2015) later carried out a twin study in Sweden, concluding that 45% of an individual's likelihood of acquiring a criminal conviction was attributable to heredity (genetic factors), with a further 27% being due to the offender's social environment for males, and 18% for females.

Adoption studies, on the other hand, tend to provide stronger evidence of an interactive effect. In one study cited by Raine (2002), Swedish male adoptees were considerably more likely to become offenders (40%) where birth parents were criminal and their upbringing was problematic, than where only one of these conditions applied (12% and 7%). A subsequent Swedish study has offered confirmation of these findings, again suggesting that both heredity and environment play a part, separately and in combination, in contributing to the likelihood of an adopted child becoming an offender (Kendler et al., 2014).

This kind of study has not passed without criticism however (see Joseph, 2001, for example), and for those attributing criminality to genetic factors, the challenge of explaining the precise distribution of the predisposition to offend amongst the population, as well as the mechanisms by which these predispositions are translated into specific offences, remains significant.

Other biological influences

Other biological factors are also believed to be associated with the likelihood of becoming an offender, including what Raine (2002: 316) describes as 'obstetric factors'. Indeed, he makes the claim that it is in this area that we can find the 'most compelling evidence' for an interaction between biological and environmental influences. By 'obstetric factors', Raine means complications during pregnancy and birth, or exposure during pregnancy to nicotine. The effects of drug and alcohol misuse during pregnancy have also been extensively researched. Portnoy et al. (2013) summarise this evidence citing several studies which show a significant representation of children in the youth justice system with 'fetal alcohol effects'. Similar effects were also reported for nicotine exposure, although outcomes appear less clear for drug use during pregnancy

(Lester et al., 2004; Oei, 2018). Portnoy et al. (2013) also suggest that birth complications may be associated with subsequent psychosocial risk factors, citing what they describe as findings which have been generated widely around the world.

Other pre-birth conditions which might be associated with behavioural differences amongst children and young people, are those associated with genetic variations, such as 'autistic spectrum disorders'. In fact, the evidence in relation to autism spectrum disorders (ASDs) and delinquency is mixed, with one study concluding that autism spectrum disorders are associated with a greater than normal risk of offences against the person and a reduced risk in relation to property crime (Cheely et al., 2012). Another review of the relevant literature has also concluded that the relationship between ASD and delinquency is 'complex', and may depend on the type of crime, as well as other intervening factors which may have an impact on young people with these conditions. Furthermore, as we discuss in subsequent chapters, there is also a strong body of evidence that young people with disabilities may be more likely to be processed through the youth justice system for a range of reasons, including the fact that they may more easily come to the attention of authorities (see Chapter 8 for further discussion).

Physiological and neurological development and delinquency

The search for physiological causes of crime also encompasses the effects of biological changes affecting children and young people, such as those associated with growth and maturation – the hormonal changes associated with puberty, for example. Here, too, neuroscience has begun to map out the ways in which brain development works, identifying particular areas associated with behavioural controls. Blakemore's (2018) *Inventing Ourselves: The Secret Life of the Teenage Brain* provides a valuable summary of the state of knowledge in relation to neurological changes during this particular life stage. Essentially, recent developments in neuroscience, including brain imaging methods, have enabled us to gain a much clearer idea about the ways in which the brain changes and develops over time. The findings of this type of research seem to suggest that there are changes specifically associated with the life stage defined as adolescence, from puberty to the late teens. So, it appears that 'risky' decision-making in adolescence can be linked with the 'slow' development of the prefrontal cortex, and other regions of the brain which govern impulsive actions, and the 'dopaminergic' system, which is particularly responsive to reward stimuli during adolescence (Blakemore and Robbins, 2012: 1189). In other words, there is a physical basis in the chemistry of the brain for the apparent propensity of adolescents to take greater risks than those in other age groups; and this is especially the case where there are immediate prospects of rewards in some form, or where peer influence may also play a significant part.

The authors report that empirical studies of brain development: 'suggest that adolescents are more likely than children and adults to make risky decisions in "hot" contexts, where emotions are at stake or peers are present and social cognition is involved' (Blakemore and Robbins, 2012: 1189).

Here, then, there appears to be a physical, neurological basis for some of the behavioural changes which are frequently associated with youth, such as impulsivity. These changes may contribute to a greater likelihood of involvement in some types of crime.

Hormonal changes, such as those associated with puberty are also believed to lead to an increase in certain types of problematic behaviour. Gender differences are also said to be significant in this respect. Pepper and Dahl (2013: 135) state:

> there is growing evidence in both humans and animals that pubertal hormones may influence (bias) some neural and neurobehavioral tendencies of social and affective processing. Examples of such neural and neurobehavioral correlates of social and affective processing include (but are not limited to) activity within the striatum during reward processing, activity within the amygdala and striatum during the processing of emotional stimuli and activity within the anterior medial prefrontal cortex and temporal-parietal junction during social-cognitive reasoning.

This evidence is taken to suggest that hormonal changes associated with puberty affect aspects of the brain, and this helps to sensitise young people 'to their social world'. They therefore become more attuned to the implications of their actions for their peer relationships, and how their behaviour appears to those around them. It also seems that certain hormones are associated with particular forms of behaviour, and studies have found links between higher levels of testosterone and increases in aggressive behaviours (Duke et al., 2014). At the same time, researchers also warn us against making simplistic causal assumptions, given the range of factors which are likely to influence young people's behaviour (Duke et al., 2014: 321). This is a rapidly developing field of research, but there seems to be a widely held view amongst scientists that the adolescent brain does have distinctive structural characteristics, which themselves are likely to be affected by age-related hormonal changes. These, in turn, are associated with particular types of behaviour and relationships which may be criminogenic; although some researchers have also acknowledged that the social context, too, might be an important associated factor (Rowe et al., 2004).

Evolution and adaptation

Another strand of thought which seeks to link biological characteristics to criminality is to be found in evolutionary criminology. Here, the suggestion is that the genetic adaptations which enable us to survive and thrive in our environment may also be supportive of deviant behaviours (Quinsey, 2002). Thus, gender and age differences in the propensity to commit crimes are attributed in part by some to the requirement for males to 'compete' with each other to ensure 'reproductive success' (p. 3); which is also a feature of a particular life stage, namely adolescence. Evolutionary theories may appear particularly plausible in terms of explaining offending by young people, because they align well with both gender differences and the 'age-crime curve' – that is, the evidence that the peak age of offending is in late adolescence. Walsh and Jorgensen (2018: 532) suggest that this is one of the great strengths of evolutionary explanations, not least because criminologists have persistently struggled to account for the continuing prevalence of offending amongst young people, at least until very recently. The correlation between certain types of behaviour found in humans and other animals, such as competition for male dominance, suggests that these may share common biological causes, they argue. Even though certain types of behaviour such as binge drinking, drug use and dangerous driving may be quite historically specific, they share the attributes of 'risky' activities which can be described as 'evolutionarily adaptive' (Walsh and Jorgensen, 2018: 533); that is, they are closely related to the kind of behaviours which most effectively support the reproduction of the species.

Physiological and lifestyle factors

Whilst the search for biological causes of delinquency may look towards generalised genetic and developmental factors, on the one hand, we might also consider other more immediate physiological influences, on the other. Thus, diet, as well as the use of substances such as drugs and alcohol, have also been identified as potential influences on young people's behaviour. Gesch (2013), for instance, has carried out research which suggests that suitable vitamin supplements can help to reduce levels of anti-social behaviour amongst convicted young offenders. Goldstein (1985) identified the possibility of direct links between the 'psychopharmacological' effects of alcohol or drugs and crime. Later studies suggest a more specific causal connection between alcohol use and violent crime (Felson et al., 2008). In a major European study, Rocca et al. (2019) offer confirmation of the association between drug and alcohol use and delinquency, although they are fairly cautious in their interpretation of these findings. Whilst they found that frequent and recent use of alcohol and cannabis were correlated with higher levels of delinquency amongst young people, they could not conclude for certain that this represented a direct causal link. However, where offences were committed under the influence of drugs or alcohol, this study found that alcohol actually 'played a greater criminogenic role than drugs', perhaps indicating that this is due to the 'exciting and disinhibiting effect' of drink (Rocca et al., 2019: 267).

This and other studies conclude that the relationship between substance use and criminal behaviour is not straightforward. Whilst it is possible to identify correlations between the two, the question of whether one causes the other, or whether there are other contributing factors – peer influence, perhaps – is much more difficult to answer with certainty. More generally, too, it is important to acknowledge unresolved questions associated with biological explanations for youth crime. These are to do with our understanding of causation, and the mechanisms which translate conditions, stimuli or characteristics into specific actions (crimes) carried out by specific individuals (offenders) at specific points in time. There is an important distinction to be made between correlations or associations and causes. It may seem logical, for instance, to assume that particular developments in the structure and processes of the brain in adolescence act as predisposing conditions for young people's deviant behaviour. However, it could be that changes in the brain are not causes but consequences of young people's experiences, actions and reactions. There is considerable evidence, for instance, that supports the suggestion that brain functioning is affected by children's early life experiences (Herzog and Schmahl, 2018), in particular those which have come to be identified as '**Adverse Childhood Experiences**' (ACEs), such as abuse and poverty (see Chapter 8 for a further discussion). Similar questions could be raised about arguments suggesting that criminality is genetically determined. If this is the case, we would expect all those with a similar genetic make-up to behave in the same way, which is clearly not the case, even in twin studies. An additional challenge for biological explanations of youth crime is to account for 'agency', and the capacity of young people to exercise choice. This, indeed, is a problem for all causal claims which assume a necessary, linear and pre-determined connection between a particular factor or characteristic and its outcomes.

Psychological explanations

Alongside those accounts of youth crime which rely extensively on biological explanations, and to some extent are aligned with them, we also find a body of ideas and evidence which locate its causes in the realms of psychology and developmental models of the life-course.

In similar fashion to some of the more purely biological depictions, psychological explanations often adopt a developmental perspective, defining adolescence as a discrete 'stage' in the life-course, with its own features and behavioural characteristics. Psychological explanations of delinquency are distinguished from sociological explanations in that they focus on individual characteristics and features, rather than examining factors which might be associated with societal or collective influences. Unlike biological theories, psychological perspectives concentrate on observable patterns of behaviour and the mental processes they represent, rather than physical or neurological evidence (although there appears to be a relatively close relationship in the latter case). The question of developmental learning and how this influences behaviour becomes important in this context.

Developmental theories

In the broader field of child development, psychologists such as Piaget, Vygotsky and Erikson have ben influential in defining distinct stages of conceptual development in childhood and adolescence, suggesting that these are associated not just with learning, but with self-awareness and social competence as well. For Piaget (1959), for instance, the stages of development are characterised by increasing capabilities to carry out complex reasoning tasks and to think abstractly. These changes are associated with greater awareness of and sensitivity to what others might think and how they see us.

Erikson (1978), similarly, thought in terms of developmental stages, across the entire life-course, identifying eight of these. In his view, though, each of these stages represented a kind of upheaval, or realignment, rather than a simple progression or accumulation of skills and traits. Adolescence, for him, is a period of 'identity vs role confusion'; and he describes adolescence as a period of stress and uncertainty which nearly everyone will experience. Indeed, Erikson appeared to see delinquency as a normal feature of youth, and to some extent as representing desirable traits and characteristics, describing young offenders as 'healthier' than more withdrawn members of their age cohort, and as demonstrating 'potential for contributing to the richness of national life' (Erikson, 1978: 104), precisely because of their energy and determination to resolve the conflicts they will inevitably experience.

Hitchcock (2001: 40) has applied Erikson's classification to gang formation, which he views as a predictable consequence of the search for identity and affirmation central to the adolescent life stage. Hitchcock describes young people as prone to feelings of 'role confusion', with a tendency to 'over-identify' with groups or individuals whose qualities offer a sense of certainty and reassurance. Hitchcock goes on to describe studies which seem to confirm the propensity for young people to develop strong and exclusive ties to their peer groups. In the Robbers Cave study (Sherif et al., 1961), for example, the mere separation of a cohort of young people into two groups led eventually to such hostility between the two that there were incidents of violence between them. This kind of process might also help to explain why the establishment of strong peer relationships may take priority for young people over their relationships with adults, including parents (Hitchcock, 2001: 44).

Kohlberg (1971) set out a similar developmental model, based on the notion of 'moral' stages of personal growth, and building on Piaget's work. Kohlberg identified six stages of moral development in childhood. At Stage One, in early childhood, the power of authority figures such as parents to determine right or wrong is unquestioned, so the child's actions will be guided by strategic choices to avoid punishment, typically. At Stage Two, a recognition that mutual cooperation can provide benefits develops, and so there emerges a wider range of incentives to behave according to the expectations of others. As the child's scope for understanding and knowing the world widens, so the capacity for moral reasoning also becomes more abstract and generalised, according to Kohlberg, so decisions about whether or not to conform to social norms and legal rules are informed by more general criteria of what is acceptable or justifiable. As children get older, then, morality becomes negotiable, and decisions about how to behave become conditional, depending on a range of considerations, incentives or pressures.

Kohlberg and others tested the model with young people who have committed offences, and findings suggested that the level of moral reasoning did differ according to whether or not young people had been in trouble. According to Veneziano and Veneziano (1988: 100), a body of research then emerged which: 'suggests that on the average, delinquents exhibit lower moral reasoning skills than nondelinquents, [although] ... there are considerable intragroup differences among delinquents'. In other words, young offenders were found to be less able than their non-offending peers to apply abstract judgements of the greater good and common interests which might dissuade them from committing crime. In their own study, Veneziano and Veneziano (1988: 111) found broad confirmation of earlier findings, although they noted that the delinquent population was 'heterogeneous'; most, too, believed that criminal acts were 'wrong', suggesting a degree of disconnection between their moral judgements and their actions.

Alongside these apparent variations, the model set out by Kohlberg has to account for the apparent differences in moral reasoning between delinquents and the conforming peers. Why do the different populations progress at different rates through the stages of moral development? Catalano and Hawkins (1996) sought to explain this by proposing a contextual basis for the development of anti-social behaviour patterns. Thus, the underlying psychological mechanisms are constant, but they are affected by the social environment (Moore, 2011).

As opposed to Kohlberg's, this model suggests a similar process of bonding and affiliation to groups and shared behaviours between delinquents and non-delinquents, determined by the distinctive stimuli and incentives on offer, rather than by different internal mechanisms. This approach also provides a greater degree of flexibility in terms of understanding patterns of change over the life-course, as suggested by Moffitt (1993), among others. In the terms set out by Moffitt, the higher rate of offending amongst adolescents can be accounted for by way of a 'temporary maturity gap'; or moral deficit in

Kohlberg's terms, which for most is redressed through maturation processes, or the resolution of intra-personal conflicts (as Erikson's theory would suggest). It is only a relatively small number of young offenders whose criminal activities persist into adulthood, for whom distinguishing influences on their behaviour need to be identified.

Social learning

Developmental models of delinquency are just one of a number of distinct psychological approaches to understanding youth crime, according to Moore (2011). These can be classified as: 'learning theories, intelligence theories, personality theories, theories of psychopathy, and cognitive and social development theories' (Moore, 2011: 226). Social learning theories, for example, are associated with Bandura (1969) in particular, and suggest a process of interaction between the individual and the context, through which behaviour can be learned, tested out and reinforced. Human behaviour can thus be seen as the product of repeated observation and experiment: Social learning theory: 'posits the interaction of (1) observation, symbolic representations and self-generated stimuli and self-imposed consequences, (2) environmental conditions and (3) behaviors in determining behavior' (Moore, 2011: 229). As Moore observes, social learning theory has been prominent in efforts to explain criminal behaviour. If learning is contextual, as suggested, then we could expect young people to be open to influence by those around them, and from this stems the idea of '**differential association**' (Sutherland, 1939). Where young people mix with criminal peers, they are therefore believed to be more likely both to observe and learn deviant behaviour, which is then reinforced and amplified within the peer network. Rebellon (2006) suggests that it is likely that, as a particular deviant activity gains attention from peers, others will intensify their own criminal behaviour to gain similar recognition and acknowledgement. Rebellon's analysis of responses from a large youth survey in the USA showed that: 'delinquency is positively related to time socializing, and this relationship would appear to reflect the social attractiveness of a delinquent' (Rebellon, 2006: 403). This, he argues, supports a 'vicarious-reinforcement' model of delinquency causation.

The influence of psychological traits

Other psychological theories of delinquency are less focused on dynamic factors of learning or cognitive development, and more on traits or characteristics, which may predetermine the likelihood of offending. 'Intelligence theories', for example, have quite a lengthy (and controversial) history, and tend to account for criminality as a function of the individual's intelligence level, often measured in the form of the IQ score. As long ago as 1929, for instance,

Milton Erickson was reporting the results of research into the supposed relationship between intelligence and delinquency. Claiming in passing that delinquency is a 'problem belonging almost entirely to the field of psychiatry rather than to the legal realm or to sociology, that field of normal human relationships' (Erickson, 1929: 593), he argued that 'fifty per cent of delinquents are definitely below normal in intelligence' (p. 595). This claim was based on an extensive file analysis of young people in penal institutions in Wisconsin, and according to Erickson this finding was supported by other studies, too. Subsequent research enabled some to claim that low intelligence could be seen as one of the major contributing factors to delinquent behaviour (Caplan, 1965), and studies such as West and Farrington's (1973) well-known *Cambridge Study of Delinquency*, seemed to give further support to this, finding that offenders averaged over five points less than 'non-delinquents' in their IQ scores.

Interest in this question was sustained, and Hirschi and Hindelang's (1977) contribution was to suggest that the relationship between low intelligence and crime was mediated by poor school performance, which, in turn, accounted for apparent racial differences. Against this, however, the controversial argument of the authors of *The Bell Curve* (Herrnstein and Murray, 1994) was that the lower IQ scores amongst Black children were sufficient in themselves to explain their higher rates of recorded delinquency. The highly controversial nature of this claim resulted in a considerable body of critical comment, challenging both the political dimensions of the Bell Curve argument and the dubious empirical analysis on which its arguments were based (Cullen et al., 1997, for example).

Personality types

Other psychological explanations of delinquency look to 'personality' types as predisposing factors which render individuals more or less likely to commit crime. Quay and Peterson (1960), for instance, claimed to be able to distinguish between 'neurotic', 'psychopathic' and 'inadequate' characteristics associated with a greater chance of becoming an offender. Thus, those from their sample identified as 'psychopathic' were those who displayed no signs of guilt for their crimes, a rebellious attitude, no empathy for others and a degree of impulsivity. Neurotic offenders, by contrast, would show signs of 'discouragement', depression and tension. Hans Eysenck is also closely associated with the idea that delinquency is strongly influenced by personality traits. According to Eysenck (1964), there are three independent dimensions or scales against which personality can be measured:

- Introversion-extraversion;
- neuroticism-stability; and
- psychoticism-normality.

These three dimensions are each independently thought to be associated with a tendency to offend. Extraverts, for example, are less likely than others to be responsive to messages which might encourage them to maintain self-control. They are less sensitive to signs of social disapproval than is the norm. Neuroticism is said to be related to highly emotional behaviour and a readiness to act in response to emotional drives without necessarily thinking of the consequences of doing so. Psychotic traits are those associated with lack of concern for others, self-obsession and non-social tendencies. In line with this, clearly, those at the extreme end of the scale are believed to act purely out of self-interest and with little regard for the consequences of their actions. The distribution of these characteristics may vary, but essentially the argument is that those at the extravert/neurotic/psychotic extremes of these scales will each be more prone to criminal behaviour.

Subsequent developments have seen alternative models proposed and tested in comparison to Eysenck's 'PEN' ('Psychoticism, Extraversion and Neuroticism') model. One Dutch study explores the question of whether this model offers a better fit with delinquent behaviour than the more recently developed 'Big Five' model (van Dam et al., 2005). This latter model also incorporates the Extraversion and Neuroticism scales, whilst adding three further measures: 'Agreeableness, Conscientiousness and Openness' (Goldberg, 1990; van Dam et al., 2005: 8). In conducting tests with offender and non-offender groups of young people in the Netherlands, the researchers found that both models were able to discriminate between the two groups: 'Analyses on single dimensions revealed that Extraversion (PEN) was higher in officially recorded recidivists compared to non-recidivists. The dimensions Psychoticism and Neuroticism (Big Five) were higher and Agreeableness was lower in self-reported recidivists' (van Dam et al., 2005: 15). However, there were also some findings which were not as predicted, with levels of extraversion being lower amongst offenders than the comparison group of students on Eysenck's scale. Typically, this kind of evidence relates to the behaviours of male offenders.

Psychological disorders

The final category of psychological theories of delinquency identified by Moore (2011) are those associated with psychopathy or personality disorder, which broadly assume that delinquency, and certainly more extreme forms of criminality, are linked with particular abnormalities of the personality. This type of disorder tends to be attributed to a small minority of 'life-course persistent' (Moffitt, 1993) and often serious offenders, who are clearly distinguishable from the population in general by their characteristics. There is: 'a relatively small group of early-onset, criminally-versatile, chronic offenders who frequently present with histories of violent behavior, comorbid attention-deficit-hyperactivity disorder (ADHD) and conduct disorder (CD)' (Howard et al., 2006: 395). Confirmation of this claim is offered by Adshead et al. (2012: 115), who state that: 'for a small number of adolescents, a diagnosis of personality disorder can be confidently made'. There appears to be a pathway into serious anti-social behaviour, grounded in a combination of predisposing factors, including genetic and early developmental problems, which result in 'callous and unemotional personality traits' (Adshead et al., 2012: 113).

We can conclude, then, that there are a number of distinct theoretical positions on the psychological origins of delinquency. These commonly draw out their conclusions from behavioural observations and self-report studies, although they face some challenges in distinguishing between what might be termed predisposing factors, and direct causes. How far, we might ask, do psychological attributes actually cause young people to offend? What relationship do these attributes have to biological or social factors? And, how do we account for young people's agency in light of these supposedly determinant influences?

Social factors

Unlike biological and psychological explanations for youth crime which highlight individual and internal drivers, social explanations look for causes in the interactions between people. They therefore depend heavily on understanding the contexts in which children and young people are brought up and live their lives; and they shift the quest for solutions from changing the individual offender to changing the influences and systems which affect them in the social world. Within the domain of social explanations, there are a number of foci of interest, including families, communities and peer groups, media and youth culture, and social structures. These are not necessarily mutually exclusive, but there are differences of emphasis, certainly; and for those concerned with 'what to do about youth crime', they may well point towards different solutions.

The family and youth crime

The family has been a major focal point for explanatory accounts. Concerns have been voiced for many years about the quality of parenting; and this was certainly a prominent issue in the minds of Victorian social reformers, for instance. May's (1973) detailed discussion of 19th-century studies of delinquency identifies some of the ways in which families were identified as potential 'breeding grounds' for crime:

> lacking affection and supervision, the juvenile delinquent in consequence displayed his independence. He was 'in general a gambler and a drunkard' with an 'unnatural' interest in the opposite sex. But 'circumstances' and parental irresponsibility rather than 'innate depravity' produced

> such outrageous behaviour: of one hundred cases examined, sixty were the offspring of 'dishonest' and thirty of 'profligate' parents. (May, 1973: 18, quoting Neale, 1840)

Consequently, parents and the family should be the targets of correctional intervention:

> Diagnosis in terms of parental neglect facilitated concrete action. It mirrored current preoccupations with the supreme importance of the home and the family in child socialisation .... Constant and vigilant parental surveillance was necessary. (May, 1973: 21)

Concern about the potential connection between the experience of family life and juvenile crime has persisted, becoming the subject of continuing research interest. The family was one of the key areas of investigation of the Gluecks (1962), who carried out a series of extensive and well-known studies of the origins of delinquency in the USA during the mid-20th century (Glueck and Glueck, 1934, 1950, 1962). Although their work came in for substantial methodological criticism (Laub and Sampson, 1988), their findings concerning the role of the family have been identified as important. Subsequent reanalysis of their data (Laub and Sampson, 1988) found evidence of strong correlations between family characteristics and the incidence of youth crime. Thus, for example, factors such as lack of parental supervision, parental criminality, parental rejection and problematic parental relationships could all be associated with a greater likelihood of offending.

Laub and Sampson concluded as a result of their review of the Gluecks' earlier findings that 'family process variables' to do with the quality of attachments and inconsistency of supervision and discipline were closely associated with delinquent outcomes (Laub and Sampson, 1988: 375). They also argued that there were identifiable links between parental criminality, for instance, and family processes of supervision and discipline, suggesting an interactive effect between a number of factors. Thus, they conclude that: 'Parental deviance of both mother and father strongly disrupts family processes of parental control, which in turn increases delinquency' (Laub and Sampson, 1988: 375).

More recently, concern has built up over the link between 'Adverse Childhood Experiences' (ACEs) and a number of harmful longer-term outcomes for children, including delinquency. The ACE model was first developed by Felitti et al. (1998) to establish links between harmful childhood experiences, such as 'maltreatment' or family disruption, and later health problems. This approach has since been developed quite widely, and has been applied to the question of youth crime. Perez et al. (2018), for instance, carried out a substantial study of young people going through the justice system in Florida, concluding that there is a correlation between earlier adversity, such as physical or sexual abuse, or parental mental health problems, and 'serious, violent and chronic delinquency'. Similarly, Craig et al.'s (2017) application of the ACEs model to the cohort on which the Cambridge Study of Delinquency was based, found a similar correlation with subsequent delinquency, across the life course.

Brown and Stillington (2017) have also identified an association between ACEs, delinquency and substance use, although they also identify a connection between 'protective adult relationships' and reduced levels of drug taking. Although the ACEs model incorporates a range of elements, some of which are not necessarily within the control of parents or other family members, most of them are framed in such a way as to suggest failures of parental care or protection; in effect, then, their association with delinquency may be taken to imply that problems within the family have a causal effect as far as young people's subsequent offending is concerned. (See Chapter 8 for further discussion about the influence of the ACE model on current practice, and some of the critiques of this perspective.)

Peer influence

Other widely held theoretical and 'commonsense' social explanations of youth crime see it as a product of peer influence. Much of what is considered youthful offending or anti-social behaviour is carried out in groups, and this perhaps encourages the view that mutual influence of some kind is a possible causal factor. Sutherland's (1939) theory of 'differential association' was an early attempt to conceptualise the peer effect. At the core of Sutherland's argument was the idea that criminal behaviour is 'learned'. Learning processes are essentially social, and they are likely to have the most impact amongst groups which associate frequently and have some sort of positive relationship. Criminality is essentially contagious, in the sense that offenders are persuaded of the desirability of criminal activity by others who have already decided that it is justifiable, or that its benefits outweigh the disadvantages.

Among others, Matza (1969) developed the idea of peer influence, introducing the concepts of 'affinity' and 'affiliation' to explain the dynamic nature of young people's journey into crime, and the part played by involvement in friendship groups. Affinity represents the kind of predisposing factors which might lead an individual to inhabit a criminogenic environment such as, perhaps, a liking for staying out late. Affiliation represents the more immediate influences and choices which determine whether someone then goes on to get involved in criminal activity; in this case, perhaps, being associated with a group involved in opportunistic crimes – such as shoplifting or criminal damage.

Matza also appears to distinguish between the concept of 'contagion' and that of 'conversion' (Beyleveld and Wiles, 1975). The former is a more deterministic process, whereby simply associating with offenders is likely to lead to someone 'becoming deviant' (Matza, 1969). The latter, on the other hand, necessitates an active and conscious process of deciding to offend, in the context of persuasion or encouragement by others, and other relevant factors, such as risks, rewards and consequences associated with the intended offence. Importantly, here, Matza is trying to bridge the gap between determinism and choice, whereby the conditions for committing a crime may be externally driven, but the decision as to whether or not to go ahead with it is a matter of immediate choice, shaped by the dynamics within the peer group at the time.

The evidence in support of the thesis that peer influence is an important factor in delinquency is not straightforward (McGloin and Thomas, 2019). Statistical associations between individuals' offending and delinquent peer groups is not hard to find: 'scores of research findings have continued to affirm that associating with delinquent friends is a strong predictor of initiation, maintenance, frequency, **desistance**, and even the types of antisocial behaviors that individuals commit' (McGloin and Thomas, 2019: 247). The problem with research findings such as these is in determining causality, partly because, as McGloin and Thomas (2019: 253) identify, most evidence is drawn from 'observational data'. That is to say, the observation that groups of young people offend together may just be the effect of prior criminal tendencies and a 'selection' effect which means that they are more likely to associate simply because of these prior inclinations.

Communities and cultural influences

The idea of peer influence links with other suggested social causes of youth offending, grounded in community contexts, rather than just interpersonal relationships. Here, the idea of 'culture' is important, and there has been considerable attention paid to the question of how particular deviant groups and identities are established and sustained. As in the case of peer-based theories, cultural theories of delinquency became prominent in the USA in the 1930s. Wirth (1931: 488), for example, asserted that there may 'be communities in which delinquency is part of the cultural tradition'. Within such communities, he believed, criminality might become a way of life. Gangs might become established with traditions and 'moral codes' of their own.

Delinquency, though, might be the result of unresolved conflicts between one culture and another; so that, rather than originating in an established tradition, it might be viewed as the outcome of clashes between competing lifestyles and norms. This may arise because of friction between the expectations of different groups within society, or in some cases because the group itself is deliberately established in opposition to 'the larger society' (Wirth, 1931: 491), as in the case of 'criminal gangs'. Cohen's (1955) influential study of 'delinquent boys' in Chicago developed this line of thought further, in pursuing cultural (or subcultural) explanations of gang formation and activity. Like much of criminology, Cohen's preoccupation was with male delinquency, and so there is an inevitable missing dimension to his analysis in terms of the question of whether cultural theories can also be applied in the same way to girls or young women.

Cohen has also been criticised subsequently for his assumption that delinquency is essentially a working-class phenomenon, and that gang culture itself is based on disaffection and rejection of middle-class norms and lifestyles which are inaccessible to the young people involved. Delinquent subculture was therefore a peer-based solution to a commonly experienced problem of social exclusion and rejection. The gang does, however, according to Cohen, provide alternative means of achieving status and power, thus providing a means towards self-expression and fulfilment. Here, Cohen was also influenced by the ideas of Robert Merton (1957) concerning anomie and the alternative means and ends to self-realisation likely to be adopted by those unable to achieve conventional markers of success and status by established routes.

Theories of delinquent subcultures and gang membership encounter problems when trying to make sense of the apparent ethnic variations in gang membership, and what factors might be associated with these. Some have tried to explain gang involvement in terms of 'multiple marginalities' (Freng and Esbensen, 2007), with the implication that cultural differences may not be so much a cause of delinquency but emerge as part of a wider response to experiences of exclusion, marginalisation and systemic discrimination (Wacquant, 2009).

Structural factors

Here, then, we are moving from what might be termed 'cultural' explanations of youth crime to those which attribute its emergence to structural factors. These can be viewed in terms of the material deprivations (poverty and homelessness, for example) which may motivate potential offenders to commit property crimes (such as theft, burglary or robbery) for money; or as the consequence of systematic patterns of exclusion, of which material disadvantage might only play a part – the process of 'othering', in Garland's (2001) terms.

Criminological concepts such as 'labelling' (Becker, 1963) and 'secondary deviance' (Lemert, 1951) articulate the mechanisms by which certain children or young people are made the subject of concern (both formally and informally), as well as processes of problematisation, which firstly identify them as potential offenders, and then through targeting them in this way, actually prompt them to (re-)offend, and accept a 'deviant identity'. Goldson and

Jamieson (2002) identify a twin-track process, whereby the impoverished material circumstances of children's families lead to both a greater likelihood of certain types of behaviour, and a response from the institutions of the state which targets these families and children and criminalises them disproportionately. As McAra and McVie (2007) have found, for example, once children become identified as offenders they are more likely to experience subsequent police and criminal justice involvement than their peers, even though their rate of offending may continue to be quite similar.

Barkan and Rocque (2018) suggest that socio-economic status and racism can be identified as 'fundamental causes' of delinquency. By this they mean that these factors have multiple consequences, working through a range of intermediate mechanisms (such as being singled out as problematic at school) (see Chapter 9 for a further discussion) to generate a higher likelihood of someone becoming involved in the criminal justice system. These mechanisms are complex and they interact in a variety of ways. Intermediate factors such as family stress and neighbourhood decline can be identified as both consequences of poverty and as helping to create the conditions under which young people are likely to turn to crime.

Researching Young People and Crime

> The Peterborough Adolescent and Young Adult Development Study (PADS+) is a prospective longitudinal study that has followed a random sample of 716 young people, who were 12 years old and living in the UK city of Peterborough and nearby villages, through adolescence into young adulthood. An initial interview was conducted with participants' parents to collect in-depth data about their families' social situations at the time of their enrolment and retrospective information on their childhood experiences and critical life events from birth. (www.cac.crim.cam.ac.uk/research/padspres)

This study is of particular interest because it did not pre-select young people as offenders or 'at risk', so there were no in-built assumptions about their level of involvement with crime. It also tried to relate individual patterns of offending to social and contextual factors, which might be helpful in making links between personal choices and wider influences.

You can read more about the study here: www.cac.crim.cam.ac.uk/research/padspres

What sort of questions might you want to ask young people taking part in this study?

There has been considerable debate, for example, about the relationship between White domination in many (particularly late-capitalist Western) societies, and the direct and indirect effects of social exclusion and racial discrimination on Black and minority ethnic communities. Much of this debate can be related to 'strain theory', and the tensions between aspirations and opportunity (Merton, 1957; Agnew, 1985; Gould, 1999). According to strain theory, deviance from expected or conformist forms of social behaviour might be prompted by the denial of legitimate opportunities to achieve socially desirable goals or economic success. Certain types of acquisitive crime might well be explicable in this way, and young people's involvement in the '**county lines**' drug distribution networks might be seen as a good example of this.

However, whilst it properly recognises young people's capacity to exercise agency and make choices (good or bad), this analysis seems to underplay the systemic effects of impoverishment, exploitation and embedded forms of discrimination. Alongside those forms of behaviour which might be termed 'adaptation', we should perhaps also consider the possibility that active forms of resistance in response to these forces may or may not be 'transgressive' (Anderson, 1999; Agnew, 2016). Equally, as Agnew (2016) points out in his detailed review of the relevant evidence, 'Race and Youth Crime. Why Isn't the Relationship Stronger?', the relationship between structural factors and specific forms of behaviour (illegal or not) must be understood in context, and in terms of the dynamic influences at play. As Agnew implies, a straightforward causal connection between structural disadvantage and crime would generate a much greater number of minority ethnic offenders than appears to be the case. This in turn suggests that the over-representation of ethnic minority young people in the criminal justice system represents the culmination of discriminatory practices and institutional racism. (See Chapter 8 for a further discussion of the over-representation of young people from ethnic minorities in youth justice systems in different countries.)

In this section, we have considered the possible influence of social factors on young people's offending, recognising that the interplay between circumstances and choice is important. The decision to offend may be shaped by a range of influences within the social environment, which may create the conditions within which this becomes more acceptable, or even necessary from the young person's perspective. We have also recognised that agencies and institutions themselves may play a part in criminalising young people, on grounds of ethnicity, for example. Social factors are less helpful, though, in helping us to determine exactly which individual will offend at which point in time.

Global Perspectives

Attention to structural factors and questions of diversity also leads us to reflect on the perspectives from which we try to make sense of young people's behaviour, and those aspects of it we find unacceptable. Much of the analysis and evidence available to us is drawn from the experience of industrialised capitalist societies; and this may lead to an overemphasis on, say, the forms of adolescence which have emerged with the development of this type of society. The rapid growth of the youth market for consumer goods, for example, is a phenomenon closely linked with post-Second World War affluence and is both historically and geographically limited. Not all young people's lives and experiences are remotely similar to this; and so there is a strong case, here, for broadening our theory base, and looking more widely than perhaps has previously been the case for youth criminologies which are capable of making sense in every context.

Carrington and Hogg (2017: 183) argue, for example, that strain theory (see above) is a clear example of partial thinking, seeking to generalise from a very specific context:

> This kind of universalising is symptomatic of western-centric or metropolitan thinking. Strain theory is inherently based on a data-driven methodological individualism that is distinctively North American .... The assumption that strain applies to 'the collectivistic orientation that characterizes many Asian societies' ... many of whose values of family and sociality are historically rooted in Confucian traditions is a quintessential piece of metropolitan thinking.

Here, the authors are asking why we should assume that the individualism which characterises Western societies under market capitalism should apply in other societies with different traditions, ways of organising and social relationships.

Acknowledging their own status as 'trespassers' (Macdonald and King, 2021), also question the apparent dominance of 'Northern' theoretical traditions at the expense of a wider understanding drawing on indigenous insights and expertise. They do not argue simply for the substitution of one set of concepts for another, or that ideas such as 'inequality' are not transferable or equally applicable in different settings. Indeed, for them, there is much common theoretical ground, in the sense that youth policy and state practices can be understood in terms of political economy, across national boundaries and global divides (a theme that will be explored in further depth in Chapter 4). Here, marginalisation, gender-based oppression, insecure education and employment, and violence appear to be common features of young people's lives (Macdonald and King, 2021: 294). Cavalcanti's (2020) account of violence and young people in Brazil, for example, offers a clear critique of theories which simply problematise youth when police and state violence is rife. 'Crime control' merely becomes a vehicle for outright repression in the circumstances she documents.

Abdullahi et al. (2016) have similarly sought to develop a contextualised analysis of youth violence, which they describe as 'rampant', in the Nigerian district of Ilorin. They draw on and integrate established theoretical traditions such as 'relative deprivation theory', 'social disorganisation theory' and 'broken windows theory', in order to link what they view as endemic forms of violence to structural factors such as poverty and social disorganisation:

> what usually inspired violence among youth has to do with poverty, economic frustration, insufficient infrastructure, political disagreement, and failure of government to punish the previous perpetrators of violence. Thus, [our] proposed model suggests urban renewal, poverty reduction strategies, slum upgrading programmes and promotion of social capital and cohesion in the neighbourhoods as a sustainable measure to ensuring peace and tranquillity in the neighbourhoods that are socially disadvantaged. (Abdullahi et al., 2016: 55)

In a rather different context, Williams and Kamaludeen (2017) consider the question of how to understand the emergence of 'hijabistas' and 'hijabsters' amongst Southeast Asian young women. As the authors observe, this particular issue has typically fallen outside conventional criminological concerns with the behaviours of young men who become involved in violent or organised crime. However, it is an example of 'non-conforming' activity or representation which is viewed as problematic amongst essentially conservative societies, where indications of cultural difference and individual self-expression may be viewed as a form of resistance or challenge. The authors cite the example of 65 young people in Indonesia being arrested on suspicion of being 'punks' in 2011 and assigned for 'reeducation' (Williams and Kamaludeen, 2017: 203).

In Singapore, where wearing the hijab is discouraged or prohibited in certain settings, the trend amongst young women to adopt its use as a form of fashion statement ('hijabistas') or to indicate independence of thought ('hijabsters') has drawn a response from conservative state agencies. Wearers of the hijab have been discriminated against, and there is a fear that they will be blacklisted by potential employers (Williams and Kamaludeen, 2017: 208). Here, then, there is a distinctive theoretical challenge in seeking to explain how a form of 'conformity' to the mainstream religion of a society itself might result in a process of exclusion, and, at the extreme, criminalisation (Williams and Kamaludeen, 2017: 210). Williams and Kamaludeen draw parallels with other work, which similarly poses important challenges to our attempts to provide neat explanations or simple pathologies of young people's (young women's) behaviours which, as in this case, appear simultaneously to challenge and yet reinforce dominant social norms, often in ways which are not articulated consistently by young people themselves.

Mendoza-Denton's account of Latina gang members and their eclectic constructions of individual and group identity appear to encompass some of the same paradoxical elements. The gang members' 'macha' identity seeks to interweave their own ideas of female strength with more conventional understandings of toughness and self-reliance (Mendoza-Denton, 2008). Gang membership is part of, but not the entirety of, that apparently deviant identity. Although this example is taken from North America, it does also help to illustrate the potential limitations of singular 'Western' explanations of young people's apparently deviant choices, how they are motivated, and how their behaviours are seen from the outside.

As Cooper et al. (2019: 41) put it:

> in the current conjuncture of economic instability it may be the global South, places where people have for centuries learnt to adapt and hustle in adversity, that generates useful insight into 'ways of being' for the world at large.

A Complex Picture – Making Sense of Alternative Explanations of Youth Crime

As we have seen in the preceding sections, the various suggested causes of offending by young people are wide-ranging and of very different characters. This may partly be attributable to the significant differences, too, in behaviours which come under the heading of 'crimes' – such as property offences, violence, so-called victimless crimes such as drug-taking, or bullying and abuse. Nonetheless, there have been several attempts to try to account for the interaction between factors and between the explanatory domains we have considered – biological, psychological and social.

The extensive work of David Farrington has contributed to detailed classifications of the factors associated with youth crime (for example, West and Farrington, 1973; Farrington, 1995; Farrington and Welsh, 2007). This work originated with the Cambridge Study in Delinquent Development (West, 1969), which followed 400 boys from six state primary schools in London from the age of 8. This was, in fact, one of a number of such studies which have sought to enumerate the factors associated with delinquency; others which have gained particular attention include the Rochester Youth Development Study (Thornberry et al., 2003), the Pittsburgh Youth Study (for example, Loeber et al., 2012) and Wikstrom's youth studies based in Stockholm and Peterborough (see, for example, Wikstrom and Svensson, 2008

Farrington and Welsh (2007) draw on a number of these studies to summarise the factors they identify as contributing to youth crime. They distinguish between 'individual', 'family' and 'socioeconomic, peer, school and community factors', arguing that taken together these can effectively establish a more or less fixed propensity for some people to be more likely to offend than others: 'Long-term criminal potential is likely to be influenced by biological, individual, family, peer, school, community and societal factors' (Farrington and Welsh, 2007: 38). On the other hand, as they acknowledge, 'short-term' influences might include specific situational factors, such as 'getting drunk' or seeing a relatively easy opportunity to profit from an offence. Predisposing factors such as 'low intelligence or impulsiveness' may reflect 'executive functioning deficits in the brain', they suggest (p. 54), but these must be viewed alongside family factors such as poor supervision or family disruption (p. 75), as well as wider social influences, such as deprivation, disadvantaged neighbourhoods or delinquent peer groups (p. 88).

As we have seen previously, there are many accounts of possible connections between aspects of young people's upbringing or their characteristics which are linked with delinquency, but relatively few of these attempt to provide an integrated analysis, in the way that Thornberry (1987) has, for example. Thornberry's argument is that there is an inevitable interaction between different factors, including delinquent behaviour itself, which both predispose certain young people to offending, and also tend to sustain this behaviour, to a greater or lesser degree. More recent studies, too, such as Wikstrom et al.'s (2018) analysis of the interplay between 'situational' and predisposing factors, have sought to develop this kind of interactive analysis.

Despite this, the precise nature of the relationship between different, incomplete ('why don't all children from disrupted families offend?', for example) and sometimes competing causal explanations of youth crime ('innate predispositions vs neighbourhood disadvantage, for instance), remains unclear, as Farrington and Welsh (2007: 89) recognise: 'It is very difficult to disentangle all these interrelationships and draw conclusions about which risk factors are causal'. In fact, they rather sidestep the question of causality, suggesting that for those concerned with preventing or responding to youth offending, 'in the present state of knowledge, it is reasonable to target all these types of risk factors in early prevention programmes'. There is, nonetheless, a risk of blurring the important distinction between identifying an association between certain characteristics or circumstances and offending, and attributing causal power to these.

The Causes of Crime in the Words of Young People

Before concluding this discussion, it will also be helpful to consider the explanatory accounts offered by young people themselves. What are the influences on their actions that they see as being important? What do they think encourages them or stops them from breaking the law?

A number of studies have sought to see the world from the viewpoint of young people identified as actual or potential delinquents. Howard Parker's (1974) in-depth study of young people in Liverpool has been seen as particularly significant because of its approach, based on participant observation, and because it represents his participants, 'the Boys', as: 'subjects and as "natural" people in their own normal social world' (Parker, 1974: 9). Here, then, the focus shifts from the attributes of the young people concerned to their perceptions, the sense they make of the world around them, and the agency they exercise in making choices, some of which involve breaking the law. Their views of an education system which has failed them are thus accepted as valid, and their choices of occupation and leisure activity are grounded in their perceptions of what is desirable and achievable. Their decision to establish an illicit business trading in stolen car radios is thus presented as a rational and in some ways quite conventional choice, given their own goals and the range of opportunities available. In this sense, Parker's analysis contrasts with deterministic explanations of youth crime, since their activities seem to be grounded in a considered assessment of the costs and benefits of crime. The 'Boys have nothing to lose from deviating .... The evidence is before their eyes – they are dispensable, there are no decent jobs and no prospects of a secure future' (Parker, 1974: 208).

John Pitts (2008) provides another insight into the kind of choices young people make about whether or not to get involved in crime in his discussion of 'reluctant gangsters'. For some, the options appear to be limited to taking part in gang activity or suffering the consequences of staying outside, and forfeiting the protections offered by membership. In this sense, choosing to take part represents the same kind of choice as deciding whether or not to take out insurance. Similar motivations are recounted in another study, this time by a young woman:

> You're in a gang, the gang becomes your family and there's a range of things you've got to do in a gang to move up, which could involve robbing; it could involve drugs, selling drugs for someone; it could involve as well, if you're going to be in our gang, you're going to prove it. You've got to go and stab her or stab him. (quoted in Cleghorn et al., 2011: 18)

In another example cited in the same study, a young woman's decision to steal clothes from a supermarket can be understood as a consequence of her being thrown out of her home by her father. However, it could also be explained by a history of family disruption, educational difficulties and social exclusion (Cleghorn et al., 2011: 19). Others in this study described crime as 'glamorous', or simply an expected feature of 'everyday life' (p. 20). In such circumstances, crime becomes unexceptional and simply a matter of the contingent choices that young people might make at any given point in time.

Importantly, this type of account, reflecting young people's own stories, sheds a different light on our understanding of causality, in the sense that the many factors associated with crime considered earlier do not appear to negate the importance of agency and subjective perceptions. This, of course, links to broader debates about determinism and free will, which themselves remain unresolved. Understanding youth crime, though, as with many other social phenomena, at least partly depends on the initial assumptions we hold about how far young people's actions are shaped by factors they cannot control (such as hormonal changes); or whether they retain the capacity to make free and rational choices about what to do in which situations. Some theorists, such as Bourdieu, have sought to provide integrated models which seek to locate choice contextually, so as to offer at least a basis for both to apply (Bourdieu, 1990; Fraser, 2013; Shammas and Sandberg, 2016). Fraser's study of youth 'gangs' in Glasgow, for example, seeks to develop this kind of framework, to illustrate the importance of context and place in shaping the manner in which young people express themselves and develop a distinctive sense of identity and culture:

> In constructing Langview as a geographically delimited area, young people are simultaneously creating a boundary within which local status and identity can be carved out; a physical and symbolic staging ground for experimentation, boundary-testing and edgework. Filtered through the prism of local forms of 'tough' masculinity, the border becomes a space in which to test individual and collective mettle. (Fraser, 2013: 982).

Conclusion

In conclusion, then, we cannot claim to have resolved the question of how to explain offending by young people. Here, we have considered a number of different frameworks within which possible explanations for young people's involvement in crime are offered. Some accounts seek individual causes, drawing on developmental, physiological and neurological analyses; whilst others look for the causes of youth crime in the social environment. Most explanations now seem to acknowledge that these factors are interlinked, and that it makes more sense to consider, and try to account for, the inter-relationships between them. Other accounts, too, note the uneven and possibly discriminatory impact of involvement with the criminal justice system and the power of labelling; indeed, it is important to remember that what is considered to be a crime varies across time and place and that accounts of 'criminality' are also reflections of this.

Therefore it is important to think in terms of complexity, and the need to incorporate alternative explanatory frameworks, not least to help us understand the many different types of behaviour which fall under the single heading of 'youth crime'.

Further Reading

Pitts, J. (2008) *Reluctant Gangsters.* London: Routledge.

This is a very readable and well-grounded analysis of the factors involved in young people's decisions as to whether or not to become involved in gang activity, making clear the considerable importance of the social context of individual choices.

Buffone, S. (2012) 'Towards an Integrative Theory of Crime and Delinquency: Reconceptualizing the Farrington Theory', *International Journal of Criminology and Sociological Theory,* 5, 2: 895–911.

An article which introduces the significant body of work of David Farrington on the factors associated with youth offending, whilst also offering a critical analysis, suggesting that an 'integrated' approach is required if we are to explain the phenomenon effectively.

3

Responses to Youth Offending

Objectives

- This chapter will explore the ideas and principles which inform different approaches to intervention with young people in the criminal justice system.
- The chapter will introduce and discuss longstanding debates between 'welfare'- and 'justice'-based responses to youth crime.
- We will also review more recently developed models of practice, such as diversion and restorative justice.

Introduction

Our starting point in this chapter relates to the aims and objectives of the agencies and services which are responsible for responding to the crimes committed by young people, and for which they are 'brought to justice'. Reflecting wider debates within criminal justice, interventions may be informed by a range of criminological theories and ideological perspectives. These apply across the range of criminal behaviour and at all ages, but they are usually modified in the case of children and young people. So, we can expect that there will be arguments for approaches and interventions tailored to young people, based on the principles outlined in the Box below:

Different Aims and Objectives of Youth Justice

- 'Just deserts' – the idea that offenders should simply 'pay the price' for their crimes;
- Deterrence – punishment should be sufficient to discourage further offences;

- Developing a sense of responsibility – offenders should be encouraged to accept their obligations towards society;
- Reform or behavioural change – interventions should be designed to directly influence the offender's actions for the better;
- Addressing 'criminogenic needs' – contextual factors contributing to offending should be addressed;
- Reintegration and personal development – offenders should be helped to reintegrate into their communities; or
- Offence resolution and problem-solving – resolving the problems associated with the specific offence should be the principal focus of intervention.

Some of these objectives align quite closely with the models of practice which apply in the context of the adult criminal justice system; whilst others, notably those which are oriented towards development and meeting welfare needs, do not necessarily have a direct adult equivalent. However, even those with adult equivalents, such as forms of custody, tend to be modified in their construction and regimes to account for the specific characteristics associated with children and young people, such as their educational and developmental needs.

We can see already, then, that youth justice is an area of practice characterised by diversity and an obvious lack of agreement as to what its core purposes and functions ought to be. It is unsurprising, then, that we should find alternative and often competing 'models' in existence at different points in time, and in different places.

Of course, any of these are unlikely to be found operating in what might be called their 'pure' form. Muncie (2002: 156), for example, has argued that youth justice in England and Wales in the early years of the 21st century could be seen as 'an amalgam' of at least six different strands of ideology and operational logic, namely: just deserts; risk assessment; managerialism; community responsibilisation; authoritarian populism; and restorative justice. These are very different and sometimes incompatible objectives.

In Muncie's view, the youth justice system effectively amounts to a composite stew of different expectations, legal requirements, professional standards and political pressures with conflict and contradiction embedded at its heart (Smith, 2011: 88). This is an important observation, and in what follows it is necessary to accept that whichever 'model' of youth justice might dominate at any particular point in time, it is unlikely to appear in its pure form. It will undoubtedly be flavoured or modified by other influences. Perhaps it is best to think of youth justice in practice as a hybrid, inevitably incorporating a range of differing and often competing ideas and operating principles. Despite this qualification, much of the available analysis of the development of youth justice, both historically and internationally, tends to represent it in terms of discernible phases, or contrasting practices across national or jurisdictional boundaries.

The History of Youth Justice and 'Periodisation'

Histories of youth justice have typically attempted to identify distinctive 'periods', represented by particular understandings of young people and crime. These, in turn, have tended to translate into specific approaches to dealing with young offenders. As noted in Chapter 1, before the 19th century, there was little differentiation between adult and child criminals, with both subject to a similar range of penalties, often particularly harsh by contemporary standards. This appears to have reflected a wider set of beliefs, in which children were viewed as 'mini-adults' (Ariès, 1962), and there was very little in the way of social differentiation according to age.

With industrialisation and the social and economic changes that followed, childhood became more explicitly recognised as a distinctive life stage, as attention became more closely focused on how to prepare a more diverse workforce for the demands of a changing economy (Hendrick, 1994). With this change of focus, reformers and political interests began to recognise, and sought to address, the problems which children experienced, and their offending began to be viewed in the context of widespread poverty, disadvantage and social dislocation. The recognition of children's vulnerability sat alongside a desire to see that they were suitably 'socialised' and prepared for the changing requirements of the labour market. We might therefore see this as a period in which 'reform' was the predominant objective of the early youth justice system, reflected in the emergence of correctional institutions with a strong educational flavour.

By the early 20th century, there had been a growth in academic interest in childhood and youth, and 'adolescence' became a distinct subject of interest and analysis. Hall (1904), in particular, believed that adolescence was a time of 'storm and stress', where biological, social and psychological influences combined to generate a state of anxiety and the risk of unstable behaviour. This shift of focus towards young people's mental state led to an interest in the adoption of psychologically-oriented methods of intervention which sought to influence and change the behaviour of offenders, although, as others have acknowledged, there remained some ambiguity in the legal framework. The introduction of the *Children Act 1908* in the United Kingdom could be seen as a continuing source of 'ambivalence' (Gelsthorpe and Morris, 1994: 951), with children simultaneously viewed as *innocent* and deserving of care and support, and *dangerous* and requiring punishment and control.

Subsequent reforms appeared to emphasise the importance of welfare-based interventions to reduce levels of disadvantage and enhance children's life chances, thereby promoting positive integration into society and reducing the risk of anti-social behaviour. The *Children Act 1948* introduced a range of such welfare measures and provided a new workforce (children's officers) to offer additional assistance and guidance to children and families. In parallel, though, the *Criminal Justice Act 1948* introduced detention centres for those aged 14–20, specifically as a deterrent. These two pieces of legislation, introduced in the same year highlight the recurrent tension between 'welfare' and 'justice' models of intervention, evident in many of the continuing debates about how children and young people who break the law should be treated, and which approach is likely to be more successful in ensuring positive law-abiding outcomes.

In England and Wales, it is commonly thought that the period up to and including the 1970s was 'the age of welfare', when both practice and policy became increasingly geared towards a needs-led approach to services for children, including those who had offended. By the 1960s, for example, a number of key policy documents (e.g., Home Office, 1968) envisaged the eventual decriminalisation of young offenders, and the *Children and Young Persons Act 1969* in fact made provision for a much-reduced role for the courts in dispensing youth justice. A change of government in 1970 meant that this legislation was never fully implemented, however, and this has come to be seen as the high-water mark for welfarism.

By the end of the 1970s, there seemed to be a renewed emphasis on holding young people to account for their behaviour ('deeds' not 'needs'), and the government gave substance to this with the introduction of the 'short, sharp shock' detention centre regime in 1980. The emphasis was very much on effective punishment and deterrence, rather than meeting children's needs, although in practice a combination of factors (progressive local practice, government funding cuts and extensive alternative-to-custody programmes) led to a reduction in the number of children and young people being prosecuted and incarcerated during the 1980s.

Since that point, there have been a number of characterisations of the dominant trends in youth justice – the 1980s were the 'decade of diversion', the 1990s witnessed the 'punitive turn', and since the mid-2000s we have observed a period of shrinking state involvement and retrenchment. Clearly, by representing the history of youth justice in this way, we can arguably identify fairly clearly critical points at which the core features and functions of the 'system' appear to herald a change of direction, sometimes apparently quite dramatic (Case and Smith, 2021). On the other hand, some authors suggest that there may be underlying trends and continuities which suggest a more linear sense of historical development and change.

Welfare and Justice – A Persistent Tension?

Hazel (2008: 6), among others, has argued that essentially the patterns of change and conflict between perspectives in youth justice can be reduced to a continuing struggle between proponents of welfare- or justice-led approaches to intervention:

> The most established differentiation between systems of youth justice around the world is that of welfare versus justice. Arguably, every other model that has been developed in the literature can be traced back to variations of these two basic types of approach. *The welfare approach* emphasises paternalism and protection, and has resulted in treatment rather than formal justice and punishment. *The justice approach* emphasises ideas of judicial rights and accountability for crimes, favouring formal justice and proportionality in sentencing [our emphasis].

In the Box above Hazel (2008) refers to models of youth justice identified from 'around the world', and therefore his claim is pretty substantial – in effect, that all youth justice systems everywhere can be reduced in essence to one of these two models, irrespective of social, economic or cultural differences, or the influences of local history and belief systems.

So, to what extent should we be ready to question this assertion?

Making International Comparisons – The Challenges of Comparing Models of Youth Justice

To support his argument, Hazel (2008) draws on an extensive analysis of youth justice systems, drawing on evidence from 93 countries. He helpfully distinguishes between what he describes as 'overall approaches' (reflected in principles, objectives and policy frameworks), 'structures and procedures' (legislative and organisational arrangements and procedures), and 'interventions' (practice realities). These are important distinctions as we shall see, and may well create real difficulties of understanding, if we too readily assume that a particular government policy is always faithfully reflected in the management and delivery of practice 'on the ground'.

Hazel also draws attention to some of the significant challenges in trying to draw parallels between different 'systems', whether in youth justice or any other area of practice, across national boundaries (see Chapter 4 for a further discussion of the challenges of comparison). Firstly, he notes the problem of actually obtaining good-quality relevant data. Each country is likely to have different tools for data collection, different methods of classification, and different frameworks for recording and analysis. Even core definitions of crime and criminality may differ. As we know, for example, in many countries an offence committed by a child under the age of 14 would not even be treated as a criminal matter, unlike the countries of the United Kingdom and a relatively small number of others, such as Thailand (where, in 2021, the age of criminal responsibility is 7) and Singapore (where moves have been made to raise the age of criminal responsibility from 7, but only to 10).

In addition, Hazel (2008: 15) points out that it may be problematic to define the appropriate geographical boundaries that apply between youth justice jurisdictions. Whereas some countries operate systems with quite centralised legislative and judicial frameworks (as in England and Wales, for example), others operate on a much more diffuse basis, with the national provisions merely establishing the outlines within which more local bodies have a great deal of autonomy (as in federal states such as Canada and the United States). Even where there is a considerable degree of centralisation, studies have consistently demonstrated substantial variation at the local level, whether in terms of the 'models' of practice in operation (Smith and Gray, 2019), or the considerable geographical divergences in terms of processes and outcomes (Bateman, 2020).

It is also important to consider the extent to which the same measure or form of practice would operate in an equivalent fashion if transferred from one national and cultural context to another. Thus, for instance, restorative justice as an idea and model of practice derives substantially from the experiences and belief systems of First Nations peoples in New Zealand and Canada. How forms of intervention such as Family Group Conferences (New Zealand/Aotearoa) or Healing Circles (Canada) might translate into more formalised adversarial justice systems is very much open to question. As Hazel (2008: 15) stresses, just because something 'works' in one setting, with all the local supporting beliefs and traditions behind it, we cannot make simplistic assumptions about its transferability or likelihood of success in a completely different environment.

A further cautionary note as far as international comparisons are concerned is to do with the horizontal or 'snapshot' character of many attempts in youth justice and other areas of practice to reach definitive conclusions about the nature of the system in any particular geographical setting. That is to say, comparative analyses usually only have the capacity to gather evidence at a particular point in time and are less able to identify trends or to account for changes in any particular system. Significant shifts in practice and underlying objectives may therefore not be easily picked up.

At the same time, it may be difficult for this kind of 'one-off' exercise to account for nuances, or aspects of national practices which are in a state of flux and perhaps disagreement, such as the nature and use of restorative approaches in Japan. Suzuki and Otani (2017), for example, argue that there are grounds for thinking that reforms to the country's *Juvenile Act* in 2000 represented a move away from approaches grounded in ideas of reconciliation and towards a harsher more punitive model of youth justice. Comparisons between national systems therefore need to take account of the capacity for change, and where possible to identify trends and inconsistencies rather than assuming that each system is fixed and entirely coherent.

Frameworks for Comparative Analysis in Youth Justice

Despite the above concerns about the limitations of drawing comparisons between youth justice systems, there is arguably still value in trying to understand the core features of different models. In order to be able to do so, it may be useful to think about the different dimensions or phases of youth justice delivery so as to help us to build up a detailed picture of each system we consider. Hazel (2008) offers one such framework, comprising the following elements:

- System models and key principles;
- The age threshold within systems;
- Prevention and early intervention;
- Investigations and decision-making processes; and
- Outcomes and disposals.

Based on an assessment of international youth justice systems using these criteria, Hazel argues that there are clearly different 'models' in place around the world (Hazel, 2008: 6), but he also accepts that these should only be seen as 'ideal types', which are not found to be reproduced directly in implementation. They should be seen rather as 'philosophical' perspectives, or alternatively as patterns of service organisation and intervention which have built up over time as conventional practices become established as the norm.

On a more practical note, Hazel argues that youth justice systems can fairly readily be differentiated on the basis of the age thresholds they set, both at the lower and higher ends of the range to which they apply. He also claims that these age differentials typically translate into differing approaches to the processing of young people reported to have offended; specialised mechanisms for dealing with their offences; and sentencing options tailored to their particular characteristics, such as their presumed lack of maturity and vulnerability.

Prevention and early intervention is also identified as an area where different approaches may be observed. Hazel (2008: 7) suggests that the distinction between early intervention and prevention itself indicates varying concerns.

Children's welfare is seen as the primary consideration if the language of early intervention tends to dominate; whereas preventive strategies are associated with a focus on 'risk' and a perceived need to target those most likely to become offenders.

In relation to the investigative and decision-making phases of youth justice processes, variations may include the presence of specialist police officers, provisions for alternative 'out of court' decision-making forums, more or less active mechanisms for diverting children and young people from formal settings such as the court, and more informal approaches at all levels of the judicial process.

Outcomes and disposals are also an important point of comparison, Hazel observes. There are very wide international variations in the use of custody, for example, which might well be seen as a critical factor in estimating how 'punitive' any particular jurisdiction might be. (However, the limitations of using custodial rates as a measure of comparison are discussed further in the following chapter, Chapter 4.) Similarly, alternative models of disposal might include a range of restorative, educational or welfare-oriented options, which could be taken to suggest a greater willingness to consider children's well-being as the principal objective of the judicial process in its dealings with young offenders.

Thus, Hazel's approach seeks to identify particular characteristics of youth justice systems in operation, and from the picture that emerges to determine where they might fit on the continuum between 'welfare' and 'justice' models. Other efforts to develop a typology of youth justice systems have tended to take the reverse approach, and develop a conceptual framework around a particular 'model', or 'ideal type' in Hazel's terms; and then attempt to identify and locate specific policies, structures and practices associated with that model. Certain countries and jurisdictions can then be associated with each of these according to our knowledge of their systems in operation.

Winterdyk (2015: 6), for example, sets out a six-fold typology, drawing on observations from 19 countries, which he has suggested could be viewed as falling at different points along a rather different continuum, running from the least to the most punitive, as follows:

- Participatory;
- Welfare;
- Corporatism;
- Modified justice;
- Justice; and
- Crime control.

These models, Winterdyk argues, can be differentiated according to a number of features, including key agencies and professional interests, practitioner roles and tasks, the predominant understanding of young people's behaviour, the purposes of interventions and the overall objectives of the system. Winterdyk goes on to suggest that particular jurisdictions can be identified with each of these models, from participatory approaches in Japan to crime-control-led systems in the United States and Hungary.

McAra (2010: 287) has been critical of attempts to oversimplify variations in youth justice practice, suggesting that it is important to recognise the 'myriad principles shaping both policy discourse in contemporary western societies [not to mention other national contexts] and the core imperatives that underpin international conventions'. Thus, for example, a 'justice' model in and of itself is neither punitive nor lenient. It simply represents an offence-based model of practice, based on ideas of due process, fairness and proportionality in sentencing, which can be more or less severe. This implies that we should be careful about making simplistic assumptions about where particular models sit on a continuum; and McAra also recognises that there is likely to be some deviation from the stated principles and overarching goals of any particular system when these are put into practice.

Despite these reservations, McAra (2010: 288) does suggest that four 'paradigms ... arguably, have come to dominate youth justice discourse: just deserts; welfare; restoration; and "actuarialism" [risk-based]. Each of these offers a different solution to the problem of balancing the needs of the vulnerable offender with the needs of society', and each tends to reflect wider social arrangements and systems of belief. McAra locates the source of these variations in the prevailing form of social relations, beliefs about 'personhood', and models of intervention actually in place. Thus, for example, our perceptions of children and childhood, and the extent to which children can be viewed as responsible for their actions, are crucial to the thinking behind different ways of responding to their criminal behaviour. To what extent do we believe that they should be held to blame for their actions, is the underlying question here.

In an influential comparative study Cavadino and Dignan (2006a, b) observe that there is a close relationship between a country's youth justice system and their wider institutional structures. In their comparative analysis, they argue that four distinct models of social organisation can be identified amongst the countries whose youth justice systems they investigated: neoliberal, conservative corporatist, social democratic, and oriental corporatist. The links between youth justice and the wider political and institutional structures are discussed further in Chapter 4.

There is a level of agreement amongst these commentators that there is potential value in seeking to differentiate youth justice systems and practices by way of some sort of typology. This usually involves classifying systems according to particular features, such as their principal objectives, operating principles and the allocation of agency responsibilities. The place and status afforded to particular 'experts', for instance, may well be indicative of the broader character of a particular system. Where social workers hold a prominent role, it seems likely that the model in place might well be geared towards welfare-based interventions. Drawing on this way of making sense of youth justice systems, we may therefore be able to get an idea about how these play out in different settings, both across national boundaries, and within individual jurisdictions

'Top Down' or 'Bottom Up'?

We turn now to consider one of the other challenges we face when trying to determine the material reality of youth justice. That is to say, what is the relationship between the 'system' as it is designed and organised, and the practices and experiences which represent the way it is enacted 'on the ground'? Phoenix (2016), for example, has been quite critical of theoretical accounts which, she believes, do not accurately represent the messy realities of practice:

> current theoretical models tend to reduce the diversity and complexity of what is done as well as render irrelevant what is said about what is being done (i.e., the connection between deeds and words). (Phoenix, 2016: 124)

Typologies based on national-level analyses may therefore be liable to oversimplification, because they tend to rely on 'official' accounts and reports, and publicly stated policy and legislative arrangements. Hence, for example, Suzuki and Otani (2017) argue that the suggestion that youth justice in Japan is largely based on restorative principles is misleading and does not sufficiently acknowledge the punitive aspects of intervention with young offenders.

Armitage and colleagues have explored this tension between formal structures and requirements, on the one hand, and the day-to-day experiences and adaptations of practitioners, on the other (Armitage et al., 2016). These every day realities may well reflect a very different 'system' to that which might be expected if we were simply to take at face value the claims made in formal documentation, legal frameworks and public representations. There is a clear tension, in Armitage et al.'s view, between the expectations placed on services and practitioners by managers and policy-makers, and the challenges faced by practitioners in getting the job done:

> This recognition demands a more nuanced understanding of 'practitioner discretion' which can account for differences between 'managerial' and frontline' experiences, and a broader definition of the youth justice field and associated actors than recent youth justice scholarship has commonly suggested. (Armitage et al., 2016: 480)

This study found, if anything, that centralised expectations and oversight were being loosened, and locally-based managers and youth justice agencies felt that they were able to exercise increasing levels of discretion in determining how to approach their roles. At the same time, however, the demands of bureaucratic accountability and formal reporting processes were experienced as constraining; for instance, by reducing the amount of time available for direct work with young people and their families. This, though, was felt to be necessary, particularly by service managers, in order to demonstrate a level of compliance with the overarching policy and operational objectives set at higher levels of the governmental structure – in this case, the Youth Justice Board and beyond that, the Ministry of Justice.

In this particular study, the comparison between two service providers at some geographical distance also offered the opportunity to consider whether different practice models could be said to operate within a single national jurisdiction. Practitioner experiences at the two sites were said to be 'very different'. One of the two appeared to be more risk-driven and concerned with procedures and formal compliance, for example ('In a phrase we heard particularly at Site A – "if it isn't recorded, it didn't happen"'); rather than the kind of relationship-based practice to which the other appeared to aspire: 'I'm not into it for ticking the boxes. I know I've got to do it but my prime focus with every case, and I will justify why certain boxes aren't ticked, is to work with young people' (Practitioner, Site B, quoted in Armitage et al., 2016: 486).

Studies by Smith and Gray (2019), and Goldson and Briggs (2021) also raise questions about the extent to which we can attribute variations in practice to the existence of national 'systems' or the uniformity of government policy within any given jurisdiction (see Chapters 4 and 5 for a further discussion). Some things are fixed, of course, such as the minimum age of criminal responsibility, but arguably these only establish the basic parameters for intervention, leaving substantial room for manoeuvre within the overarching framework. Smith and Gray (2019) developed a threefold typology of local youth justice systems within England, namely: 'offender management'; 'targeted intervention'; and 'children and young people first'. This typology was based on an analysis of local youth offending service strategy documents, and closer analysis of practitioner and manager accounts of their practice orientation.

The *offender management* model draws heavily on the kind of procedural and routinised form of practice associated with managerialism, and standardised targets and performance measures. The focus is on delivering prescribed interventions consistently with the expectation that these will achieve the projected outcome, whether that might be a reduction in reoffending levels, compliance with statutory orders, or perhaps even a reduction in the number of prosecutions. In this sense, the test of whether or not the specified intervention 'works' depends on its defined objectives alone; and it is not necessarily informed by any particular underlying philosophy (Gray and Smith, 2019). In the course of their study, for example, Gray and Smith found one 'offender management' service which was adopting this approach effectively to reduce the level of statutory interventions and achieve targets associated with reducing the number of young people going through the courts.

Typically, though, we would expect offender management-type services to emphasise compliance and control in the administration of youth justice interventions. Thus, for example, regular reporting and monitoring techniques would be at the core of formal supervision of the offender; and programmes would be determined by their capacity to impose timeframes and routines, rather than necessarily seeking to build relationships with young people or explicitly seek to change their behaviour. So, for instance, emphasis would be placed on physical attendance at specified places and times; with an active threat of breach for failure to comply.

Bateman (2011a) has commented on what he describes as a particular 'practitioner culture' associated with a noticeable increase in readiness to use powers of breach where young offenders were believed not to be complying with the requirements of court orders. He identified this emerging culture with a distinct break with previous practice, linked to the influence of national practice standards, and the desire of the New Labour government to be seen to be 'tough' on crime (Bateman, 2011a: 125). For many practitioners involved in supervising young offenders in the community, as Bateman observed, this represented a significant shift away from previous guiding principles, quoting one youth justice professional as saying: 'I used to … argue to keep young people out of the criminal justice system'. Instead, he found that practice was, in the view of respondents to his survey, now much more about enforcement and compliance:

> The logic that had militated against breach while avoiding custody was the 'the major *raison d'être* of the job' [youth justice worker], no longer prevailed. … 'Our workers take the young people back to court at the earliest opportunity for non-compliance. As they are told to do' …. In at least some areas, breaching a child was 'now considered a success factor! …' (Bateman, 2011a: 126)

Although none of the three 'types' identified could be said to exist in its pure form, there are clear and identifiable differences of approach, and the *targeted intervention* model can be distinguished by its preoccupation with risk and those who carry it. Thus, targeted services set out to identify those young people who are most at risk of becoming involved in crime or becoming persistent offenders, and then aim to take action to reduce or remove the factors and influences which give rise to such risks. This approach then translates into a number of distinct strategies, including the development of tools to identify and quantify 'risk', the establishment of specialised techniques and tools for managing risk, the design of mechanisms for selecting and isolating those who are believed to pose the greatest risk, and the provision of specific specialist services for this group alone.

Risk assessment tools are by now quite widespread in criminal and youth justice. Notably, in England and Wales, the Onset, Asset and later AssetPlus tools have been deployed at various times in order to seek to evaluate the criminogenic risks associated with young people identified as offenders, across a range of aspects of their lives. These tools have then been used to generate predictions of future behaviour, and prescriptions for the type of intervention likely to reduce the potential for further offending. As such, they have been subject to considerable research and critical evaluation, with substantial concerns raised both about their levels of accuracy, and the danger that they will cement in place certain stigmatising assumptions about young people who score highly and are therefore singled out for intervention (Almond, 2012).

Because assessments draw on a wide range of predictive factors, the types of programme designed to address the identified risk factors can vary quite widely. Typically, though, they maintain a focus on achieving changes in the young person's attitudes or belief systems, or in those contextual circumstances which are believed to be influential. So, interventions may be designed to change beliefs, change behaviours, change interests, change expectations and goals, change parenting styles, or change social networks and peer influences. Ross et al. (2011) have identified a number of such approaches which share the objective of reducing the likelihood of the child or young person reoffending, and are believed to be effective in doing so, including: child skills training, behavioural parent training, multi-systemic therapy, family functional therapy and multidimensional treatment foster care.

In terms of selection, practitioners appear to operate according to a range of formal and informal criteria, in order to judge whether a young person should be engaged with a targeted programme. In the case of 'radicalisation', youth offending practitioners found themselves being faced with a new responsibility without much preparation; and in some instances, at least, they adopted a strategy of selection and specialised provision: 'We have a sort of profile of the sort of young person who we think we want to get to, so it is about the troubles about identities, sense of grievance, interested in theological debates ...' (youth justice practitioner, quoted in Hirschfield et al., 2012: 36). Similar approaches could be identified, too, in the Knife Crime Prevention Programme, developed by the Youth Justice Board for England and Wales. Young people convicted of an offence involving a knife, or thought to be 'at risk' of carrying a knife could be referred to the programme, specifically tailored to this type of offence (Farag, 2013). In practice, it could be observed, selection for the programme extended well beyond the specified criteria, highlighting one of the significant challenges of adopting a 'targeted' approach to youth offending in general; or to any category of offending behaviour, in particular (Farag, 2013: 11).

In this case, the programme seemed to be geared towards achieving changes in young people's knowledge and attitudes relating to knife crime, by focusing on the harms caused and effects on victims, and in some instances this could be viewed as having some effect:

> I've been stabbed a couple of times so I used to carry a knife for protection, and for some people you don't have a choice as you're mixed up in all sorts [...] but I realise now that you don't need to carry a knife to protect yourself; being a man doesn't mean you have to be tough, avoiding the situation makes you stronger. (young person, quoted in Farag, 2103: 18)

This is clearly consistent with the overarching notion of a targeted form of intervention, with a precisely defined programme, clearly formulated practitioner roles and specific objectives. Interestingly, though, at the delivery level, there was some variation of approach between youth offending services, perhaps reflecting differing levels of commitment to a pure targeted approach (Farag, 2013: 22).

The third practice model identified by Smith and Gray (2019) is defined as *children and young people first*, and this clearly finds echoes in the influential 'Children First' strategy in youth justice, drawing on experience in Wales (Haines and Case, 2015) and subsequently endorsed with some enthusiasm by the Youth Justice Board (2021). Youth offending services which adopt this perspective can be clearly distinguished from targeted services because they start from a position of seeking common ground between young people in trouble with the law and their peers, rather than marking them out as different and then constructing interventions on this basis. Because of this, 'children and young people first' approaches argue that young people whom come into conflict with the law should be dealt with primarily on the basis of their status as children, and, as far as possible, in the same way as other children. Interventions should therefore seek to engage them (or re-engage them) with universal services, and provide assistance and support to enable them to thrive and achieve beneficial outcomes – which, it is argued, will also coincidentally reduce the incentives for involvement in anti-social or criminal behaviour.

Here, the main aim is to work in an integrated way across service boundaries, rather than to concentrate on specialisation and the creation of atomised services and programmes which set problematised children and young people apart: 'What distinguishes a "Children First" area is that the organisational structure created for the delivery of services is a secondary matter. What comes first are the needs of children and the type and range of services that are required to promote the best possible outcomes for children' (Haines and Case, 2018: 143).

At the level of practice, we might expect to find 'Children and Young People First' work to concentrate on establishing positive relationships with children and their families in order to understand their circumstances and address factors in their lives which might be associated with offending. At the same time, this kind of holistic approach would also necessitate close collaboration between different agencies, including schools, children's services, and the police, in order to promote social inclusion and strengthen the networks of support around the child or young person.

Diversionary initiatives might feature strongly in those areas which pursue children and young people first objectives, although these would differ from those adopted by proponents of offender management approaches. Both would be geared to reducing the potentially harmful effects of involvement with the justice system, such as 'labelling', and social exclusion, but, in the latter case, **diversion** would simply involve achieving the aim of '**minimum intervention**'; that is, reducing the levels of formal processing of children through the justice system. 'Children first' diversion, on the other hand, would also seek to ensure that children and young people were diverted 'into' alternative services and networks of support, as in the case of the 'Swansea Bureau' (Haines et al., 2013).

Here, a close collaboration between agencies was developed under the remit of the Safer Swansea Partnership to support police decisions to deal with young people's offences in ways short of prosecution. Instead:

> Where there is a mutual recognition that support is appropriate, an individualised package is developed. These services may be delivered by the YOS [Youth Offending Service] or by a range of community-based organisations such as: schools, youth groups or community projects. Services are typically informal and young people are often integrated into existing community programmes/provision. (Haines et al., 2013: 174)

As this account of the Swansea Bureau (and see Chapter 5 for a further discussion) makes clear, the shift of focus from dealing with young people who commit crimes simply as offenders to considering other factors and the wider context also creates space for alternative forms of offence resolution, such as restorative justice. The Bureau thus developed the capacity to include consideration of victims' interests and wishes in the process of dealing with the offence, with the subsequent option of enabling the young offender to make an apology or to meet the victim face-to-face in a 'Restorative Conference' (Haines et al., 2013: 173).

Whilst restorative practices are certainly to be found operating within broader children first frameworks, Smith and Gray (2019) also suggest that there may be 'outlier' youth justice services which at least claim to be fundamentally driven by restorative principles. In other words, in these relatively few cases, interventions are determined principally by the aim of resolving any issues surrounding the offence, including consideration of harm done to any victims, the possible need for the offender to acknowledge responsibility and put things right, and the opportunities for forgiveness and 'healing' of damaged relationships within the community. Services organised on this basis are more apparent in contexts where there is an indigenous tradition of similar models of offence resolution, which have played a powerful part in influencing developments such as the Family Group Conference model originating in New Zealand and drawing substantially on Māori history and conventions. The Box below provides an outline of restorative practice in New Zealand.

Youth Justice in New Zealand

Youth justice principles

The object of the *Oranga Tamariki Act 1989* (OTA) is to promote the well-being of children, young persons and their families, whānau, hapū, iwi and family groups (In Māori culture multiple groupings of whānau makeup clans or sub tribes called hapū. Multiple groupings of hapū makeup tribes called iwi. Groups of hapū and iwi all have multiple ancestral houses called marae. Multiple Iwi make up Māori society.)

There are four primary considerations for matters relating to the Youth Court:

- the well-being and best interests of the child or young person;
- the public interest (which includes public safety);
- the interests of any victim; and
- the accountability of the child or young person for their behaviour.

General principles under s 5 OTA provide that wherever possible family and whānau should be involved in decisions affecting the child or young person, that those relationships should be maintained and strengthened, and that timeliness is important.

Youth justice principles under s 208 OTA guide decision-making.

For further information see: https://youthcourt.govt.nz/youth-justice/youth-justice-principles-and-processes/

Other 'outliers' identified by Smith and Gray (2019) included a more explicit 'children's rights' model, which was espoused at least in principle by one youth offending service in England. This kind of approach would prioritise ensuring that children and young people's voices would be heard and acted upon during the criminal justice process, and that their rights would be prioritised and protected. Thus, for example, youth justice practitioners might be viewed as advocates, acting to safeguard children's access to education and training opportunities, to ensure fair treatment in judicial settings, to protect them from exploitation and abuse, to challenge discriminatory practices, and to pursue their entitlements to care and support where necessary.

It is difficult to identify this kind of advocacy-based approach within mainstream services for young people in trouble with the law, not least because of the varying and sometimes conflicting accountabilities of agencies and practitioners concerned with the delivery of youth justice. Children's rights projects therefore tend to operate outside these structures, hosted by non-governmental organisations (NGOs) in order to ensure their independence and capacity to speak out and challenge institutional practices which may compromise children's rights or best interests. Just for Kids Law, for example, is an organisation in England which offers independent advice and support for children and young people who are unfairly treated in the criminal justice process (www.justforkidslaw.org/about-us).

The Local and the National: Convergence or Divergence?

Whilst the models we have previously considered can certainly be described in terms of quite different characteristics and, indeed, service priorities, the question still remains as to the extent to which they do represent different ways of 'doing' youth justice; or are these variations rather more superficial? Are different approaches and the grand claims about their distinctiveness no more than window-dressing for what we might rather see as constant and immoveable core realities which have always and will always lie at the heart of youth justice, and its inherent conflicts and challenges. Hazel (2008), for one, has suggested that the dynamic tension between 'welfare' and 'justice' perspectives effectively shapes all possible approaches to dealing with the crimes of the young, as we have seen.

On the other hand, there has been a considerable amount of comparative work which suggests that youth justice systems are very different across international borders, in particular; and that they are likely to be shaped by cultures and traditions which are also quite distinctive. Thus, for example, Goemann (2018) explicitly outlines the developing New Zealand model of youth justice as a counterpoint to contemporary mechanisms and processes across the United States. In particular, she pinpoints the growing awareness of racialised systems and practices as a trigger for a sustained programme of reform, leading to the increasing integration of Māori dispute resolution methods at the heart of the judicial process:

> The Rangatahi Courts work within the Youth Court framework established by the Act – operating with the same laws and consequences – but are informed by Māori values and are meant to reduce the overrepresentation of Māori youth in the youth justice system. Youth can choose to have their Family Group Conference plans monitored by a Rangatahi Court. If they do, then all subsequent Court appearances until the plan is completed are held on the marae venue – a Māori community hub – and Māori elders are involved in follow-up activities where appropriate. … It has been described as a way for Māori youth to learn about who they are, where they are from, and where they fit in as young Māori people in New Zealand. (Goemann, 2018: 11)

Goemann does acknowledge, though, that these shifts in organisation and delivery of youth justice have not brought to an end the racial disparities in the relative proportions of young people brought to court in New Zealand, despite a very substantial overall reduction in the number of prosecutions and the increasing centrality of restorative practices in the judicial process.

By contrast, in other jurisdictions where patterns of unequal treatment can also be observed, the form of intervention may be very different. In the United States, for instance, some state jurisdictions apply an extremely stringent approach to juvenile 'corrections', with little scope for ideas to do with restoration or rehabilitation to influence practice. Here, instead, the emphasis is on surveillance and managing behaviour, drawing on principles of 'crime control' (Case et al., 2017) rather than engagement and problem-solving.

Hughes et al. (2020), for example, describe the close relationship between police and schools which has developed in many US states, where the lines between school discipline and criminality have become blurred. Here, there is an emphasis on controlling and monitoring behaviour, with the result that relatively minor infringements of educational requirements may be criminalised, and act as the trigger for more severe forms of sanction. Failure to complete homework, for example, may be treated as a breach of probation, with revocation and 'time in a detention facility' as a possible consequence (Hughes et al., 2020: 76). Teachers take direct responsibility for evaluating school students' behaviour and the ready availability of police attached to the school means that it is relatively straightforward to make requests for police intervention. Police become routinely involved in arresting students 'to calm them down', or because teachers have requested they get involved (Hughes et al., 2020: 73). In this context, the relationship between criminal justice agencies (and schools) and young people becomes one of surveillance, control and rapid intervention.

As the authors note, there are further consequences, in terms of embedded and systematic discrimination against Black children and young people from ethnic minorities, whilst the environment becomes one in which students 'feel scared and mistrusted'. The authors note that this is not a uniform picture, with some areas attempting to introduce restorative forms of practice into the school environment, amidst wider dissatisfaction with the dominant model of intervention (Hughes et al., 2020: 76).

This accords with the 'crime control model' attributed to the United States by Winterdyk (2015: 9), whereby the maintenance of order and extensive use of mechanisms of surveillance, behaviour management and discipline are the norm. This approach is characterised by some in terms of a 'school to prison pipeline', in which 'school authorities and school-based police officers rely on suspensions, expulsions, and criminalization as responses to student misconduct' (Benekos and Merlo, 2015: 388). The cumulative effect of this approach, including suspensions for 'minor discretionary infractions' which are not in themselves criminal is an increased level of school dropout and involvement with the formal justice system. It is noted that even where levels of violence in schools were in decline in the early 2010s, the number of school suspensions actually increased, as routinised surveillance triggered this kind of sanction (Benekos and Merlo, 2015: 389). (See Chapter 9 for further discussion about the overlap between school disciplinary measures and the criminal justice system.)

Similarly, the readiness of some US jurisdictions to transfer young offenders to the adult court also suggests a 'crime control' philosophy. In practice, transfers of this kind have been shown to lead to 'longer sentences, increased potential for victimization and disruptions in personal development' (Benekos and Merlo, 2015: 389). Although this model is described as pervasive and highly influential within the United States, it is also observed that other models are adopted in some areas, and in some state jurisdictions, given that individual states have a great deal of latitude under a federal system of government. Thus, for example, some attempts have been made to develop a 'psychoeducational' form of intervention in a group setting to enable young offenders who have been exposed to violence to understand the origins of their problems, and to initiate 'the changes that are needed to manage problems better' (Benekos and Merlo, 2015: 386).

In other jurisdictions though, the framework for intervention with young people does seem to be very different, and we can observe a sense of alignment between dominant understandings of the causes and nature of crime on the one hand, and the most appropriate ways in which to respond, on the other. The Nordic countries are often viewed as quite distinctive in terms of their criminal justice systems and practices, which are described by some as 'Nordic exceptionalism' (Lappi-Seppälä, 2012). Although Scandinavian countries have long been associated with well-developed welfare states which prioritise children's well-being, they have also increasingly been concerned about the impact of any form of institutional or criminalising intervention on children and young people (Lappi-Seppälä, 2019).

Typically, then, Scandinavian states have sought to develop 'community-based' programmes of intervention to address young people's offending. Sweden, for example, provides for courts to order programmes of 'Youth Care', involving social service interventions to 'promote the young offender's social development and re-integration' into the community (Lappi-Seppälä, 2019: 110); or a Youth Service, which involves a period of unpaid work by the young person on behalf of the community, as well as a programme of education or preparation for employment. Norway, on the other hand, has also sought to develop community-based sanctions, but geared more towards restorative practices. In place of imprisonment the expectations placed on young offenders and the support available to them are decided according to a 'mediation meeting', and this can involve quite stringent requirements, in terms of programme attendance or community service.

The Nordic states have been 'exceptionally successful' in restricting the use of custodial sanctions for young offenders; and it is claimed that they 'share a progressive orientation to juvenile justice', combining social work support and treatment with other forms of community-based intervention, such as requirements to undertake unpaid work (Lappi-Seppälä, 2019: 123). Although we are also cautioned to be critical of the extent to which supposedly 'welfare' interventions actually translate into punitive measures, especially from the point of view of young people experiencing them, the approach adopted by Scandinavian countries does appear distinctive. Winterdyk (2015: 10) refers to Norway's approach as a 'welfare-modified justice model', which seems to capture quite well the aim of providing a range of community-based interventions within an established criminal justice framework; and he describes Denmark's approach as 'a combination of the penal system and the social welfare system'.

This common orientation to welfare-oriented models of reintegration is typified by programmes such as 'MultifunC', a programme of residential 'treatment' and aftercare offered in Sweden, Norway and Denmark. Here, children are supported initially in a residential setting, but one which is connected to the community, where a 'holistic' programme is designed to support behaviour change, reintegration into educational settings, family and community engagement, and employment preparation. Following the residential element of the programme, young people are also provided with continuing aftercare support to consolidate improvements in their lives and ensure effective reintegration into the community.

Significantly, the young person and family members are closely involved in all aspects of planning and decision-making, and the aim is to support change across all key aspects of young people's lives, including family, school, peer groups and educational settings (Hayes, 2020). The intervention is grounded in cognitive behavioural and social learning theories, and it is provided by an integrated 'treatment team' which is responsive to the issues and needs affecting each young person. The objective of reducing reoffending is viewed as most likely to be achieved when all aspects of the young person's life are considered and 'criminogenic' and other needs addressed in tandem. Löfholm et al. (2020) found some limited indications of successful outcomes, in that participation in the MultifunC programme led to a reduced reliance on 'locked settings' or other 'out of home' placements for young people, although it did not seem to affect reoffending rates or use of psychiatric care.

Global Youth Justice?

Up to this point, we have been considering the development of youth justice practices and approaches as shaped by alternative 'models' with different characteristics and driving principles. This does seem to suggest a relationship between underlying philosophies, policies and practices, although we have also acknowledged that these are subject to considerable variation and other influences, such as practitioner power and community interests. It is also important to accept that the dominance of certain 'ways of seeing' and patterns of resourcing might mean that we tend to overlook or even discount certain approaches because they do not fit within a predominantly Westernised world view.

Restorative approaches, for example, have been seen as very influential and have been widely adopted and adapted across the range of youth justice systems. They have been accommodated within different models, certainly, although this may be at the expense of certain key principles, such as the absence of coercion and effective victim participation.

Indigenous traditions of restorative practice may well indicate distinctive understandings of youth crime and methods of dealing with it, although Cunneen (2007) cautions against the tendency to romanticise these, and we must be careful not to assume that they are necessarily child-friendly.

Amongst other 'restorative' forms of youth justice, we can find the example of the 'peacemaker process' as practised traditionally amongst the Navajo people (Nielsen, 1999). Here, the role of the peacemaker is to convene a meeting attended by the alleged offender and all those affected by the reported offence, where each is entitled to play a part. Everyone is invited to have a say, and to state their expectations and desired outcome. The peacemaker's role is to oversee the discussion and direct the meeting towards an agreed resolution. This model appears to have much in common with the Māori approach to dealing with the reported crimes of young people, discussed previously. A key question, though, concerns the extent to which this kind of conciliatory, problem-solving mechanism, relying on established community institutions and understandings, can supplant more formalised state-led mechanisms for dispensing justice to young people. For instance, the Referral Order in England and Wales has been established since 1999, ostensibly as a restorative mechanism to be implemented at the discretion of the court:

> Referral Orders directly involve the local community, by means of volunteer youth offender panel members and as beneficiaries of reparation. Youth offender panels conduct meetings in accordance with restorative principles and practice. These meetings enable children to recognise the consequences of their offending and to be accountable for their actions. A 'contract' is agreed between the child and the youth offender panel. The contract will include a range of goals and activities, with the aim of supporting the child towards living a safe and crime-free life and making a positive contribution to society. (Ministry of Justice, 2018: 7)

Thus, youth offender panels are intended to operate as the focal point for restorative engagement with those affected by an offence, particularly victims, whose 'voice' is 'central' (Ministry of Justice, 2018: 7). In this sense, the format and processes may appear similar to those described above, which originate in the form of community forums and are grounded in history and established social traditions. However, their location within the criminal process, the ideas of 'contracts' and 'accountability', and the exclusively child-focused outcomes suggest something rather different. This is further exemplified by the requirement for professional oversight of the process through the Youth Offending Team; and the capacity to return children to court for 'non-compliance' with the terms of the contract agreed at the youth offender panel meeting. This form of 'restorative justice' aligns much more closely with the 'corporatist' model identified by Winterdyk (2015: 6) than the 'participatory' approaches developed by the Navajos and attempted in New Zealand. The aim is correctional, and is focused on 'retraining' (Winterdyk, 2015: 6) the child to become a law-abiding and productive citizen.

Conclusion

This chapter has explored the idea of 'models' of practice in youth justice, and their use as the basis for international comparison between youth justice systems. We have explored a number of ways in which youth justice systems can be classified into different types, such as those developed by Winterdyk (2015) and McAra (2010) and we have considered the implications of these typologies for approaches to the organisation and delivery of youth justice. Whilst this has often led to attempts to classify whole countries or youth justice jurisdictions as operating in a uniform fashion, it has also been shown to be important to recognise differences in philosophy and practice at the local level, as in the case of the typology developed to account for variations across England and Wales (Smith and Gray, 2019). Changes over time are also important to acknowledge, especially given the 'lag' which is often apparent in the task of collating and disseminating material internationally.

We have also been able to reflect on the risks of applying classification systems based on one perspective, which might be relatively insensitive to historical and cultural variations, as in the case of 'restorative justice', for example. Restorative justice has become widely known and adopted in a relatively short period of time; but, at least partly for this reason, the term has been applied relatively uncritically to cover what are in fact very different forms of practice, as we have seen. Similar concerns might also apply to attempts to generalise about other forms of intervention, too, such as 'welfare' interventions which rely heavily on residential/institutional provision, and may be experienced by young people themselves as punitive rather than beneficial.

Further Reading

Sherman, L., Strang, H. and Newbury-Birch, D. (2008) *Restorative Justice.* London: Youth Justice Board.

Overview report commissioned by the Youth Justice Board which summarises evidence, ideas and approaches to practice which are intended to achieve restorative justice.

Smith, R. (2018) *Diversion in Youth Justice.* Abingdon: Routledge.

Extensive review of historical development of diversionary approaches to youth justice, contemporary practices, and potential future contribution of diversion to progressive practice in future.

Thorpe, D., Smith, D., Green, C. and Paley, J. (1980) *Out of Care.* London: George Allen & Unwin.

This is a key source highlighting the tensions between 'welfare' and 'justice' orientations to youth justice, whilst also drawing attention to the risks of 'unintended consequences' of pursuing particular ideological objectives.

4

Comparative Youth Justice

Objectives

- This chapter explores how youth justice has been studied in comparative contexts.
- Readers will be introduced to some of the key comparative studies.
- The chapter will help the reader to understand some of the methodological challenges of comparative research.
- The chapter will also enable readers to critically explore the dominance of accounts centring on the 'Global North' in criminological research.

Introduction

This chapter explores youth justice within comparative contexts. The field of comparative research has grown in recent years, and there are many examples of texts which compare youth justice in different contexts. These include earlier publications such as Muncie and Goldson's (2006) *Comparative Youth Justice: Critical Debates*, which explored a number of trends in youth justice across several Western countries. Looking at and comparing how other youth justice systems operate can help us to challenge taken for granted assumptions about the way a system works and what could and should be done differently.

However, some of the challenges of comparative research are also explored in this chapter, including the methodological and epistemological challenges – such as are we comparing like with like, and can we sufficiently understand another system in order to make meaningful comparisons? The chapter also explores some approaches to comparative research which have attempted to address these issues through different approaches. The use of children's rights standards as a frame of comparative reference (discussed further in Chapter 5) as well as challenges in addressing the dominance of the Global North in studies of youth justice are also critically explored.

Comparing Different Systems

One of the most influential early comparative criminological studies is Downes' (1988) work exploring the different trajectories of penal policies and practices in the Netherlands and England and Wales in the post-war period. The starting point for this analysis was the different rates of imprisonment (that is the number of people imprisoned per 100,000 people in the population) between the two jurisdictions. At the times of Downes' study (the mid-1980s), the rate of imprisonment in England and Wales was four times that of the Netherlands, whereas in the immediate post-war period the rate of imprisonment in the Netherlands had been much higher but had since declined. One of the novel features of Downes' research was the fact that it explored the experiences of prisoners in the different countries by carrying out interviews with English people held in Dutch prisons and Dutch people who had served time in English prisons (Downes, 1988; Kruttschnitt and Dirkzwager, 2011). Several of the people interviewed had also served time in both systems. By analysing prisoners' perspectives on their quality of life in prison Downes found that the conditions in prisons in the Netherlands (including rights and privileges and material conditions such as in-cell sanitation) were superior to those in English prisons. Downes (1988) also explored the differential crime rates and sentencing trends for specific crimes, and he concluded that there were different attitudes towards crime and punishment (he coined the phrase 'Contrasts in Tolerance', which is the book's title), which impacted on criminal justice policies.

Cavadino and Dignan's (2006a, b) analysis of penal systems and their relationship to **political economy** is another of the most well-known comparative studies. In their research they explored the systems of what they characterised as 'contemporary capitalist countries' (2006b: 422). They concluded that the political economy in each country impacted on the **punitiveness** of the penal culture and differential rates of imprisonment across countries. The political economy means the interrelationship between economic and political (e.g., law and government) institutions. Punitiveness is understood to encompass approaches favouring expressive forms of punishment. (For general discussions about the concept of punitiveness and some of the difficulties in measuring it see Matthews [2005] and Hamilton [2014].) The 12 countries included in Cavadino and Dignan's analysis and the different political economies they delineated – neo-liberal, conservative **corporatist**, social democratic and oriental corporatist – are outlined in Table 4.1.

Table 4.1 Political Economies and Penal Ideologies

	Type of Political Economy			
	Neo-liberal	**Conservative Corporatist**	**Social Democratic Corporatist**	**Oriental Corporatist**
Economic and social policy organisation	Free market; minimal or residual welfare state	Status-related, moderately generous welfare state	Universalistic, generous welfare state	Private sector based, welfare corporatism, bureaucratic, paternalistic
Dominant penal ideology	'Law and Order'	Rehabilitation/ Resocialisation	Rights-based	Apology-based rehabilitation and restoration
Examples	United States, England & Wales, Australia, New Zealand, South Africa	Germany, France, Italy and the Netherlands	Sweden and Finland	Japan

Source: Adapted from Cavadino and Dignan (2006b: 441).

According to Cavadino and Dignan (2006b), one of the key distinguishing features of countries with higher levels of punitiveness was the extent to which their political economy could be characterised as 'inclusive', rather than 'exclusive' towards people who came into conflict with the law. Countries with neo-liberal economic policies, which are broadly defined as favouring free-market capitalism, and with minimal state interventions in relation to welfare were considered the most exclusionary in their typology. Cavadino and Dignan (2006a) included the following countries in this category: United States, England and Wales, Australia, New Zealand and South Africa; whereas countries with a social democratic corporatist model, characterised by universalist welfare provision and a left-wing political orientation, were considered the most 'inclusive'. Cavadino and Dignan (2006a) included Sweden and Finland in this category.

Cavadino and Dignan (2006a, b) considered rates of imprisonment to be one of the key indicators of punitiveness. They established that countries with neo-liberal political economies had the highest rates of imprisonment, while social-democratic countries (and countries with an 'oriental corporatist' political economy, of which Japan was the only example included in their study), had the lowest rates of imprisonment. Exploring the possible links between different political economies and punitiveness, Cavadino and Dignan (2006a, b) hypothesised that neo-liberal states may be *criminogenic* (meaning causing crime), because poor welfare provision and more manifest inequality can be linked to higher incidences of crime. However, they also noted that there was not necessarily a *causal* link between rates of crime and rates of imprisonment.

They argued that different forms of political economy embody certain attitudes towards individuals, which then translate into a range of policies, both in the criminal justice system and in wider social policy. So, for example a neo-liberal orthodoxy might suggest that some people are more deserving than others, and that success is linked to personal ambition and drive rather than structural conditions such as the availability of meaningful employment. This form of thinking can lead to policy formation which links welfare to deserts – meaning judgements about who is considered 'deserving' of state support, and by implication who is 'undeserving'. It also places responsibility firmly on the shoulders of individuals rather than on the state. Such a perspective, Cavadino and Dignan (2006a, b) argue, also translates into criminal justice policies which are more punitive. In relation to England and Wales, they note for example the retraction of welfare supports and the rise of 'law and order' rhetoric and harsher criminal justice policies from the 1990s onwards.

On the other hand, more inclusionary models recognise the state's role in providing for all citizens (a universalist model of support) and more *penal-welfarist* approaches within the criminal justice system. Penal-welfarism is associated with less harsh penal policies, and an emphasis on rehabilitation rather than punishment (Garland, 1985). Such approaches favour alternatives to custody rather than immediate recourse to, or excessive use of imprisonment. This model recognises that exclusionary approaches do not lead to reduced reoffending, as countless studies of the impacts and efficacy of imprisonment attest. In Cavadino and Dignan's typology, the two Nordic countries included in their study (Sweden and Finland) were considered exemplars of this approach.

Comparing Youth Justice Systems

In their consideration of the impact of political economy of different penal systems, Cavadino and Dignan (2006a) also explored the different approaches to youth justice in the countries included in their study. They noted the fact that differential responses to youth offending, that is responses that were distinct from adult criminal justice systems, which emerged across many countries in the late 19th century in the context of industrialisation and urbanisation, were evidence of a globalising tendency within criminal justice policy (a topic explored in Chapter 1). These globalising effects included the transfer of policy ideas and approaches such as institutions including industrial and reformatory schools, that were specifically targeted towards children. However, notwithstanding the fact that similar institutions emerged in different countries in the late 19th century, there were notable differences in the way that the youth justice systems evolved. This, Cavadino and Dignan (2006a) argue, was a result of different political economies.

As well as different political economies and the extent to which countries adopted 'inclusionary' or 'exclusionary' social and criminal justice policies, as described above, Cavadino and Dignan (2006a) also argued that when considering variations in youth justice systems in different countries it is important to take into account philosophical underpinnings (such as how child and adult criminality is differentiated, and how youthful offending is understood), as well as the institutional arrangements and the systems and processes in which children and young people are dealt with. Based on these factors they identified five models of youth justice:

1. Welfare Model;
2. Justice Model;
3. Minimum Intervention Model;
4. Restorative Justice Model; and
5. Neo-Correctionalist Model.

Some of the key identifying features of each model and their institutional arrangements are outlined in Table 4.2.

Table 4.2 Youth Justice Models

Models	Philosophical Assumptions	Institutional Arrangements
Welfare Model	Crime is caused by factors in the child's environment. Children are dependent and should be subject to protections. Focusing on needs rather than deeds.	Welfare-oriented – children can be dealt with through welfare and child protection services.
Justice Model	Children have free will and are responsible for their actions. Children should be held accountable for wrongdoing. Focusing on deeds rather than needs.	Children dealt with in youth courts (modified criminal courts).
Minimum Intervention Model	Contact with the criminal justice system has negative 'labelling effects' that lead to 'deviancy amplification' and potential net-widening.	Diversionary approaches, alternatives to prosecution, community-based interventions.
Restorative Justice Model	Focus on reparation and reintegration, paying attention to all parties involved in the harms caused by offending.	Restorative justice conferences; family-welfare conferences; mediation.
Neo-Correctionalist Model	Children and their parents are responsible for offending. Prevention of offending is a primary goal. Children should be held to account for offending.	Court responses (and more alignment with adult courts). Civil measures (including preventative orders).

Source: Adapted from Cavadino and Dignan (2006a: 201).

For Cavadino and Dignan (2006a) the *welfare model*, whose key philosophical underpinnings and institutional arrangements are outlined in Table 4.2, is based on an understanding that children and young people's behaviour is influenced (some would say determined) by their upbringing and the circumstances in which they live. Such an orientation by implication views children as less responsible for criminal behaviour and underscores an approach whereby the care and protection of children is the responsibility of adults. This is not to say that welfarist approaches do not apply in the adult criminal justice system also (such as penal-welfarism as described above), but in the case of children there is a clear recognition that adults, including parents and society more generally, are responsible for ensuring that children's needs are met; and where they are not being met then the onus falls on state agencies to intervene to provide a safety-net of support.

In many discussions of youth justice, welfarist approaches are contrasted positively with justice approaches (which hold young people accountable for their offending and respond accordingly) (see, for example, Smith, 2005). However, as Cavadino and Dignan (2006a) and many others have noted, just because welfarist interventions are justified based on children's needs, their impacts are not necessarily experienced benignly. Long periods of detention in secure facilities for instance could be justified on the basis that this is the only way that a child's needs can be met, whereas if the same child was dealt with through criminal proceedings, there would necessarily be limits on the range of sanctions or interventions that could be imposed as these would be bound by *rule of law* principles. In historical contexts there is ample evidence of interventions justified based on a child's welfare legitimising highly intrusive interventions. These after all were the key arguments made in the *Gault* case in the American Supreme Court in 1967, which held that children cannot be detained indeterminately and are equally entitled to due process in criminal proceedings (Platt, 2009).

The Case of Jerry Gault

Jerry Gault was a 15-year-old, living in Arizona in the United States, who was accused of making an obscene phone call to his neighbour in June 1964. Gault and his friend were arrested and taken to a Children's Detention Home. When Jerry was arrested his parents were at work, and the police did not inform them of the fact that he had been placed in the Children's Detention Home. His parents were also not properly informed about a subsequent hearing in the juvenile court. The case against Jerry was unclear and there were conflicting accounts regarding the obscene phone call. There was no proper record of the legal proceedings. Nonetheless at the conclusion of the hearing the judge committed Jerry Gault to juvenile detention for six years. An adult convicted of a similar crime would have received a maximum sentence of a $50 fine or two months in jail. Jerry's parents eventually appealed his case to the Supreme Court of the United States (*In re Gault*, 387 U.S. 1, 20 (1967)), where the Court examined the juvenile justice system in depth and found that, as in the adult criminal court, the juvenile court had to respect 'due process' rights and follow procedural rules.

You can read more about this case, the legal opinion and its significance here: www.uscourts.gov/educational-resources/educational-activities/facts-and-case-summary-re-gault

In contrast to welfare models, *justice models* in youth justice are underpinned by an understanding that children should be held accountable for their behaviour, and indeed that doing so within the criminal justice system (albeit through the modified format of a youth court), is one way to educate children and to prevent further offending (see Chapter 3 for a further discussion of different models). This model is sometimes associated with more punitive attitudes towards children and young people (in part because of the focus on children's deeds rather than their needs), but, as noted above, justice approaches also necessitate application within a legal framework which means that children must be accorded *due process rights*. This means that children should have the right to legal representation, they should know the legal case against them, and they can only be tried and sanctioned in relation to their offence and not based on wider considerations, such as their welfare needs. As Cavadino and Dignan (2006a: 202) elaborate, under a justice model:

> Punishment should be apportioned in accordance with the seriousness of the offence and the offender's corresponding 'just deserts'. Because the system is acknowledged to be unequivocally engaged in the administration of punishment that often entails a loss of liberty, and that cannot be assumed to be benign 'treatment' that is in the interests of the offender, there is a greater emphasis – formally at least – on the need for procedural rights of 'due process' and for appropriate constraints to be placed upon the punitive power of the state.

Minimum intervention models of youth justice are those that recognise the harmful effects of criminal justice system contact on young people. Countries which adopt minimum intervention approaches tend to have higher minimum ages of criminal responsibility, with the obvious effect that if a child cannot be held legally responsible, then they cannot be dealt with in the criminal justice system. Such models also favour diversion without sanctions or diversions with services offered outside of the criminal justice system. Cavadino and Dignan (2006a) note that elements of the 'minimum intervention' model are seen in Scandinavian countries and in aspects of the German juvenile justice system.

Restorative justice models of youth justice use restorative approaches such as family conferences and victim-offender mediation to bring parties who have been harmed by offending together. As the name would suggest, such models are influenced by restorative justice principles, which include an emphasis on repairing harm, promoting reconciliation and building positive relationships (Bazemore and Schiff, 2001; Doak and O'Mahony, 2011). Furthermore, restorative justice is associated with 'reintegration' of the young person back into the fold of their community, as opposed to more 'disintegrative' approaches, such as incarceration, which involves the removal of young people from their communities (Braithwaite, 2000). As noted in the previous chapter, countries such as New Zealand have been at the forefront of implementing restorative justice approaches in their youth justice system (Lynch, 2012). Northern Ireland has also used restorative approaches extensively in the youth justice system, going so far as to mandate this approach within legislation (Doak and O'Mahony, 2011). (See Chapter 6 for further context on the youth justice system in Northern Ireland.)

Finally, Cavadino and Dignan (2006a) associate a *neo-correctionalist* model of youth justice with countries they categorise as 'neo-liberal' in their typology of political economies. They identify the United States as an exemplar of this model and describe two characteristics evident in the youth justice systems across the United States. Firstly, an increased tendency to blur the boundaries between juvenile and adult courts, and secondly evidence of an increasingly punitive approach towards juvenile offending. Of course, it is important to note that the United States is not a unitary entity in relation to systems of youth justice, as there are significant inter-state variations in policies and practices. For example, there are notable differences between states in the minimum age of criminal responsibility and ages of criminal majority, as well as when children's cases can be heard in adult courts, and the range and severity of sentences that a court can impose (Brown, 2012; Merlo and Benekos, 2016). However, Cavadino and Dignan (2006a) observed these broad trends across many of the states in the United States.

A further feature of this neo-correctionalist model is the shift from considering children as potentially vulnerable and requiring protection, to a view that juvenile offenders are rational actors that should be punished according to 'just deserts' principles. In other words, the distinction between juvenile and adult offenders has been increasingly eroded. Another important point to note in respect of this increased punitiveness, is its highly disproportionate effects. In the United States young people from ethnic minorities, most prominently African American and Hispanic young people, are disproportionally represented in the juvenile justice system, particularly among the population of young people who are incarcerated (Dillard, 2013).

It is important to note that these models described by Cavadino and Dignan (2006a) are to some extent *heuristic devices* (Bruce and Yearley, 2006: 162). This means that the models they propose are not necessarily all seen in true forms in specific countries, but rather they help us to think about different approaches to youth justice and how these may be impacted by different political economies (i.e., the extent to which wider social policy including welfare provision is inclusionary rather than exclusionary). It is also worth observing that approaches to youth justice can change across time and place (this will already be evident from the discussion of historical approaches to youthful offending outlined in Chapter 1), and that we may see a melding of these models in different contexts.

For example, some countries may generally adopt restorative approaches, but at the same time enact justice-based (or punitive) responses to more serious offending, as is the case in New Zealand (Lynch, 2012). Exploring trends in youth justice, John Muncie, for instance, describes approaches to youth justice across the four different nations of England, Wales, Scotland and Northern Ireland as representing 'an amalgam of rationales oscillating around, but also beyond, the caring ethos of social services, the neo-liberal legalistic ethos of responsibility and the neo-conservative ethos of coercion and punishment' (2006: 771). He also identifies the impacts of globalisation as influencing youth justice policy and practice.

Challenges of Comparison

Comparing different countries' systems and approaches in criminal justice is not a straightforward task. David Nelken (2009), a scholar who has written extensively about comparative criminal justice, notes some potential pitfalls when comparing different criminal justice systems and practices. Firstly, there is the risk of being *ethnocentric* – that is, viewing the world from the point of view of one's own position and assuming that position is the benchmark against which other countries should be measured. Or secondly, falling foul of *relativism*. This means adopting a position where you consider that comparison is futile because you will never be able to grasp the specificities of another context, and so you don't even bother. Nelken (2015) also cautions against what he calls 'foil comparisons', that is overly simplistic interpretations, that are then used to justify arguments for the adoption of approaches used in another jurisdiction, without a sufficient understanding of the conditions and contexts in which they apply. He warns:

> A focus on other jurisdictions as being better models of what the observer believes her system is already doing, but would like to do better, can even lead to drawing quite opposite lessons from that warranted by any serious study of the actual practices in the foreign jurisdiction concerned. (Nelken, 2015: 528)

He cites the example of Italian approaches to juvenile justice being viewed as a positive model in the English context, but without fully appreciating the limitations of this system and the importance of contextual issues such as other mechanisms of social control (e.g., the family and the church). He cautions that to avoid these pitfalls '... requires a careful mix of explanatory and interpretative strategies' (Nelken, 2009: 492).

Such strategies include moving beyond a simplistic analysis of, for example, rates of imprisonment in different countries (a measure that is often used to compare the 'punitiveness' or 'leniency' of different systems) (Cavadino and Dignan, 2006a, b; Nelken, 2009). The fact that certain countries may imprison more people per 100,000 of the population might indeed be an important indicator of how their criminal justice system functions, but it does not tell us about the *experience* of imprisonment in that country (Nelken, 2009), and we know from a range of international research that conditions of imprisonment vary markedly (Fair and Walmsley, 2021). Equally, countries may have low rates of imprisonment, but operate under regimes of restriction or confinement which are experienced as punitive by those who are subject to them, but which do not figure in traditional accounts of punishment. For example, Sweden is often seen as an exemplar of 'Scandinavian Exceptionalism' (Pratt, 2008; Pratt and Eriksson, 2012) and as having a relatively mild penal regime, but it operates a system of compulsory detention for people with drug and alcohol difficulties. (On the broader question of the use of the term 'exceptionalism', Nelken [2017: 421] makes the important point: 'If we write about "exceptional" places (and the list of places described in this way grows ever longer) we beg the question of what we are taking to be "normal" and why'.) There are also well-documented concerns regarding the treatment of migrants in detention centres in Sweden (Barker, 2013).

Similar issues pertain in relation to comparisons of youth justice systems. For instance, countries with higher minimum ages of criminal responsibility cannot detain children under criminal justice legislation, but compulsory detention may be mandated on the grounds of child protection. In Denmark for example, where the age of criminal responsibility is 15, very few minors are placed in custody, but a substantial system of secure care exists allowing for the detention of young people for behavioural reasons or on the basis of their own protection (Henriksen and Prieur, 2019). This is similarly the case in Finland, where the minimum age of criminal responsibility is also 15, but where concerns have been raised about the powers of judges in child welfare proceedings to order confinement of young people without sufficient due process protections (Abrams et al., 2018). Nelken (2009) therefore argues that careful attention must be paid to these contextual factors, and that such understandings can only be gleaned from careful study and familiarity.

Comparative Case Study: When Children Kill Children: Penal Populism and Political Culture

David Green adopted a comparative case study approach to examine very different responses to two cases of children who killed children in Norway and in England and Wales. Many people will be familiar with the case in England and Wales, where two 10-year old boys were found guilty of the abduction and murder of 2-year-old James Bulger in Liverpool in 1993. The case was covered widely in the media, and it provoked a public outcry at the time. Court cases involving children are usually held in camera (meaning that the public are not allowed to attend, and the media cannot identify child defendants), however, in this case media outlets asked if they could identify the two 10-year olds, on the grounds of 'public interest'. Controversially, a judge granted this request, and pictures of the faces of the two boys appeared on newspaper covers and television screens across the country.

The boys were convicted of kidnapping and murder and were sentenced to be 'detained at Her Majesty's pleasure'. This sentence is the equivalent of a life sentence for under 18s. In such cases the sentencing judge sets a 'tariff', which is the minimum period a person should spend in prison before being considered by the Parole Board for release. The trial judge initially set the 'tariff' for the two boys at eight years. This tariff was subsequently raised to 10 years by another judge, and more controversially it was raised again to 15 years, by the then Home Secretary Michael Howard, following a public petition organised by *The Sun* newspaper. This intervention by the Home Secretary was the subject of an appeal, and the boys' tariff was again reduced. The treatment of the boys in the criminal justice process (i.e., in particular the failure to give due account to their age and ability to understand the court proceedings), was the subject of a further appeal to the European Court of Human Rights (*T* v *United Kingdom*; *V* v *United Kingdom* (2003) 30 EHRR 21). (The role and jurisdiction of the European Court of Human Rights (ECtHR) and the particular issues raised in this case are discussed further in Chapter 6.)

As Green and others (e.g., Haydon and Scraton, 2000) have observed, this case left an indelible mark on attitudes and responses to offending by young people. It ultimately led to legislative changes in England and Wales including the lowering of the age at which a child can receive an indeterminate sentence (from 14 to 10 years), and the length of custodial sentences that children can receive. Five years after this case the Crime and Disorder Act (1998) abolished **doli incapax** provisions (that is the provision which recognises that children below a certain age, but older than the age of criminal responsibility, may still be unable to understand the wrongfulness of their behaviour) (Fitz-Gibbon, 2016). This fixed the minimum age of criminal responsibility (MACR) at 10 years. Since then, calls to raise the MACR in England and Wales (which is well below the European average) have been resisted and this case is frequently cited as the reason why (Goldson, 2013).

In his comparative case study, Green (2008) contrasts the media coverage of the Bulger case and the public and political response with another case involving the death of a child at the hands of other children, which occurred in Norway in 1994. In this instance, Silje Marie Redergård, a five-year-old, was killed by three 6-year-old boys while they were playing together. She was beaten by them and left unconscious in the snow and as a result died from hypothermia. In this instance the boys were not prosecuted, as they were below the MACR, which in Norway is 15 years. Their case was therefore dealt with by child welfare services, rather than in the criminal justice system. Although there was ample press coverage of the case in Norway, the identities of the children were never made public and Green (2008: 7) notes the following distinction between this and the Bulger killing:

> There was no mass outpouring of anger or outrage from the family, the community, or the press, no cries for vigilante justice, and no political manoeuvring by any party's politicians to politicize the incident.

How to explain the marked differences between these two cases? One explanation of course is the different ages of the children involved. The MACRs of the two countries are also different (10 compared to 15 years), and this reflects different cultural attitudes and understandings of childhood. Green (2008) argues, however, that different political and media cultures are more salient explanations of the differential responses in these cases. He argues that English tabloid culture in particular 'present selectively homogenized accounts of crime and punishment issues' (Green, 2008: 11) and that politicians engage with these in a cycle of increased punitiveness. Moreover, the type of democratic systems in the two countries (majoritarian in the case of England and Wales, and consensual in the case of Norway), create the conditions for more or less penal populism.

Which Level of Analysis?

A further challenge raised in comparative research is choosing the level of analysis. Frequently, studies take countries as their unit of analysis, which leads to what is sometimes referred to as 'methodological nationalism' (Beck, 2002; Friedrichs, 2011; Dollinger et al., 2021). So, for instance, we may see the youth justice system in France compared with that of Belgium or the system in Finland compared with that of Spain. However, a range of research also points to significant local variation in youth justice practice. For example, if we look at England and Wales, which comprises one legal jurisdiction, we see that the practice of youth justice and the experiences of young people in the system in England or Wales may be very different, not least because child welfare and protection policies are devolved matters, and the Welsh government has adopted a different approach to children's rights (Goldson and Briggs, 2021) (see Chapter 6 for a fuller discussion of the differences in youth justice across the nations of the United Kingdom).

But even at a more granular level we can see that practices within one country can vary. For instance, and as discussed in Chapter 3, taking the example of England, there are significant variations in the approaches to youth justice taken in different parts of the country. For example, in an analysis of practice models in different Youth Offending Services in England, Smith and Gray (2019) found that some areas adopted offender-focused, risk management approaches, while in other areas more universalist child welfare models were applied. This led the authors to question 'monolithic' accounts of the youth justice field (Smith and Gray, 2019: 556), and to caution for the need for more nuance in comparative analyses. A further critique of the 'nation state' approach to comparative research is that this can potentially elide trends that do not stop at national borders. Muncie (2015) therefore advocates maintaining a focus on different levels of analysis.

Paying attention to context and nuance and to the potential contradictory nature of youth justice policies, practices and experiences in comparative analyses is therefore critically important. These contexts include the shape of legislation and broader political structures such as those described by Cavadino and Dignan (2006a, b) above. David Garland (2013) has also pointed towards the need to study the relationships between different aspects of state and legal processes more carefully. Garland (2013) does not specifically address youth penality in this work, but arguably these considerations are even more important in relation to youth justice, where there are often very significant overlaps with other areas of state intervention (e.g., education and child protection and welfare systems) (see Chapter 9 for a fuller discussion of these overlapping systems). Garland (2013) directs particular attention towards the relationship between the state and civil society (e.g., the influence of non-state actors and interest groups). In the context of youth justice, one example of this could be the role and influence of Children's Commissioners and children's rights bodies in the scrutiny of the youth justice system, or advocacy organisations which represent children's interests and campaign for change (see Chapter 5 for more discussion of this topic).

Garland (2013) also points towards the need to carefully study the interrelationship between other state agencies and institutions to explore who exercises control of decision-making. Again, thinking specifically about the youth justice system, this might mean the interrelationships between government policy on youth justice and a central organisation such as the Youth Justice Board in England and Wales and the interface with locally delivered services (see Chapter 6). Critically also, there is a need to explore the modes and means through which penal power is exercised. In other words, what is the youth justice system *like in practice and how do young people experience it?* All of this suggests the need for detailed empirical research that explores *both questions* – what Goldson and colleagues (2021: 13) characterise as the *'higher narratives'* of legislation and policy and the *'finer-grained'* contours of localised practice.

Youth Justice in Comparative Contexts

One example of a comparative study of different juvenile justice systems is research carried out by Field and Nelken (2007, 2010), comparing the operation of youth justice in England and Wales and Italy. Italy has traditionally been considered a relatively 'lenient' youth justice system (Nelken, 2006), particularly when contrasted with England and Wales, which at the time of Field and Nelken's research had one of the highest rates of young people in custody in Europe, and one of the lowest ages of criminal responsibility. The MACR in England is 10 years, while in Italy it is 14 years. However, moving beyond this simplistic comparison of rates of detention and differential ages of criminal responsibility, Field and Nelken (2010) found that, from the standpoint of actors involved in the system, their intentions were not punitive per se, and that many believed that directing children and young people through the youth justice system was a means through which they could access services. This of course, speaks to the availability of more universalist services and wider government policy. Nonetheless, it does show that merely characterising a system as 'punitive', without understanding the intentionality of actors or the experiences of young people, does not necessarily advance our analysis.

A further important issue noted in Field and Nelken's (2007, 2010) comparative work was the relevance of different cultural attitudes and understandings about children and their development. So, for example, in England and Wales a more interventionist approach was favoured based on an understanding that intervention would set children on the right path, whereas in Italy a non-interventionist approach was supported based on a belief that children will eventually grow out of delinquency. In Italy the youth justice system is overseen by a specialist professional youth justice magistracy and the main system response is to avoid conviction, so a case could be considered successful if a child ultimately does not receive a conviction. This contrasts with a system where success is measured based on targets such as 'offences brought to justice' as operated in England and Wales in the 2000s, and which led to more numbers of young people being drawn into the system (Bateman, 2014). Again, these are important cultural differences which are essential to understand when comparing different systems.

However, notwithstanding these important differences, Field and Nelken (2010) also reported that some of these broader trends they saw did not necessarily operate in the same way for children from ethnic minority backgrounds. In Italy for instance, children from gypsy or immigrant backgrounds were more likely to be viewed as 'risky' because of wider prejudices, and their parents and family groups were viewed as somehow 'lesser' than traditional Italian family structures. These attitudes permeated through to the decision-making processes and ultimately to outcomes for children and young people:

> Magistrates and social workers share the view that social intervention for these groups is likely to be ineffective because the subjects do not have the 'normal' Italian family and community backgrounds which would enable supervision ... to function effectively. (Field and Nelken, 2010: 290)

In Italy, as in many other countries, children from minority ethnic groups were over-represented in the custodial population, with one explanation being that they and their family situations were constructed differently, and they were therefore considered unamenable to interventions that would have been offered to other children. As a result they did not benefit from diversion, so therefore they were propelled more quickly through a system.

Comparing Countries with a Common Legal Heritage

Goldson et al. (2021) have more recently undertaken a comparative study of criminal justice and 'penality' between England and Wales and four Australian States: New South Wales, Victoria, Western Australia and Queensland. The authors explain their choice of these four States for the study: New South Wales has the highest rate of child detention in Australia; Western Australia has the highest rate of Aboriginal and Torres Strait Islander children as prisoners; Victoria has the lowest detention rates, while Queensland is a 'middle-range' jurisdiction (Goldson et al., 2021: 3). They define the frame of 'penality' used in their study as:

> ... the whole system of punishment, ranging from its philosophies, laws and methods, to its material effects and the wider social, cultural and political and environments in which it is located. (Goldson et al., 2021: 1)

Part of their initial motivation for undertaking comparative research was the fact that despite a common legal heritage, the patterns of the use of youth custody in Australia and England and Wales had diverged markedly over time. By 2010 the rates of juvenile detention were lower in Australia than in 1981, while over the same period in England and Wales the numbers of children in custody had more than doubled. Moreover, the patterns of decline in youth detention in Australia diverged from an expanding adult prison population, while in England and Wales both the youth and adult custody populations had both risen in the same period (before the youth custodial population in England and Wales began to decline from 2008 onwards).

Some of the notable differences between the Australian states and England and Wales include the different arrangements for the administration and governance of youth justice. In Australia youth justice is coordinated at State and Territory level, meaning that each State or Territory might have different structures and therefore different approaches and outcomes. Whereas in England and Wales youth justice policy is overseen by a central Youth Justice Board, which is a non-departmental public body sponsored by the Ministry of Justice (MoJ) and delivered at local level through over 150 Youth Offending Teams (YOTs). However, despite such central structures attempting to homogenise approaches, there were still significant variations in local practices (see Chapter 6 for a fuller discussion). As these researchers observe, these dimensions of complexity, both in institutional arrangements, but also in approaches and practices on the ground – 'makes the task of a *comparative* endeavour all the more complex and challenging' (Goldson et al., 2021: 10). However, they also go on to state:

> But recognising complexity and the need to engage caution does not, in itself, render comparative research impossible or signal the spectre of some infinite phenomenological regress. (Goldson et al., 2021: 12)

By this, the authors of this study seem to be echoing some of the challenges raised by Nelken (2009, 2015) (e.g., *ethnocentrism, relativism* and *foil comparisons*), while still making the argument that comparative research can yield valuable insights and is worthwhile.

Goldson et al.'s (2021) comparative study finds a greater emphasis on diversion and decarceration in Australia over time, while in England and Wales the emphasis on diversion has waxed and waned, particularly in the context of an increased politicisation of the issue of youth crime in England and Wales in the 1990s and up to the early 2000s. The authors argue that from the early 2000s up to the present day, there is increased evidence of contradictory priorities in youth justice. As well as points of divergence this comparative study also notes some points of convergence between the different contexts:

- Some minority groups are disproportionately impacted by youth justice interventions. In Australia Aboriginal and Torres Strait Island children are detained in custody at much higher rates. In England and Wales children from Black and minority ethnic backgrounds are also disproportionately represented in the youth custodial population.
- In both contexts there is an over-representation of children and young people who are known to child protection and welfare services (including children in care); and children and young people with mental health disorders and/or cognitive/neuro-disabilities. There is also a predominance of children who are living in acute poverty.
- In both England and Wales and in Australia the rate of girls and young women being detained has risen markedly. (See Chapter 8 for a broader discussion of the characteristics of young people who come into contact with youth justice systems.)

Children's Rights as a Framework for Global Comparisons

The United Nations Convention on the Rights of the Child (UNCRC) is a global rights convention to which all countries in the world (bar the United States) are signatories. The UNCRC sets out a series of rights principles that should apply to all children, which it defines as people under the age of 18 years. Alongside the UNCRC there are several rights instruments which apply specifically to the area of juvenile justice and children who come into conflict with the law. These include standards on the administration of juvenile justice, standards for children held in detention, and standards for promoting early intervention and diversion from the system (these rights instruments are discussed in depth in Chapter 5).

As children's rights standards are intended to have a global application, they have provided a framework for a body of comparative juvenile justice research. For instance, Goldson and Kilkelly (2013) have explored the application of children's rights standards in relation to child detention, focusing on the findings of rights inspections' bodies such as the UN Committee on the Rights of the Child and the Committee for the Prevention of Torture (CPT). In this work they have noted the dissonance between countries signing up to rights standards and practice on the ground, including in areas such as the separation of child and adult prisoners, the provision of 'child-appropriate regimes' and the protection of children's rights in prison.

The UNCRC and the UN Committee on the Rights of the Child have also set out standards in relation to the minimum age of criminal responsibility (MACR). Variations in MACRs in the global context have provided a further framework for comparative analysis in juvenile justice. Cipriani (2009/2016) for example has published a worldwide analysis of MACRs and their intersection with children's rights. In this wide-ranging analysis Cipriani (2009/2016) notes some of the historical antecedents of different MACRs, including the legacy of different legal systems and social and cultural conceptions of childhood and the different ages at which children are held to have reached a sufficient level of understanding and capacity to understand the difference between right and wrong and the implications of their behaviour. He highlights the legacies of European colonial law and Soviet law in different countries, and different schools of thought within Islamic law regarding the ages at which children are deemed to have the capacity for intelligent reason (*akl)* and the ability to exercise free choice. This work serves to highlight that comparative research needs to take into account differences across both *time* and *place* as well as paying attention to wider dynamics regarding conceptions of childhood and other salient issues such as gender (Staines et al., 2021). For instance, Staines et al. (2021) note that Iran has a different MACR for girls and boys (9 compared to 15 years). While in some countries offence categories are gender-based.

As well as comparative work focusing on variations in MACRs, there has also been research which has explored differences in the age of criminal majority (ACM) in different countries. The ACM is the age at which young people can be dealt with in the adult criminal justice system rather than in the youth justice system. One such example is a comparative study by Abrams et al. (2018) which explored the different boundaries between MACRs and ACMs in four different jurisdictions: Argentina, Belize, England and Wales, and Finland. The aim of this research was to explore how the category of 'juvenile' was constructed in law and policy and what these boundaries mean for children's rights. In this research the category of 'juvenile' was understood to be the age group in the boundaries between the MACR and the ACM. Table 4.3 shows the variations in MACRs and ACMs in the countries included in the research.

This research notes some of the different legal, socio-cultural and political contexts that can explain variations in these age thresholds. For example, in Argentina the age of legal adulthood was lowered from 21 to 18 in 2011. While the MACR and ACM are both 16, and there is no separate juvenile court for 16–18-year-olds (i.e., those young people above the MACR and below the ACM), some range of protections apply. For instance, young people in this age category are not incarcerated in adult prisons, but there is some lack of clarity as to whether sentences which could be imposed on adults (e.g., life sentences) apply. Meanwhile in Finland, the relatively high MACR (when compared to the European average of 14 years) reflects a longstanding socio-cultural tradition regarding the status of children (Lappi-Seppälä, 2006). This means that children under the age of 15 who come to the attention of the authorities because of concerns regarding their behaviour are dealt with in the child protection and welfare system. As in Argentina, there are no separate juvenile courts in Finland, and children between the ages of 15 to 17 years may be dealt with in adult courts (but there are also provisions allowing judges to waive criminal justice proceedings altogether for young people in this age category). In Finland, young adults are legally defined as those aged between 18 and 20, and while their cases will be tried in adult criminal courts, they can only be sentenced to two-thirds of the sentence of an adult (i.e., someone over the age of 21).

Table 4.3 Variations in MACRs and ACMs

Country	MACR	ACM
Belize	9 years	16/18 years
England and Wales	10 years	18 years
Argentina	16 years	16 years
Finland	15 years	21 years

Source: Abrams et al. (2018: 115).

As Abrams et al. (2018: 124) note, these 'age parameters create a "wider" or "narrower" net for bringing youth into the justice system'. But perhaps, more importantly, the different contours of youth justice systems in these different countries tell us something more broadly about the way in which childhood and (young) adulthood is constructed and understood, and indeed speak to the wider polity and political economy that Cavadino and Dignan (2006a, b) argue are particularly salient variables.

Dominance of the Global North in Comparative Studies

As Franko (2017) observes, for much of history criminal justice and criminal law has been bound to the idea of the individual nation state. However, with the increasing nature of challenges that transcend national borders, such local responses cannot meet the scale of global challenges. Responses to climate change, or indeed more recently the global Coronavirus pandemic, provide stark illustrations of the limitations of the conceptual frame of the nation state. In the sphere of criminal justice, phenomena such as cybercrime, transnational terrorism and people trafficking have also destabilised the idea of the nation state as the locus of response. More fundamentally, perhaps, Franko (2017) argues that our conceptions of the role of states (i.e., what governments should be doing and how) are informed by geographic and historical specificities. These conceptions of the nation state are also bound up with histories of conquest and colonialism (Connell, 2007).

Much of the literature written about youth justice, including the comparative work we have discussed in this chapter and the examples we draw on throughout this book, focuses on the Global North. Although, some texts, such as Winterdyk's (2014) edited collection *Juvenile Justice: International Perspectives, Models and Trends* (including chapters on youth justice in Austria, Australia, Brazil, Canada, China, Iran, Japan, Namibia, the Netherlands, Scotland, Slovakia, South Africa as well as on England and Wales and the United States) and Cox and Abrams' (2021) *International Handbook of Youth Imprisonment* (including contributions exploring the context of youth imprisonment in Colombia, Ghana, India, Malawi, and Sweden as well as in England and Wales and the United States), have a much broader coverage, there is a predominance of work focusing on juvenile justice in Europe and the US contexts. This reflects a wider pattern in criminological scholarship and knowledge production which focuses on the 'Global North' (that is Western Europe and North America) as the referent to which other contexts are compared. As Connell (2007) demonstrates in her influential text, *Southern Theory*, this is also part of the legacy of colonial on systems of knowledge production, including the fact that the English language dominates academic publishing.

Taking forward Connell's (2007) arguments about the need to redress this imbalance in the ways in which knowledge is produced, including what is studied and how, Carrington et al. (2016) have made the case for 'Southern Criminology', that is:

> ... a more transnational criminology that is inclusive of the experiences and perspectives of the Global South, that adopts methods and concepts that bridge global divides and that embrace the democratization of knowledge production as a political aspiration. (Carrington et al., 2016: 1)

Carrington et al. (2016) argue that much of extant criminological theory generalises from experiences in the Global North, and fails to take into account different historical trajectories, including the impacts of colonialism and resource extraction. Moreover, this occlusion has failed to account for different patterns of crime and justice.

It is important to consider the extent to which these critiques also apply to the sphere of youth justice (which they undoubtedly do). Our conceptions of the status of childhood are culturally, socially and historically specific (as the discussion in Chapter 1 has illustrated). So too, are ideas about what constitutes criminal behaviour and how we should best respond to address this. While international children's rights standards articulate a particular 'universalist' vision of childhood and about the delivery of youth justice, we need to be mindful of the knowledges upon which such claims are based. (children's rights standards and youth justice are discussed in depth in Chapter 5.)

Conclusion

This chapter has explored some of the frames through which youth justice has been studied in comparative contexts. This has included the location of different responses to children who offend in the context of broader political and social systems, such as in Cavadino and Dignan's (2006a, b) work on political economy and punishment. Some of the challenges of engaging meaningfully in comparative research, including questions regarding what is being compared and how, have also been discussed. Some examples of comparative research adopting methods such as comparative case study approaches have been described. The frame of international children's rights standards as a means of exploring similarities and differences between countries has also been used as an approach to comparative analysis; although, as highlighted, some approaches which focus on countries or nation states as the unit of analysis may miss important inter-state differences. Moreover, as with much academic scholarship in criminology, as well as in other disciplines, there has been a predominant focus on the Global North. This means that there is still much to research and learn about approaches to children who come into conflict with the law in many other contexts.

Further Reading

Goldson (2019) (Ed.) *Juvenile Justice in Europe: Past, Present and Future.* London: Routledge.

This edited collection explores the history of youth justice in different contexts in European countries as well as current approaches to youth justice in different contexts. It includes thematic analyses of important topics such as race, ethnicity and social class and the intersections between the 'refugee crisis' and juvenile justice.

Cox, A. and Abrams, L. (Eds.) (2021) *The Palgrave International Handbook of Youth Imprisonment.* London: Palgrave Macmillan.

This handbook explores youth imprisonment in a broad range of countries. It also includes thematic chapters on topics such as gender and sexuality, as well as accounts of young people's experiences of youth custody in different contexts.

5

Children's Rights and Youth Justice

Objectives

- This chapter provides an overview of the importance of children's rights principles in youth justice.
- Readers will be introduced to the key rights instruments relating to young people who come into conflict with the law, and the youth justice system.
- The chapter will help the reader to identify the processes through which rights compliance is monitored.
- The chapter will also enable readers to explore aspects of disjuncture between rights in principle and the reality of practice.

Introduction

Children's rights principles are particularly relevant in the area of youth justice where the state can intervene in a child's life to impose a penalty or mandate treatment when a child is deemed to have contravened the law. International rights standards, such as the United Convention on the Rights of the Child (UNCRC), specify that the system of justice for children should be separate from that for adults and that a 'child's best interests' should guide all decisions. Alongside the UNCRC, a range of international rights instruments specific to juvenile justice outline further key principles for the administration of youth justice and the treatment of children who are its subjects. At the European level the Council of Europe has also developed Guidelines on 'Child Friendly Justice' that draw on international principles and insights from cases raised in the European Court of Human Rights (ECtHR). These range of rights instruments provide consistent messages regarding diversion (meaning to divert children from being dealt with in the criminal justice system), minimal intervention, age-appropriate treatment and reintegration (Kilkelly, 2008), and as such serve as a potential counterpoint against more punitive trends towards children and young people (Goldson and Muncie, 2015). Children's rights standards are increasingly referenced by organisations working with children and young people and are drawn upon in legal judgments concerning children's rights.

However, at the same time, there are gaps between rights rhetoric and reality seen in the failures to uphold children's rights and in examples of rights' transgressions, including where children are subject to inhumane and degrading treatment within the youth justice system. This chapter provides an overview of the key rights instruments in juvenile justice before proceeding to an exploration of the application of rights in practice. The chapter concludes by considering some of the limits of children's rights standards and outlining areas of current debate.

Children's Rights Standards and Youth Justice

This section sets out the key children's rights standards and draws out their specific relevance to youth justice.

United Nations Convention on the Rights of the Child (UNCRC)

The United Nations Convention on the Rights of the Child (UNCRC) is a comprehensive, internationally binding agreement on the rights of children, which was adopted by the United Nations General Assembly in 1989. It is the most ratified human rights instrument globally. All countries with the exception of the United States have ratified the UNCRC. This means that they have entered a binding agreement to meet its provisions and obligations. The UNCRC defines a child as a person under the age of 18. The Convention includes a number of articles (40 in total) that address different aspects of children's rights. There are four key principles outlined in the Convention:

1. Non-Discrimination: That all rights guaranteed by the Convention must be available to all children without discrimination of any kind (Article 2);
2. Best Interests: That the best interests of the child must be a primary consideration in all actions concerning children (Article 3);
3. Right to Life: That every child has the right to life, survival and development (Article 6); and
4. Right to be Heard: That the child's views must be considered and taken into account in all matters affecting him or her (Article 12).

The UNCRC applies to all children, but there are two Articles that specifically address children in the youth justice system: Article 37 and Article 40. Article 37 refers to Torture and Deprivation of Liberty, and states that:

> No child should be subjected to torture or other cruel, inhuman or degrading treatment or punishment. Neither capital punishment nor life imprisonment without the possibility of release shall be imposed for offences committed by persons below eighteen years of age. (Article 37, a)

Article 37 further elaborates that no child should be deprived of their liberty unlawfully or arbitrarily and that if they are arrested or detained, this should be in accordance with the law and should be 'only as a measure of last resort and for the shortest appropriate period of time' (Art. 37, b). If a child is deprived of their liberty they should be treated with humanity and dignity, and in a manner that takes account of their age. Children deprived of their liberty should have the right to maintain contact with their family.

Article 40 of the UNRC refers to the Administration of Juvenile Justice and outlines that States Parties (that is, individual countries and legal jurisdictions) should have separate laws, procedures and institutions for dealing with children who come into conflict with the law. In other words, countries should have separate youth justice systems. Such systems should provide different ways for dealing with children, for example through guidance and supervision or education and vocational training programmes. All countries should establish a minimum age of criminal responsibility (MACR), which is the age at which a child can be held responsible for a criminal offence. Due process rights should apply to children who come into conflict with the law (see also Chapter 4 for a discussion of the *Gault* case). This means that children should have the right to the presumption of innocence until proven guilty, the right to legal representation and appropriate assistance and to have their privacy respected at all stages of the proceedings.

International rights guidelines on juvenile justice

Alongside the UNCRC, there are a number of United Nations rules and guidelines that specifically address the youth justice system and young people who come into conflict with the law. These include guidelines on the administration of the criminal justice system, the prevention of juvenile delinquency and the treatment of young people who are deprived of their liberty:

- *United Nations Minimum Rules for the Administration of Juvenile Justice (The Beijing Rules) 1985;*
- *United Nations Guidelines for the Prevention of Juvenile Delinquency (The Riyadh Guidelines) 1990;*
- *United Nations Rules for the Protection of Juveniles Deprived of their Liberty (Havana Rules) 1990.*

The *Beijing Rules* were published in 1985, so they predate the UNCRC. These rules encourage countries to develop social policies aimed at preventing juvenile delinquency. They outline that countries should develop separate responses to children who come into conflict with the law, and that approaches to children should be proportionate and focus on welfare rather than punishment. Children who break the law should be afforded the same legal rights as adults and be subject to a fair trial. The rules favour diversionary approaches for young people in order to avoid the stigmatising effects of contact with the criminal justice system. This means that children should be dealt with through less formal measures where possible. The rules further advocate that people working with the juvenile justice system, including the police, receive specific training to equip them for this role.

Detention pending trial should be a measure of last resort, and children's cases should be adjudicated by a competent legal authority. Children have a right to legal representation and to be accompanied by parents and guardians during legal proceedings. The sentencing of children should be proportionate and take into account their needs. Deprivation of liberty should be used as a measure of last resort and for the shortest time possible. Capital punishment is prohibited for children, as is corporal punishment. The rules outline certain measures that may be suitable for young people in order to avoid institutionalisation measures. These broadly include using community sentences such as probation, care and supervision orders and orders to participate in counselling or treatment in the community.

The *Beijing Rules* advocate that cases involving young people should be dealt with quickly without any unnecessary delay. The need to process juvenile cases quickly is given particular emphasis because of young people's development, and the need to intervene expeditiously in order to provide support and prevent further offending. The commentary on Rule 20 on 'Avoidance of Unnecessary Delay' states:

> The speedy conduct of formal procedures in juvenile cases is a paramount concern. Otherwise whatever good may be achieved by the procedure and the disposition is at risk. As time passes, the juvenile will find it increasingly difficult, if not impossible, to relate the procedure and disposition to the offence, both intellectually and psychologically.

This emphasis on the need to deal with children's cases quickly points to an understanding that young people need to relate the consequence with the action. If too much time passes between the commission of an offence and the subsequent disposal (i.e., how the young person is dealt with), a young person may not understand the reasoning for intervention and/or have become involved in further offending.

The *Beijing Rules* also address the issue of criminal records acquired as a juvenile and state that these should be 'kept strictly confidential and closed to third parties'. Records acquired as a juvenile should not subsequently be disclosed in any proceedings as an adult. While the *Beijing Rules* are clear that detention should be used as a measure of last resort, they also elaborate that where a child is subject to detention, the objective should be 'to provide care, protection, education and vocational skills, with a view to assisting them to assume socially constructive and productive roles in society' (Rule 26.1).

Further elaboration on the treatment children in detention is provided in the *Havana Rules (United Nations Rules for the Protection of Juveniles Deprived of their Liberty)*, which were adopted in 1990. These rules reiterate the principle that the detention of children is a measure that should be used sparingly and that the focus of any detention should be educative rather than punitive. The *Havana Rules* also provide more detailed guidance on the management and administration of detention facilities, noting for instance that children should not be detained with adults. Children should be provided with suitable clothing and their basic needs should be met (including food and access to drinking water) as well as the provision of education and training opportunities. Children should not be made to work in forms of child labour while in detention. They should have access to recreation and medical care and provision should be made for religious observance. The use of physical restraint is prohibited except in exceptional circumstances (such as in order to prevent injury). Detention facilities should be subject to inspection and children should have the opportunities to make requests and complaints.

The UNCRC is not incorporated directly into domestic law in the jurisdictions of the United Kingdom, as it has been in Iceland (in 2013) and elsewhere (see Lundy et al., 2013), but the principles of the UNCRC are intended nonetheless to guide domestic law and practice and are referred to by the courts when interpreting obligations imposed by human rights (House of Commons Joint Committee on Human Rights, 2015). Furthermore, the United Kingdom is subject to periodic inspection by the Committee on the Rights of the Child to assess its compliance with children's rights in accordance with these international standards.

United Nations Committee on the Rights of the Child

The United Nations Committee on the Rights of the Child is a body of independent experts that monitors the implementation of the UNCRC in different countries. The Box below provides further detail on the composition and role of the Committee.

United Nations Committee on the Rights of the Child

The United Nations Committee on the Rights of the Child comprises 18 democratically elected expert members drawn from the States Parties that have ratified the Convention. It monitors the implementation of the UNCRC by States Parties. It also monitors the implementation of two Optional Protocols to the Convention, on the involvement of children in armed conflict and on the sale of children, child prostitution and child pornography. In 2011 the UN General Assembly approved a third Optional Protocol which allows children to submit complaints regarding specific violations of their rights under the Convention and the Optional Protocols. Further detail on the UN Committee on the Rights of the Child is available here: www.ohchr.org/en/hrbodies/crc/pages/crcindex.aspx

The Committee carries out periodic reviews of States' compliance with the UNCRC. To date the United Kingdom (which consists of the legal jurisdictions of England and Wales, Scotland and Northern Ireland, as well as Overseas Territories and Crown Dependencies) has been subject to five periodic reviews, the last of which was in 2016. As part of the review, parties such as the Children's Commissioners prepare a report on their assessment of the UK's compliance with the UNCRC, highlighting any issues of concern. Each of the jurisdictions of the United Kingdom (England and Wales, Scotland and Northern Ireland) have an independent Children's Commissioner. The precise legal roles of the Children's Commissioners in each of the UK jurisdictions varies, but generally their roles are to safeguard children's rights and to carry out reviews and investigations where there are rights breaches (Thomas, 2011). As well as the report from the Children's Commissioners and other interested parties (e.g., non-governmental organisations working in the area of children's rights), the government submits a report to the Committee on its compliance with the UNCRC.

For the last periodic review, the Children's Commissioners highlighted a number of areas of concern regarding the United Kingdom's compliance with children's rights standards (UK Children's Commissioners, 2015). The negative impact of austerity measures on children's health and well-being during the period since the last review (2008–2015), and the consequential impacts on record levels of child poverty and the provision of services to children in general was noted:

> Austerity measures have reduced provision of a range of services that protect and fulfil children's rights including health and child and adolescent mental health services; education; early years; preventive and early intervention services; and youth services. (UK Children's Commissioners, 2015: 2)

The effects of austerity were evident for all children and in relation to youth justice specifically a number of criticisms were made. These included the fact that the minimum age of criminal responsibility (MACR) remains low across the UK jurisdictions (see further discussion below), and that some cases involving children charged with serious offences are routinely dealt with in higher courts that are not sufficiently adapted for children. This impacts on children's ability to understand proceedings and to meaningfully participate. Further concerns were raised regarding the fact that in certain circumstances reporting restrictions can be lifted in court cases involving children, meaning that children can be publicly identified in the media. This contravenes rights standards which recommend that proceedings involving children should be held in private in order to prevent the negative impact of further stigmatisation. Further negative effects of stigmatisation are seen in the application of the criminal record regime in the UK jurisdictions, where criminal records acquired as a juvenile may be subject to disclosure many years after the commission of the offence, and in some cases for the rest of a person's life (UK Children's Commissioners, 2015).

Particular concerns were also raised by the Children's Commissioners regarding the over-representation of children from Black, Asian and Minority Ethnic (BAME) backgrounds in the youth justice system. In England and Wales children from BAME backgrounds constitute 38% of the custodial population, despite comprising less than 14% of the general population (this issue is discussed in further depth in Chapter 8). Looked After Children (LAC), i.e., children who are in the care of social services for reasons of child welfare and protection, are also over-represented within the youth justice systems of the different UK jurisdictions. (The reasons for the overrepresentation of LAC in the youth justice system are complex and are discussed in further depth in Chapter 9.)

While overall the numbers of children in custody have declined across the UK jurisdictions there is still clear evidence that custody is not being used as a measure of last resort for all children (UK Government 2014; Committee on the Rights of the Child, 2016). For instance, new presumptive custodial sentences for knife crime introduced in England and Wales in 2014 mean that children convicted of such offences would automatically be sentenced to custody. Further still, the conditions of custody including access to education and the use of physical restraint have been critiqued by the Children's Commissioners (UK Children's Commissioners, 2015).

The Committee on the Rights of the Child considered all of the evidence they received in relation to the United Kingdom's compliance with the UNCRC, including the government's own assessment (UK Government, 2014), and it published its Concluding Observations in 2016 (Committee on the Rights of the Child, 2016). Whilst noting some of the positive achievements in relation to the realisation of children's rights in the United Kingdom, the Committee made strong criticisms of the continued use of force against children within the youth justice system. This included the use of Tasers, and in Northern Ireland the use of accentuating energy projectiles (rubber bullets), by police against children. On this specific point, the UK report to the Committee on the Rights of the Child had stated:

> The UK Government has carefully considered the Committee's recommendation that it should end the use of Tasers and Attenuating Energy Projectiles (AEPs) on children. While we support the recommendation in principle, we believe it is impractical to implement it while [the] Taser is in use for other age groups and officers' first priority must be to defend members of the public or themselves. A similar approach is taken in Northern Ireland, Scotland and Wales. (UK Government, 2014: 47)

The Committee was also critical of the use of physical restraint on children to maintain good order in Young Offender Institutions (YOIs) and the use of pain-inducing techniques on children in institutional settings in England, Wales and Northern Ireland (see Shenton and Smith, 2021). The Committee recommended that the MACR should be raised across the jurisdictions in line with children's rights standards; that the mandatory imposition of life imprisonment for some offences when committed by someone under 18 should be abolished; and that the principle that detention should be a measure of last resort should be established in legislation (Committee on the Rights of the Child, 2016). It is worth noting that a number of these recommendations echo similar issues raised in previous periodic reviews (e.g., the recommendation to raise the MACR).

A review of the various reports produced by the Committee on the Rights of the Child on the United Kingdom's compliance with the UNCRC shows that there have been repeated criticisms of aspects of the youth justice system over the years in which the periodic reviews have been conducted (i.e., between 1994 and 2016). Apart from expressing concerns about these issues and prompting countries to change aspects of practice and legislation, the Committee on the Rights of the Child has no way of forcing rights compliance, for example through sanctioning countries who do not comply. More fundamentally, the UNCRC has not been incorporated into domestic law in any of the jurisdictions of the United Kingdom. Therefore, it is not **justiciable**. This means that an individual cannot go to a court in the United Kingdom to complain about a breach of any rights in the Convention. Courts have however, drawn on the principles of the UNCRC in their judgments, and the European Court of Human Rights has increasingly done so in cases involving children (Kilkelly, 2001; Nolan and Kilkelly, 2016) (see further discussion below).

Committee on the Rights of the Child – General Comment on Juvenile Justice

Based on their experience of conducting periodic reviews of countries' compliance with the UNCRC across the world, the Committee on the Rights of the Child has noted several areas where further elaboration and guidance is required. In 2007 the Committee on the Rights of the Child published its General Comment on Juvenile Justice (General Comment No. 10) (Committee on the Rights of the Child, 2007), and observed the following:

> ... many States parties still have a long way to go in achieving full compliance with CRC, e.g., in the areas of procedural rights, the development and implementation of measures for dealing with children in conflict with the law without resorting to judicial proceedings, and the use of deprivation of liberty only as a measure of last resort .... The experience in reviewing the States parties' performance in the field of juvenile justice is the reason for the present general comment, by which the Committee wants to provide the States parties with more elaborated guidance and recommendations for their efforts to establish an administration of juvenile justice in compliance with CRC. (Committee on the Rights of the Child, 2007: 1)

The General Comment provides further guidance on areas such as the need to actively ensure non-discrimination in juvenile justice systems. It notes for instance that discrimination and disparities on the basis of race, ethnicity, gender and disability may occur because of a lack of specific policies tackling these areas or because of a lack of training for those working with young people. Significantly, the General Comment provides a more specific recommendation on an appropriate MACR. The UNCRC merely states that countries should establish a MACR and the *Beijing Rules* says that the MACR, should 'not be set at too low an age'. However, the Committee goes further and states:

> ... *a minimum age of criminal responsibility below the age of 12 years is considered by the Committee not to be internationally acceptable.* States parties are encouraged to increase their lower MACR to the age of 12 years as the absolute minimum age and to continue to increase it to a higher age level. (Committee on the Rights of the Child, 2007: 11, emphasis added)

The Committee is currently drafting a new General Comment (General Comment No. 24), which when ratified will replace the existing General Comment (General Comment, No. 10) (Committee on the Rights of the Child, 2018). This proposes a higher minimum age of criminal responsibility, recommending 14 as the minimum age:

> In the original general comment No. 10 (2007), the Committee had considered 12 years as the absolute minimum age. However, the Committee finds that this age indication is still low. *States parties are encouraged to increase their minimum age to at least 14 years of age.* (Committee on the Rights of the Child, 2018: 9, emphasis added).

The proposed change to the recommended MACR shows a shift in thinking regarding the appropriate age at which children should be dealt with within justice systems, even where these systems are specifically adapted for young people. However, the persistently low MACR within the UK jurisdictions (see further discussion below), provides one of the clearest examples of the gap between rhetoric on children's rights and lived reality.

Council of Europe – Child-Friendly Justice

In addition to global standards such as the UNCRC, there are a range of European-level standards and guidelines that are relevant to children in the youth justice system. The Council of Europe has also developed rules that advocate rights-based approaches for children who come into conflict with the law. (See the Box below for an explanation of the background and role of the Council of Europe.) These have been outlined in a range of recommendations and guidelines including Council Recommendations addressing juvenile delinquency, the rights of children living in residential institutions, the European Prison Rules, and the European Rules for Juvenile Offenders subject to sanctions or measures (Recommendation Rec (2003) 20 Concerning new ways of dealing with juvenile delinquency and the role of juvenile justice; Recommendation Rec (2005) 5 on the Rights of Children Living in Residential Institutions; Recommendation Rec (2006) 2 on the European Prison Rules; Recommendation CM/Rec (2008) 11 on the European Rules for Juvenile Offenders subject to sanctions or measures).

What is the Council of Europe? A Brief Explanation

The Council of Europe comprises of 46 member states (it had included the Russian Federation amongst its members until March 2022, when a decision was made by the Committee of Ministers to exclude Russia following the invasion of Ukraine). Twenty-seven of the Council of Europe members are also members of the European Union. However, the Council of Europe should not be confused with the European Union, which it predates. The Council of Europe was established in 1949 after the

Second World War to promote democracy and protect human rights and the rule of law in Europe. The European Convention on Human Rights is a Council of Europe treaty adopted in 1953, which sets out a number of fundamental rights and freedoms (right to life, prohibition of torture, prohibition of slavery and forced labour, right to liberty and security, right to a fair trial, no punishment without law, right to respect for private and family life, freedom of thought, conscience and religion, freedom of expression, freedom of assembly and association, right to marry, right to an effective remedy, prohibition of discrimination). Member states of the Council of Europe are required to secure these rights and freedoms for everyone living in their countries. The United Kingdom incorporated the European Convention on Human Rights into domestic law through the Human Rights Act 1998. This means that the government and public bodies must uphold human rights in laws and decision-making, and failure to do so can lead to legal challenge. If these issues are not resolved at the domestic level (i.e., in the UK courts), then a case can be brought before the European Court of Human Rights (ECtHR), which is based in Strasbourg. The ECtHR was established to ensure that there is an enforcement mechanism for the European Convention of Human Rights. There have been a number of cases brought before the ECtHR concerning the treatment of children in the justice system in different member states. While the UNCRC is not directly justiciable (i.e., a person cannot challenge a government on the basis of failing to uphold the UNCRC), the ECtHR has taken note of the UNCRC in its interpretation of the European Convention on Human Rights. Once the European Court of Human Rights issues a ruling, the parties to a case must abide by the judgments of the Court and take all necessary measures to comply with them. While, following Brexit, the United Kingdom has left the European Union, it is still a member of the Council of Europe. This means that cases can still be brought before the European Court of Human Rights and the United Kingdom is still obliged to follow the judgments of the Court.

In 2015 the Council of Europe published its guidance on '**child-friendly justice**', which draws together the various principles outlined in the UNCRC and other rights instruments relating to children in the juvenile justice system (such as the *Beijing and Havana Rules*) and children's rights more generally (Council of Europe, 2015). Part of the motivation for developing this detailed guidance was a recognition of the gap between *law and policy* and *practice* in the implementation of children's rights. In other words, a gap between what's written on the page, and what happens on the ground:

> While a number of legal instruments exist at the international, European and national levels, gaps remain both in law and in practice, and governments and professionals working with children are requesting guidance to ensure the effective implementation of their standards. (Council of Europe, 2015: 37)

Some of the evidence in the gaps between rights on the page and rights and practice is derived from inspections and reports published by European Committee on the Prevention of Torture (CPT), a Council of Europe body that visits places of detention in different member states, including prisons, juvenile detention centres, police stations, immigration holding centres and psychiatric hospitals, and produces reports containing findings and recommendations. Further evidence of the gap between policy and practice is seen in the cases brought before the European Court of Human Rights, where member states' compliance with the European Convention on Human Rights has been challenged. Some of these cases relate specifically to the treatment of children in the criminal justice system in different countries. See the Box below for a discussion of a case involving children.

Case Study: *T* V *United Kingdom and V* V *United Kingdom* (European Court of Human Rights, 1999)

T and V were aged 11 in November 1993, when they were tried in the Crown Court for the murder of 2-year-old James Bulger. They were convicted of murder and sentenced to detention at 'Her Majesty's Pleasure'. This is a sentence in lieu of a life sentence, which is the automatic sentence that an adult would receive for such an offence. Following an intense level of publicity, which was in part fuelled by the fact that the trial judge had ruled that both defendants could be publicly identified, which is not ordinarily allowed in cases involving juveniles, the Home Secretary Michael Howard made a decision that the boys should serve a minimum of 15 years in prison before they could be considered for release (see also Chapter 4 for a discussion). This decision was appealed in the domestic courts, and their case was subsequently appealed to the European Court of Human Rights, where representatives for the two boys argued that their treatment in the court system had contravened their human rights under the European Convention of Human Rights. Namely, they argued that Article 6 (the right to a fair trial) of the ECHR had been contravened because the public trial where the children had been identified had been intimidatory. Furthermore, their treatment had not been impartial because the Home Secretary had been influenced by a public campaign to imprison the boys for a lengthy period of time. *The Sun* newspaper had run a campaign encouraging readers to submit coupons to the Home Secretary advocating that the boys should be detained for life (Haydon and Scraton, 2000).

The European Court of Human Rights ruled that T and V's right to a fair trial had been compromised by their treatment as their ability to participate effectively in their trial had been impaired. For instance, insufficient adaptations had been made to take account of their young age and their capacity to understand the court proceedings. The Court also ruled that the Home Secretary's involvement in setting the minimum time they would spend in custody (this period is referred to as the 'tariff') was also a breach of their rights. A number of other rights violations had been alleged (including that the children were subjected to inhumane and degrading treatment), but these were rejected by the Court (Haydon and Scraton, 2000). Nonetheless, this judgment of the European Court of Human Rights (ECtHR) underscored some important issues regarding the need to ensure that systems of justice are sufficiently adapted to allow for a fair trial for children, and this case has subsequently been referenced as an important legal benchmark (Council of Europe, 2015).

Case Reference: European Court of Human Rights (Grand Chamber) judgment of 16 December 1999, T. v. UK, No. 24724/94, and judgment of 16 December 1999, V. v. UK, No. 24888/94

Discussion points

- What do you think about the principle that children's legal proceedings should be held in private?
- What sort of adaptations would children and young people require to participate effectively in legal proceedings?

The above case predates the Council of Europe's *Guidelines on Child-Friendly Justice*, but, as mentioned earlier, is one of a number of cases that influenced their development. The Council of Europe's Guidelines on 'child-friendly justice' conceptualise justice quite broadly. The Guidelines address children's contact with justice systems in the context of child protection and welfare, and as victims and witnesses of offences as well as potential perpetrators. In other words, they address children's interactions with criminal, civil or administrative law. This encompasses children who are prosecuted for offences, and children who are subject to child protection measures and care proceedings. It also includes children's rights in family law proceedings such as divorce and separation. In all cases, the Guidelines outline that 'child-friendly justice' should apply, defining this as follows:

> 'Child-friendly justice' refers to justice systems which guarantee the respect and the effective implementation of all children's rights at the highest attainable level ... giving due consideration to the child's level of maturity and understanding and the circumstances of the case. It is, in particular, justice that is accessible, age appropriate, speedy, diligent, adapted to and focused on the needs and rights of the child, respecting the rights of the child including the rights to due process, to participate in and understand proceedings, to respect for private and family life and to integrity and dignity. (Council of Europe, 2015: 17)

Five fundamental principles underpin 'child-friendly justice':

1. Participation – Children have the right to be informed about their rights, and they should be given appropriate ways to access justice and to be consulted and heard in proceedings which affect them.

2. Best interest of the child: This should be the primary consideration in all matters involving or affecting children.
3. Dignity: Children should be treated with care, sensitivity, fairness and respect. Particular attention should be paid to their specific needs.
4. Protection from discrimination: The rights of all children should be secure without discrimination.
5. Rule of law: The rule of law principle should apply fully to children as it does to adults.

(Council of Europe, 2015: 17–19)

While the Guidelines are not legally binding, Liefaard (2016) argues that they have broader legal and political relevance. For instance, they have been incorporated into the Council of Europe's children's strategy and they have also been included as part of the European Union's 'Agenda for the Rights of Child', in the development of EU legislation and as a reference point in ECtHR case law. (The EU Directive (2016/800) on Procedural Safeguards for Children who are Suspects or Accused Persons in Criminal Proceedings specifically references the *Guidelines on Child-Friendly Justice* and was officially adopted by the European Parliament on 11 May 2016. Member states are required to transpose the directive into national law by 2022.) The Guidelines elaborate how child-friendly justice should be achieved, and, at almost 100 pages, are more comprehensive than the UN Guidelines on juvenile justice referred to earlier. As well as articulating general principles, they address specific areas including legal counsel and representation, the organisation of proceedings to allow children to effectively participate and the use of evidence and statements from children. However, the statement on MACR is weak, merely specifying that 'the minimum age of criminal responsibility should not be too low and should be determined by law' (Council of Europe, 2015: 25). And while the need to provide for legal counsel for children as a core principle of 'child-friendly' justice is underlined, the Guidelines fall short of requiring states to provide free legal aid to all children (Liefaard, 2016). (On the issue of free legal aid, the Guidelines state: 'Children should have access to free legal aid, under the same or more lenient conditions as adults' (Council of Europe, 2015: 27).) Furthermore, they do not consider the transition of children into the adult criminal justice system, an issue that has become increasingly prominent in the context of wider research exploring maturation and extended transitions to adulthood (Pruin and Dünkel, 2015).

Children's Rights Standards – Rhetoric and Reality

Taken together, this body of children's rights instruments at the global and European level shows an increasing emphasis placed on the need to recognise the rights of children in general and the need to safeguard the rights of children who come into conflict with the law specifically. First and foremost, the UNCRC explicitly states that a child's welfare should be the paramount consideration in all matters that affect them. In other words, the welfare and needs of the child should be the first consideration of any institution dealing with children. Children rights' standards are also clear that there should be separate justice systems for children and adults, and that where possible youth justice systems should favour diversionary approaches, meaning that a child should have minimal contact with formal processes. This might mean for instance that a child is dealt with by way of a police warning, rather than by being required to appear in court (see Chapter 3 for further discussion of diversionary approaches).

Furthermore, where children are dealt with more formally within the youth justice system, an emphasis should be placed on their welfare, education and rehabilitation as opposed to further punishment. Several commentators have noted that children's rights instruments have had a positive impact on youth justice systems by establishing a set of norms and standards through which we can assess the treatment of children who come into conflict with the law (Kilkelly, 2008; Goldson and Kilkelly, 2013; Goldson and Muncie, 2015). Children's rights instruments have also helped to inform and shape domestic policy and legislation (Lynch and Liefaard, 2020). For example, youth justice legislation in the Republic of Ireland specifically references the principle set out in Art. 37 of the UNCRC, that detention should be a measure of last resort, and for the shortest time possible. While in Scotland children's rights, along with insights from research on the potentially negative impacts of children's contact with the criminal justice system (McAra and McVie, 2007), have been instrumental in leading to a change in the MACR. However, it is also evident that there are limits to the reach of rights within the youth justice system, and many examples of gaps between rights rhetoric and reality (Smith, 2010). The next section of this chapter explores some of these gaps, with specific reference to the minimum age of criminal responsibility (MACR) and the treatment of children in detention.

Minimum age of criminal responsibility

There is a wide variation in the minimum age of criminal responsibility globally. Some countries have MACRs as low as 7 years (e.g., Brunei Darussalam, Egypt, India) and some countries do not even have an established legal MACR (e.g., Cuba, Malaysia, Mozambique) (Cipriani, 2009/2016). The range of MACRs varies in Europe, where the average minimum age of criminal responsibility is 14 years (Goldson, 2013). Some countries apply different MACRs according to the seriousness of the offence. For instance, in the Republic of Ireland, the MACR is normally 12 years, but is only 10 for serious offences such as murder or rape. This is a somewhat incongruous position, as from a children's rights perspective, it is not clear why a child should be held more responsible based on the nature of the wrongdoing.

Article 40 of the UNCRC refers to the minimum age of criminal responsibility (MACR), but the wording in the Convention is weak, as it merely specifies that States Parties should establish 'a minimum age below which children shall be presumed not to have the capacity to infringe the penal law' (Art. 40,3(a)). Part of the reason that the UNCRC does not specify a MACR is because the Convention was intended to have international applicability, and at the time of drafting it was impossible to fix a MACR that would be acceptable to all signatories (Cipriani, 2009/2016). However, this lack of specificity has been criticised (Goldson, 2013). As noted earlier, the General Comment (No. 10) (2007) from the Committee on the Rights of the Child has since recommended that the MACR should be 12, and the updated Comment has recommended that the MACR should be raised to 14 years.

However, the MACRs of the jurisdictions of the United Kingdom still remain comparatively low, despite continued sustained critique (Goldson, 2013). In England and Wales and in Northern Ireland the MACR is 10, while in Scotland the MACR has recently been raised to 12 years under the *Age of Criminal Responsibility (Scotland) Act 2019*. Prior to this the age at which children in Scotland could be held criminally responsible was 8 years. England and Wales and Northern Ireland are therefore outliers when compared to other countries in Europe. The refusal of the Westminster government and the Stormont Assembly (the legislatures responsible for justice matters in England and Wales and Northern Ireland respectively), to raise the MACR despite repeated calls from a range of quarters, including children's rights charities, Children's Commissioners and penal reform organisations, has been the subject of sustained critique (Goldson, 2013; Brown and Charles, 2021; UK Children's Commissioners, 2015). The United Nations Committee on the Rights of the Child has consistently criticised the low MACR, and in its last periodic review stated that the UK jurisdictions should:

> Raise the minimum age of criminal responsibility in accordance with acceptable international standards. (UN Committee on the Rights of the Child, 2016: 22)

The fact that the MACR has not been raised despite a clear iteration in international children's rights standards that 10 years is considered too low, demonstrates some of the limitations of children's rights principles in practice. It is worth noting that every periodic review conducted by the UN Committee on the

Rights of the Child on the United Kingdom's compliance with the Convention, has made the same point about the unacceptably low MACR and pointed to other shortcomings, such as the failure to use detention as a last resort for the shortest time possible.

Children's rights in detention

While children's rights standards have served an important role in providing clarity and guidance on the roles and responsibilities of states when dealing with children who come into conflict with the law (Kilkelly, 2008; Lynch and Liefaard, 2020), the extent to which a failure to implement standards can be meaningfully challenged is limited. As noted earlier, standards such as those enshrined in the UNCRC are 'permissive' and failure to implement them or more even flagrantly breaching them does not attract any formal sanction (Goldson and Muncie, 2015).

The issue of child detention provides another illustrative example. The body of children's rights standards clearly emphasise that custody should only be used 'as a measure of last resort' and for the 'shortest time possible'. Furthermore, where children are detained the regimes should be 'child appropriate' and focused on education rather than punishment. Children should not be subject to inhumane or degrading treatment, and the use of corporal punishment of any kind is explicitly prohibited. We see however, from global figures on juvenile detention that it is estimated that 410,000 children are deprived of their liberty in pre-trial detention facilities and prisons per year (and this figure is likely to be an underestimate) (Nowak, 2019). This clearly illustrates a gap between the rhetoric of 'detention as a last resort' and the lived reality of many children's lives (Goldson and Kilkelly, 2013).

Furthermore, in many cases across the globe there is unfortunately ample evidence of children being subject to violence and degrading treatment within such facilities (Nowak, 2019). The United Nations' *World Report on Violence Against Children* (Pinheiro, 2006), noted the particular vulnerability of children detained in custodial facilities to violence and mistreatment. Meanwhile inspection reports of custodial institutions in England and Wales consistently point to serious concerns regarding safety, including incidents of bullying, the use of pain-based restraint techniques and excessive use of violence and force in some institutions (HM Inspectorate of Prisons, 2019). Of particular concern was the fact that in the latest round of inspections, facilities that were ostensibly aimed at catering for younger and more vulnerable children (Secure Training Centres) were often performing worse in relation to children's safety than those accommodating older children (Young Offender Institutions) (HM Inspectorate of Prisons, 2019).

Secure Training Centres

The following is taken from the HM Chief Inspector of Prisons' report into treatment of children in secure training centres:

- Outcomes for children in all three STCs remained a cause for concern.
- We continued to find high levels of violence and use of force.
- All three centres had experienced significant staff turnover, and systems to manage children's behaviour were undermined by inconsistent application by staff.

Extract from: *HM Chief Inspector of Prisons for England and Wales, Annual Report, 2018–2019* (p. 60).

A recent report published by the Council of Europe's Committee for the Prevention of Torture (CPT) following its visit to institutions of detention in the United Kingdom in 2019, noted serious concerns in respect of juvenile justice facilities (CPT, 2020). It documented a range of issues in Young Offender Institutions (YOIs) and Secure Training Centres (STCs) in England and Wales. This included reports of ill-treatment of young people by staff in YOIs, including excessive use of force and the use of insulting language by staff towards young people. The use of pain-based restraint techniques (such as wrist flexion, which is applied by taking hold of the thumb and forefinger and, with the elbow bent pressing the hand downward) on children was still occurring in YOIs and STCs, despite previous recommendations that this should cease, and the CPT recommended that this should 'be abolished in law and practice' (CPT, 2020: 60).

The endemic problems evident in youth detention across time and place have led some commentators to observe that while children's rights standards may provide a framework to 'pacify the more problematic excesses of child imprisonment' (Goldson and Kilkelly, 2013: 345), the fact that these problematic excesses continue to occur in the face of international standards, routine inspections and oversight, is evidence of the limitations of 'rights-based approaches to the penal detention of children' (p. 345). This has led some to argue that the abolition of penal detention for children (something which the UNCRC and associated standards do not explicitly advocate), would be the only way to effectively achieve rights compliance in this domain (Goldson, 2009; Goldson and Kilkelly, 2013).

The Limits of Children's Rights Standards in Youth Justice

While international standards on children's rights and specific guidelines on youth justice play an important role in establishing norms and benchmarks for how children should be dealt with in the criminal justice system, as the previous section demonstrates, there are limits in their reach and clear gaps in how these standards are realised in practice. As O'Brien and Fitz-Gibbon (2018: 218) observe:

> ... it is increasingly apparent that the ubiquity of rhetoric about child rights and child friendly justice does not, in any automatic sense, ameliorate, or even mitigate, the brutal conditions endured, at times, by children in conflict with the law.

Some of the reasons for this gap between rhetoric and reality include failures to implement children's rights standards in legislation and practice. For instance, Australia maintains a reservation to Article (37, c) of the UNCRC, which is the requirement that children should be detained separately from adults, and it has faced repeated criticism for this stance (Cunneen et al., 2016; O'Brien and Fitz-Gibbon, 2018). The consequences of detaining children with adults have led to situations where children have been assaulted and suffered serious injury, and where children have suffered harm as a result of being subject to control and restraint techniques that are not approved for use on children (O'Brien and Fitz-Gibbon, 2018). We have also seen, as in the instance of MACR discussed earlier, that there was a certain amount of vagueness in the formulation of the original wording of the UNCRC in relation to establishing a specific minimum age of criminal responsibility. This lack of specificity provides room for varying interpretations of what 'constitutes too low an age'. At the same time, it is recognised that countries have diverse historical, cultural, societal and legal traditions and that rights instruments cannot be totalising.

There has also been concerning evidence of reversals to progress made in relation to children's rights in some countries. For example, while children's rights standards have consistently advocated higher MACRs, some countries have seen attempts to lower the MACR as a result of internal political pressures. For example, in 2010 Denmark reduced the MACR from 15 years to 14 years, only to raise it again to 15 in 2012, when a new government came to power. In the Philippines the MACR has recently been reduced from 15 to 12 years following the election of Filipino President Rodrigo Duterte and his pursuit of a 'law and order' agenda (UNICEF, 2019). These examples highlight some of the tensions between children's rights and the wider politicisation of crime and punishment, an issue we discussed in detail in Chapter 4. While in some cases children's rights can act as bulwark to punitiveness (as in the example of Denmark above where the policy on MACR was reversed), in other instances children's rights can still be restricted in the face of wider currents of policy or popular opinion.

While there has been noted progress in certain areas of children's rights in youth justice, there are also thornier areas, which potentially underscore some of the limitations of children's rights standards. Lynch and Liefaard (2020) have described a range of issues that have often been placed in the 'too hard basket'. These include examples such as children who commit serious offences (such as murder, rape and terrorist offences), and where the discourse around children's rights comes up against pressures to focus more on public protection. Some analysis has also explored the particular effects of high-profile cases in shaping public attitudes towards youth justice (Hamilton and Harvey, 2004; Green, 2008), and there is some evidence to suggest that the intense media focus on the killing of James Bulger in 1993 by two 10-year-olds has formed part of the resistance within England and Wales towards raising the MACR (Cipriani, 2009/2016) (see also the discussion in Chapter 4).

This is not to say that issues concerning children's rights do not apply in such 'hard cases' (Lynch, 2018), arguably they apply even more so, but that conceptions of children's rights typically envisage a particular type of relatively minor juvenile transgression, that these more serious cases problematise and disrupt. Some countries even apply exceptions in legislation that allow children to be tried as adults in such cases and/or allow for the imposition of harsher sentences than would otherwise be permitted. England and Wales, Scotland and Northern Ireland still allow for the imposition of mandatory life sentences for children under 18 for murder, a fact that has been consistently criticised by the UN Committee on the Rights of the Child (2016). (In England and Wales life imprisonment can be imposed on children in the form of 'detention at His Majesty's Pleasure'. In Northern Ireland this is allowed at the 'pleasure of the Secretary of State', while Scottish legislation allows for 'detention without limit of time'. Such sentences are mandatory for murder committed while the offender was under the age of 18.)

Arguments to extend the reach of the youth justice system beyond 18 years in recognition of the fact that youth transitions to adulthood have become more extended also push up against the limits of children's rights (Lynch and Liefaard, 2020). As noted at the outset of this chapter, children's rights standards explicitly define a child as a person under the age of 18. However, insights from neurodevelopmental research have shown that many young people take longer to attain cognitive maturity and impulse control (Delmage, 2013), and this has formed part of the rationale for arguments that the reach of the youth justice system should be extended (Pruin and Dünkel, 2015). However, there are obvious tensions with this position from the perspective of children's rights. For one, this could lead to a situation where children are detained with adults (albeit young adults), a situation incompatible with children's rights standards. Secondly, arguments that children and young adults lack capacities based on developmental maturity is potentially at odds with broader children's rights scholarship which advocates for increased autonomy and agency for children (Hollingsworth, 2013; Lynch and Liefaard, 2020).

Conclusion

The articulation bulwark against punitive impulses, which foreground punishment and stigmatisation of children while neglecting their rights and welfare. At an international level the UNCRC and the associated juvenile justice rules and guidelines provide a clear statement of principles regarding the treatment of children who come into conflict with the law. Acting in the 'child's best interests' should serve as the guiding principle, children should be diverted from formal judicial mechanisms and detention should be used as a measure of last resort and for the shortest time possible. In the European context these principles have been further articulated in the *Guidelines on Child-Friendly Justice* (Council of Europe, 2015), which apply across justice, civil and administrative proceedings.

At the same time, as this chapter demonstrates, there are both limits to rights instruments – for instance the opacity regarding the MACR, or the continued disproportionate use of detention for minority populations – and their application in practice. The periodic reporting to the UNCRC demonstrates some of the continued areas of concern. The need for more robust data and research in this field is also highlighted. While rights approaches clearly provide a compass to orientate policy and practice towards a child's best interest, any consideration of whether youth justice systems are rights compliant must also consider the wider purview of children's lives beyond these systems, a subject that we consider in further chapters throughout the book.

Further Reading

Cipriani, D. (2009/2016) ***Children's Rights and the Minimum Age of Criminal Responsibility: A Global Perspective.*** **London: Routledge.**

This book provides a comprehensive overview of the minimum age of criminal responsibility (MACR) globally. It notes some of the tensions between welfare and justice arguments and places the analysis in the context of children's rights principles.

Stalford, H., Hollingsworth, K. & Gilmore, S. (Eds.) (2017) ***Rewriting Children's Rights Judgments: From Academic Vision to New Practice.*** **Oxford: Hart Publishing.**

This book re-writes existing case law from a children's rights perspective. The authors highlight the potential for using children's rights principles in practice, and the importance of using child-friendly procedures and child-friendly language. The book covers different areas, including children's rights and family life and children's rights and medical decision-making. There is a section devoted to children's rights and criminal justice, which covers a range of international judgments.

6

Comparative Youth Justice in the United Kingdom

Objectives

- This chapter will provide an outline of the different systems of youth justice across the United Kingdom.
- Readers will be introduced to the histories of these systems, as well as their key characteristics.
- The chapter will help the reader to identify some of the key differences in these systems.
- The chapter will also enable readers to develop an understanding of the different political contexts in which youth justice policy and practice has developed in the United Kingdom.

Introduction

The different countries of the United Kingdom (England and Wales, Scotland and Northern Ireland), have different youth justice systems. This is a consequence of diverse legal systems and different political, cultural and historical trajectories that have led to the development of distinct approaches to children who come into conflict with the law. These divergent approaches are also partly the result of the devolution of law-making powers to local governments that have led to the development of national approaches to policy-making. The processes of devolution that have taken place in the United Kingdom since the late 1990s have had profound effects on the governance of the different jurisdictions, including the criminal and youth justice systems. In 1998, the United Kingdom parliament passed three devolution acts: the *Scotland Act*, the *Government of Wales Act* and the *Northern Ireland Act*. These pieces of legislation paved the way for the establishment of local assemblies in

Holyrood, Cardiff and Stormont and the transfer of some powers and functions from Westminster to the devolved governments. Since then there have been further changes, including the devolution of policing and justice powers to the Northern Ireland Assembly in 2010, a referendum on the devolution of primary law-making powers to the Welsh Assembly in 2011 and a referendum on Scottish independence in 2014 (in which the majority voted that Scotland should remain in the United Kingdom).

However, reflecting different histories and political legacies, the processes of devolution have not been symmetrical. For instance, Scotland has had a long-standing distinct legal system that predates the re-establishment of the Scottish parliament in 1999 (Mooney et al., 2015), while the devolution settlement in Northern Ireland has taken place against a backdrop of transition from a violent political conflict which has posed particular challenges for the legitimacy of the criminal justice system (McAlinden and Dwyer, 2015). Meanwhile, Wales has experienced a different trajectory, as policing and criminal justice powers remain under the remit of the UK government in Westminster. That said, there are distinct features of the youth justice system in Wales, as policy-making in relation to youth justice extends to areas within the scope of devolved policy-making powers such as education and social services provision (Jones, 2020).

Questions regarding devolution and the balance of powers between national governments and Westminster remain live issues that have been brought into even sharper focus by Brexit. The result of the 2016 Brexit referendum saw an overall majority of the United Kingdom vote to leave the European Union (52% to 48%), however, within both Scotland and Northern Ireland a majority of people voted to remain (62% and 56% respectively). This has led to renewed calls for a further referendum on independence in Scotland and a 'border-poll' in Northern Ireland to explore the electorate's appetite for a 'United Ireland' (Garry et al., 2020). Meanwhile, the Welsh political party, Plaid Cymru, has renewed its calls for Welsh independence (Greer, 2018).

It is hard to predict where these various campaigns may ultimately lead; however, it is certainly the case that the constitutional future of the United Kingdom remains unsettled (Bogdanor, 2019), and this may result in further impacts on different spheres of government policy-making and practice, including in the area of youth justice. Indeed, some initial commentary suggests that the government's focus on Brexit, and more recently the focus on the response to the public health crisis caused by the Coronavirus, has diverted attention away from youth justice as an area of policy concern (Case et al., 2020). At the same time, writing about the different youth justice systems of the United Kingdom McAra (2017a) has argued that the field of youth justice has become a ground where claims regarding distinct national approaches can be staked. For instance, Scotland has operated a '**Children's Hearing System**' since the early 1970s which has traditionally foregrounded a welfarist approach (McGhee and

Waterhouse, 1998), while in Northern Ireland the youth justice system was subject to reform following the Good Friday peace agreement when a restorative justice model was instituted as the main response to juvenile offending (Doak and O'Mahony, 2011). Meanwhile, in Wales in recent years there has been a greater emphasis placed on children's rights in youth justice, and some commentators have described this as evidence of the 'dragonization' of youth justice (Edwards and Hughes, 2009; Drakeford, 2010).

However, while there are evidently divergences in practices and approaches to youth justice across the United Kingdom, some have questioned whether these differences are in fact illusory, given the fact that to some extent the same underlying logics, such as the targeting and responsibilisation of certain groups, apply (Muncie, 2011). Meanwhile, others have pointed to significant intra-jurisdictional variation (that is, differences in how policy is implemented within the same country), signifying less coherency than official rhetoric might suggest (Smith and Gray, 2019; Goldson and Briggs, 2021). For instance, research which has explored the implementation of youth justice practice on the ground has noted that different practice cultures and the operation of practitioner discretion mean that there is considerable variation in how youth justice operates, and consequently how young people experience the 'system' within different countries (Field, 2007; Hamilton et al., 2016; Goldson and Briggs, 2021). This suggests that taking a country or jurisdiction as the unit of analysis may obfuscate important differences.

Bearing all of this in mind, this chapter will explore the different systems of youth justice in each of the jurisdictions of the United Kingdom and critically consider the extent to which they constitute distinct approaches. It will also explore some of the intra-jurisdictional differences and changes to the youth justice systems over time. It will also critically consider Muncie's (2011) claim that the different approaches are merely 'illusions of difference' which serve to mask what are ultimately the same underlying logics. The chapter begins with a discussion of the contours of each system in turn – Wales, England, Scotland and Northern Ireland – before turning to these broader debates.

'Children First' in Wales: A Distinct Approach to Youth Justice?

As noted at the outset of this chapter, 'England and Wales' is a distinct legal jurisdiction, and policing and criminal justice powers remain under the jurisdiction of the Westminster parliament despite the fact that the Welsh Assembly has been operational since 1999 and has its own law-making powers. Some commentators have observed that one of the results of the aggregation of 'England and Wales' as a legal jurisdiction, is a 'presumed policy linearity' (Brewster and Jones, 2019: 365) between England and Wales and a subsumption of the distinct character of Welsh criminal justice policy and practice under a dominant 'anglocentric narrative'. Jones (2020: 4) therefore observes:

> The legacy of this anglocentric narrative is that, so long as the England and Wales system remains intact, it is deemed perfectly acceptable for criminologists to speak on behalf of Wales through the dominant position of England.

While youth justice is a non-devolved policy domain, meaning that criminal justice legislation pertaining to young people in England and Wales is passed in Westminster, many of the areas impacting on the lives of children and young people fall under the policy-making remit of the Welsh government (e.g., health, housing, education and training, and child protection and welfare services). In recognition of this fact the Welsh government committed to a 'Children First, Offender Second' approach within the youth justice system in the *All Wales Youth Offending Strategy* published in 2004 (Drakeford, 2010). This strategy articulated that the youth justice system should aim to achieve a balance between the interests of the child or young person and the interests of the wider community; that the welfare of children should be promoted in a way that reduces the risk of re-offending and in so doing protects the public; and that the principle of treating young people as 'children first, offenders second' should be promoted. The articulation of these principles was viewed by some as evidence of the 'dragonization' of youth justice in Wales, i.e., as the emergence of a distinctly 'Welsh' approach to youth justice (Edwards and Hughes, 2009; Drakeford, 2010). However, the extent to which the approach in Wales differed substantively from England, particularly given the fact that much of the legislation and institutional architecture was the same, has been the subject of some debate (Haines, 2010).

The *Crime and Disorder Act 1998* established a new institutional framework for youth justice in England and Wales. This legislation introduced a range of new sentences for young people who came into conflict with the law, and provided for the establishment of multi-disciplinary local **Youth Offending Teams** (YOTs) in each of the Local Authority Area across England and Wales. There are currently more than 150 YOTs across England and Wales. YOTs are multi-agency partnerships that deliver youth justice services at local level. Their statutory partners are the Local Authority and Police, Probation and Health Services. This means that each one of these bodies has a legal duty to participate and provide funding to the YOT in their area. YOTs also receive a proportion of their funding through grants administered by the Youth Justice Board (YJB).

The *Crime and Disorder Act 1998* also led to the establishment of the Youth Justice Board for England and Wales (YJB). Part of the rationale for the establishment of the YJB was 'to produce a consistent and coherent system of youth justice across England and Wales' (Souhami, 2015: 115). The YJB does not have any direct management responsibility for YOTs; however, it does have responsibility for defining the duties and targets of YOTs through the promotion of particular types of practice (e.g., standardised assessment tools) and 'evidence-based' approaches and through the monitoring of their activities (Field, 2011; Souhami, 2015). These centralising tendencies or 'micro-management' (Field, 2011: 312) have been subject to some critique, not least because of the fact that in the period following the establishment of the YJB and the implementation of other elements of the *Crime and Disorder Act 1998*, the numbers of young people processed through the youth justice system in England and Wales rose dramatically. Between 1998 and 2008 the average daily population of young people in custody rose from approximately 2,500 to over 3,000. Various analyses of the role of the YJB has noted the extent to which the approach taken by the Board, in the early years of its existence at least, was predicated on a particular risk-based approach towards children and young people (Case, 2007; Bateman, 2011b).

One of the distinctive features of YOTs is that they are multi-disciplinary by design, with staff from education services, housing, health, probation, social work and policing seconded to work within the teams which are housed in Social Services departments. This means that within YOTs staff are drawn from areas for which the Welsh Assembly had devolved responsibility (e.g., health, education and housing), and perhaps more importantly the majority of their budgets are outside of the control of central government. Drakeford (2010: 139) estimates that in 2007–2008 between 50% and 70% of YOT budgets in Wales were funded by services under the policy remit areas of the Welsh Assembly Government. Therefore at a practical level the work of youth justice teams on the ground was potentially influenced by different imperatives (notwithstanding the fact that part of the rationale for the introduction of YOTs was to achieve greater standardisation of approaches towards young people who offended).

In 2004, the Welsh Government published an *All Wales Youth Offending Strategy (AWYOS)* which was jointly agreed by the Youth Justice Board (YJB) and the Welsh government.

The AWYOS articulated the principle that, alongside balancing the interests of public protection and child welfare: 'young people should be treated as children first and offenders second' (Welsh Assembly Government, 2004). Some of the impetus for a different approach to youth justice in Wales has been driven by broader social policy agendas, including a commitment to children's rights and the principles of *universalism* (i.e., that supports and services should be available to all children). The Welsh Government's 'Extending Entitlement' youth inclusion strategy (National Assembly Policy Unit, 2000) established that all children and young people aged 11–25 should have unconditional access to universal entitlements including education, training and employment, housing and recreation (Case and Haines, 2015).

In 2004 the Welsh Assembly unanimously voted to formally adopt the United Nations Convention of the Rights of the Child (UNCRC) as the basis for policy-making in matters affecting children (see Chapter 5 for a discussion of the UNCRC). The rights-based principles enshrined in the UNCRC are specifically referenced as a guiding framework within the *All Wales Youth Offending Strategy* (Drakeford, 2010). However, as the previous chapter (Chapter 5) exploring the influence of children's rights in the youth justice arena demonstrates, there are frequently gaps between policy rhetoric on children's rights and practical implementation. Moreover, as Haines et al. (2013: 171) observe: 'The distinctiveness of Welsh policy is no guarantee of effective or consistent practice ...'. Nonetheless, there have been some examples of distinct approaches to youth justice in Wales, including the Swansea Bureau, an initiative established to undertake a 'new approach to diversion'.

The Swansea Bureau

The Swansea Bureau is an initiative developed by South Wales Police and the Swansea Youth Offending Service (YOS) in 2009. The key aims of the Bureau are to divert young people from the formal processes of the youth justice system (see further discussion of diversion in Chapter 3); reduce the number of first-time entrants in the youth justice system; treat young people as 'children first and offenders second' and to provide programmes that address offending behaviour through the promotion of positive and prosocial behaviour (Haines et al., 2013). The promotion of diversion was aimed at avoiding a criminal record. According to Haines et al. (2013), who were involved in the development of the Swansea Bureau and some of the evaluations of the project, the focus on 'children first' entailed the following:

> Crucially, the Bureau is designed to be *children first* through its foci on: *(re-) engaging parents/carers* in the behaviour of their children, giving explicit place to hear the *voices of young people* and decoupling the *needs of the victim* from the responses to the child. (Haines et al., 2013: 171, original emphases)

The Bureau process involves a number of stages. Firstly, if a young person is arrested and is eligible (i.e., they have admitted the offence, the offence is of a certain level of seriousness and they are a first-time entrant or have not been dealt within the past two years), they and their family are then assessed. The next stage of the process involves an assessment of the needs of any victims of a Victim Support Officer working in the YOS. The views of the victim are incorporated into the Bureau report. A Bureau panel meeting then takes place with the Bureau Coordinator, a police sergeant and community representative. The Panel consider the report prepared on the young person and decide on the disposal (e.g., non-criminal disposal, warning or prosecution) and any supports the young person may require. This Bureau Panel is followed by a Bureau Clinic where members of the Panel and the young person and their parent/carer attend. The participation of the young person is encouraged at the Clinic, and the aim is to agree an outcome (Haines et al., 2013).

An evaluation of the Swansea Bureau conducted between 2009 and 2012 showed that, following the introduction of the scheme, the number of First Time Entrants (FTEs) into the youth justice system decreased. However, this decrease took place against a wider backdrop of a decline in the numbers of young people entering into the youth justice system across England and Wales (Bateman, 2014). Nevertheless, there was clear evidence that more young people were being diverted from the system through the Bureau (the number of cases with no criminal disposals rose markedly). Furthermore, this did not merely result in a delay in these children eventually entering into the system, as there was an overall decrease in the reduction of the level of offending by young people more generally (Haines et al., 2013).

The *Children and Young People First, Offenders Second* (Youth Justice Board and Welsh Government, 2014) youth justice strategy continues the rhetorical emphasis on children's rights. This emphasis has now been incorporated more fully into the wider work of the Youth Justice Board and into the youth justice system in England. The articulation of 'children first' principles has since been seen in the Youth Justice Board's Strategic Objectives for 2020 to 2021, and in the *Youth Justice Blueprint for Wales* (Ministry of Justice and Welsh Government, 2019). The *Youth Justice Blueprint for Wales* (2019) sets out aims to prevent children from entering the criminal justice system, as well as minimising their contact with it and maximising the opportunities for diversion. The *Blueprint* references the *Social Services and Well-being (Wales) Act 2014* and the *Well-being of Future Generations (Wales) Act 2015*, which require the provision of social services to prevent children from offending and to promote their future welfare.

The *Blueprint* places emphasis on the importance of a 'Whole-System Approach', involving a broad range of services in children's lives, and across different areas of intervention, from prevention of offending and pre-court diversion, through to community and custodial sentences, as well as resettlement supports for children when they leave custody. In addition to articulating a 'children first' approach to youth justice, the *Blueprint* also promises to deliver a 'trauma-informed approach' throughout the various stages of the youth justice system. This approach is underscored by research which has shown that children involved in the youth justice system are often likely to have experienced a range of Adverse Childhood Experiences (ACEs) (Glendinning et al., 2021), and therefore require responses that recognise the impact of childhood trauma (see Chapter 8 for further discussion of ACEs and trauma-informed practice).

Youth Justice Blueprint for Wales – Guiding Principles

The Youth Justice Blueprint for Wales (2019) sets out the following vision for youth justice in Wales.

> It will:
>
> Take a 'children first' approach to youth justice, ensure that it is child-centred rather than service focused, ensure that it meets the individual needs to children and responds to their best interests.
>
> Take a trauma-informed approach throughout the various stages of the youth justice system, from prevention and early intervention to resettlement from custody, recognising and responding to ACEs and indicators of complex need.
>
> Embed trauma-informed approaches into community and custodial practice to effect cultural and systemic change and deliver consistent approaches in meeting children's needs.
>
> Align devolved and non-devolved services through a shared vision, values and approach which underpins the design and delivery of services.

Source: *Youth Justice Blueprint for Wales* (Ministry of Justice and Welsh Government, 2019).

Overall then, as we have seen, there have been claims that there is a distinctly 'Welsh' form of youth justice, and some have argued that this represents a form of 'dragonization' of youth justice; although others have noted that the extent to which Welsh youth justice is distinct from English practice remains a contested debate (Goldson and Briggs, 2021). The most emblematic difference is the earlier adoption of the 'Children First, Offender Second' approach in youth justice services in Wales, which was in part influenced by the Welsh government's explicit commitment to children's rights and responsibility for intersecting devolved areas of social policy. The wider Youth Justice Board for England and Wales has since adopted a 'children first' approach in its policies and strategic objectives, so to some extent this could be seen as the Welsh approach informing the strategic direction of wider youth justice policy in England and Wales. Although it also remains an open question as to what adopting a 'children first' approach means in practice.

Youth Justice in England – from Micro-Management to Localism?

As noted above, until relatively recently, youth justice 'overviews' have tended to treat England and Wales as sharing a common history, culture and ideological perspective on young people and crime. Instead, however, and increasingly following devolution, England must be understood as having a distinctive place in the youth justice domain, exhibiting a particular 'trajectory' in terms of historical and contemporary developments. McAra and McVie (2019: 82), for instance, contrast the emergence of a 'systems management' approach to diversion in England with a more clearly 'welfarist' approach in Scotland during the 1980s. Certainly, this coincides with a wider view that recent developments in England can be understood in terms of a series of distinct phases, each with its own characteristics. See the Box below for an overview of these phases.

Recent Phases in Youth Justice in England

- The 'decade of diversion' in the 1980s;
- The 'punitive turn' and increasing reliance on more severe sanctions of the 1990s;
- Micro-management, actuarialism (Smith, 2006) and 'mission creep' in the early 2000s;
- State withdrawal, pragmatism (Goldson, 2020) and localism from around 2008 onwards.

In seeking to make sense of these shifts, commentators have sometimes sought to identify particular influences or currents of thought as principal drivers of change (or continuity), whilst others have attributed change to a combination of factors. Muncie (2006), for example, views youth justice as it is delivered as the product of a series of influences and beliefs working in combination and sometimes at odds with each other, including:

- Just deserts;
- Risk management;
- Managerialism;
- Community responsibilisation;
- Authoritarian populism; and
- Restorative justice. (Muncie, 2002: 156)

Interestingly, he does not include 'welfarism' in this list, although by contrast, Hazel (2008) sees English (perhaps all) youth justice at any point in time as the evolving outcome of a continual battle between advocates of 'welfare' and 'justice' (as discussed in Chapter 3).

Certain aspects of the English system may well reflect different elements of this catalogue of potential influences, whilst we must also be careful to distinguish between 'top-down' policies and monitoring mechanisms (the YJB, OFSTED and the Prisons Inspectorate) and 'bottom-up' activities, such as the creativity (and constraints) of local systems. Thus, the MACR set at 10 in England (and Wales) is untypically low and represents an unequivocally 'just deserts' framing of young people's problem behaviour in legislative and overarching policy terms, particularly in light of the abolition of the presumption of *doli incapax* under the *Crime and Disorder Act 1998*. Against this backdrop, it becomes more straightforward to invoke a spirit of 'authoritarian populism' aimed towards children and young people who become legally defined as 'criminal' and indistinguishable from adult offenders, to the extent that they are assumed to be responsible for their actions.

Although public attitudes to young offenders are rather less well-researched than might be expected, it is consistently found to be the case that people overestimate the level and seriousness of youth crime (Roberts and Hough, 2005; Jacobson and Kirby, 2012), at least by comparison to recorded crime rates. The detailed analysis carried out by Roberts and Hough (2005) suggests that there is a persistent tendency for the public to 'misperceive' both trends and patterns of youth crime, with respondents reporting rising levels of crime, even at the time of a sustained fall in rates of offending across all measures.

As Jacobson and Kirby (2012: 7) have observed, based on a focus group study, there is a general sense of unease about the apparent threat posed by young people 'hanging about' the neighbourhood. This is linked to concerns about vandalism and graffiti, and damage to cars and windows, routinely attributed to young people (Jacobson and Kirby, 2012: 8). To this extent then, it is understandable that the justice system itself should be influenced by or at least take account of these widely held views. We have observed distinct shifts in practice and decision-making over time, which appear to represent a direct response to public concerns, at least so far as this is interpreted and represented through the media, as in the 1990s following the killing of James Bulger (Goldson, 2013), and later, in the aftermath of the 2011 'riots' (Roberts and Hough, 2013).

At the same time, however, studies have demonstrated that more nuanced explorations of young people's infractions produce a rather different response (Hough and Roberts, 2005; Jacobson and Kirby, 2012). Here, we find that there is more appetite for tailored responses which address the specific concerns of the communities affected and individual 'victims'.

These findings interestingly coincide with ideas of 'community responsibilisation' to use Muncie's term; that is, the idea that those affected by crime should be more closely involved in dealing with it and deciding what should happen as a result.

Hence, for example, government introduced revised legislation (the *Anti-social Behaviour, Crime and Policing Act 2014*) to devolve powers to respond to anti-social behaviour to localities, whereby 'victims' and their communities are put 'at the heart of the response to anti-social behaviour' (Home Office, 2022: 4). This measure might well be seen as part of a wider government strategy associated with 'localism' (Tait and Inch, 2016) on the one hand, and as a systematic process of withdrawal of state investment and involvement in local communities on the other (Vizard and Hills, 2021).

A shift towards localism?

In this way, we can begin to map out the ways in which broader government policies and changing ideas about how services should be organised have exerted an influence on the shape and character of youth justice services and delivery arrangements, whilst perhaps also creating the space for local creativity to generate quite diverse innovations at the level of practice (Kelly and Armitage, 2015; Smith and Gray, 2019). Notably, the idea that offences should be resolved locally, and with the full involvement of those most directly affected, has prompted interest in developing 'restorative' models of intervention. This, too, has been underpinned by changes in policy and legislation at the national level; and in this sense can be traced back to the New Labour government's introduction of the Referral Order under the *Youth Justice and Criminal Evidence Act 1999*. This initiative has subsequently been reinforced in various ways, including the Youth Restorative Disposal (Community Resolution) for relatively minor offences and the explicit endorsement and encouragement of restorative justice innovations by government. Although the extent to which restorative approaches have become embedded across local youth justice systems is unclear, it is certainly the case that in some areas services have adopted explicitly 'restorative' principles at the core of their practice (Smith and Gray, 2019).

Despite the relatively wide endorsement of such approaches at the more minor and earlier stages of the criminal process in England, they tend to be superseded by a focus on risk and offender management as offending is identified as more serious. Here, we see evidence of risk assessment models such as 'triage' in relation to diversion programmes (Smith, 2018), the continuing use of routinised assessment tools to assist with sentencing decisions and the 'bifurcation' of interventions according to the level of risk associated with particular young people (Day, 2022). As Day demonstrates effectively, for youth justice practitioners the feeling is that they are exposed to mixed messages from policy-makers and monitoring agencies, and that this has been exacerbated by the reassertion of 'child first' principles by the Youth Justice Board in particular.

Certainly, the mid to late 2010s can be identified as a period of liberalisation in youth justice policy, with the publication first of the *Taylor Review of Youth Justice* (Taylor, 2016), and the subsequent adoption of 'child first' principles by the Youth Justice Board itself (Youth Justice Board, 2021), apparently influenced by earlier developments in Wales, as some have argued (Case and Browning, 2021). In concrete terms, this strategic shift has underpinned the commissioning of the first 'secure school', which title is intended to signal a shift away from punitive custody to a secure setting which prioritises the well-being and personal development of those held there (Taylor, 2016). At the time of writing, this apparently radical shift in emphasis at the institutional policy level could not be expected to have had a substantial or permanent effect, despite clear statements of intent, so careful monitoring is certainly required. Critical observers, though, might wonder whether the announcement of a supposedly novel and more progressive form of custodial provision for children might be more likely to achieve beneficial outcomes than its predecessors with similar aspirations, dating back to the 19th century: reformatory and industrial schools, borstals, approved schools and secure children's homes, for example.

An amalgam of influences

This overview of recent and current developments in English youth justice does, then, suggest that there is an amalgam of influences on policy and practice, in much the way that Muncie (2002) has set out. Recent initiatives, however, suggest that the principles of child welfare and even children's rights have also retained a place, and if anything support for these perspectives had increased by the early 2020s. The relaxation of state control and managerialism has enabled local agencies and collaborations to adopt a variety of models (Smith and Gray, 2019) and approaches, emphasising children's rights, restorative practice and inclusive interventions; in light of which, it would be difficult to state clearly that there is a uniform and distinctive *English* youth justice.

Goldson (2020) has described this as an era of 'pragmatism' as opposed to, say, the welfarism of the 1960s/1970s or the punitive period between 1992 and 2008. Day's (2022) position, on the other hand, is that practice remains bifurcated, with a relatively benign and quite diverse approach to the minor infringements of young people who offend or are deemed problematic contrasted with a risk-oriented and controlling framing of interventions with the minority of persistent, serious or dangerous offenders.

It is important to note here, too, that there are other consequences of changing practices which might also be viewed as representative of the system of justice experienced by young people. Thus, for example, the progressive developments from 2008 onwards reflected in increasing levels of diversion and community resolution of offences are mirrored by the negative impacts of an increasingly disproportionate treatment of Black young people in terms of prosecution, custodial outcomes and oppressive treatment (HM Inspectorate of Prisons, 2021). Here, also, the tension between policy and aspiration and practice realities becomes clearer. The Mayor of London's (2020) progressive strategy for tackling the 'disproportional' treatment of young Black people in the justice system stands in stark contrast to persistent reports of insensitive and oppressive treatment at the threshold of the system (Children's Commissioner, 2022) (see Chapter 8 for a further discussion).

At this point in time, if anything, we are led to conclude that youth justice in England is disparate and to some extent contradictory. As the policy rhetoric has become increasingly 'child friendly', recognising the social harms experienced by many children in conflict with the law, so practice has become both fragmented geographically and increasingly 'bifurcated' (Day, 2022), to the detriment of many Black young people who still appear to be targeted for controlling and sometimes oppressive interventions. Many of the wider uncertainties and social changes impacting on both agencies (cuts and retrenchment) and young people (austerity and marginalisation) resonate within the distinctive sphere of youth justice. Some of these impacts have perhaps informed strong and distinctive policy commitments (by the YJB and the London Mayor, for example) to 'do better' for children and young people and adopt a 'child first' approach. However, for those most severely disadvantaged there remain unresolved questions about whether the youth justice system is capable of offsetting entrenched social inequalities.

Scotland – from Kilbrandon to Getting It Right for Every Child (GIRFEC)

Historically, the youth justice system in Scotland has been characterised as adopting more of a 'welfarist' approach than other UK jurisdictions (McAra and McVie, 2010b; Muncie, 2011). This is best exemplified by the 'Children's Hearing System' (CHS). The Children's Hearing System was established following the publication of the *Kilbrandon Report* in 1964. Following the publication of this report, the *Social Work (Scotland) Act 1968* abolished existing juvenile courts and established the Children's Hearing System as the new institutional framework for youth justice (McAra and McVie, 2010b). The CHS involves an approach whereby children who come to the attention of authorities because of either their offending behaviour or welfare concerns are responded to on the basis of their needs, rather than simply their 'deeds'. This system involves children being assessed by a 'Lay Panel' and a plan being put in place to respond to their particular situations. In practical terms this means that children under the age of 16 were effectively removed from the court system and dealt with through the hearing system. As Croall (2006: 590) explained it:

> Children's Hearings, in which cases are dealt with by lay panels, are not courts deciding guilt or innocence and their decisions are guided solely by the needs of the individual child. Under the 'Kilbrandon philosophy', children who offend are not differentiated from other children who require care.

Under the Children's Hearing System, children who offend, or for whom there are child protection concerns, can be referred to a 'Children's Reporter'. The Children's Reporter will investigate the case and draft a statement of grounds and decide whether a child or young person needs to be referred to a Hearing. The hearing takes place at a Hearing Centre, and typically involves the following attendees: child and/or parents and carers, a Children's Reporter, three voluntary panel members (who receive specific training on this role) and a social worker. A child may also elect to bring a family friend or professional to support them. At the hearing the panel members review the information, and they will also seek the views of the child or young person, their parents or carers and other professionals (such as teachers). The hearing must decide whether compulsory measures of supervision are needed for the child and, if so, what they will be. All decisions should be in the best interests of the child or young person.

In most instances the outcome of a case will be decided at the hearing. However, in some cases decisions cannot be made at the hearing and the case can be sent to the Sheriff Court. (The Sheriff Court in Scotland is the principal local civil and criminal court. It is broadly equivalent to the Magistrates' Court in England and Wales and the District Court in Northern Ireland.) This can happen because the child or young person or their parents/carers do not agree or do not understand the grounds for the hearing. In such instances after the Sheriff has heard the evidence they can either decide that the grounds are correct and send the case back to another Children's Hearing or decide that the statement of grounds are not correct, in which case there will not be another hearing. If the hearing decides that compulsory measures of supervision are necessary it will make a Supervision Requirement, which the Local Authority is responsible for overseeing. In most cases this will still involve children living at home, however, in some cases it could involve placement in a residential school or secure accommodation. The majority of children dealt with in the CHS are under 16. So, despite the child centred approach of the CHS, most 16- and 17-year-olds who come into conflict with the law are dealt with in adult courts (CYJS, 2022).

Since the establishment of the Children's Hearing System in 1971, there have been changes to its operation that have to some extent watered down its original welfarist approach (McAra and McVie, 2010b). The original legislation allowed for the right for children who had committed the most serious offences (such as a rape or murder) to be prosecuted in criminal courts. But further legislation (*Children (Scotland) Act*), introduced in 1995 allowed public protection concerns to be considered in deciding which approach to adopt in responding to young people (McGhee and Waterhouse, 1998). This followed from criticisms that the CHS was 'too soft' an approach for young people involved in serious offending (Croall, 2006).

Following devolution in Scotland in 1999 it might have been anticipated that the gaps between Scottish and English and Welsh approaches to youth justice would have widened. However, a number of analyses highlight points of both convergence and divergence in youth justice (Mooney and Poole, 2004; Croall, 2006; Muncie, 2011). As McAra and McVie (2010b: 71) observe:

> Indeed it is somewhat ironic that the full-flowering of devolution (which might have been thought to nurture all things Scottish) led to a degree of policy convergence with the system south of the border in England and Wales ...

This was partly due to the political parties in power at the time. At the point of devolution a Labour and Liberal Democrat coalition was in power in Scotland, and this government adopted some of the same policy approaches as the Labour government in Westminster, which was particularly active in the criminal justice policy arena. The Blair-led Labour government had placed youth justice firmly on the policy agenda by introducing the *Crime and Disorder Act 1998* in England and Wales (as discussed earlier in the chapter), and it also targeted so-called 'anti-social behaviour' through the introduction of 'Anti-Social Behaviour Orders' (ASBOs). Anti-Social Behaviour is defined in legislation as 'behaviour which is likely to cause alarm and distress'. Therefore its assessment is based on the subjective opinion of others. Typically, anti-social behaviour (such as playing loud music in a residential area), would not meet the threshold of a criminal offence. ASBOs were introduced in Scotland in 2004 following the passage of similar legislation in England and Wales.

The introduction of standards and key performance indicators, as well as a new institutional infrastructure, were other points of convergence between Scottish and English and Welsh youth justice systems in the early 2000s (McAra and McVie, 2010b). The first two governments of the Scottish parliament were Labour and Liberal Democrat coalitions (1999–2003 and 2003–2007) (Mooney et al., 2015). In 2007 the Scottish National Party (SNP) formed a majority government for the first time. Some analysis suggests that the SNP's primary focus on the 'constitutional question' (i.e., the ambition for Scottish independence), has taken attention away from areas such as justice (Mooney et al., 2015). Some have even argued that since this time there has been a 'retartanization' of justice policy (i.e., more of a focus on welfare than justice), although the extent to which this is more perception than actuality is contested (Mooney et al., 2015).

Getting It Right for Every Child (GIRFEC) and the Whole System Approach (WSA)

In 2011 a new national infrastructure for the Children's Hearing System (Children's Hearing Scotland) was created. The aim was to establish consistency across the system, which includes more than 2,500 volunteer panel members (Robertson, 2022). There has also been a renewed emphasis on prevention and early intervention across children's services, including in youth justice in recent years. In 2008 the Scottish Government published *Preventing Offending by Young People – A Framework for Action*, which eventually led to the development of the *Whole System Approach (WSA) for Children and Young People who Offend*, which was implemented in 2011. Alongside this, a national policy framework for improving children's well-being – Getting It Right for Every Child (GIRFEC) – was implemented. Coles et al. (2016: 339) explain the GIRFEC philosophy and approach in the following terms:

> Underpinned by a set of common values and core components, the GIRFEC approach is intended to provide a coherent strategy and program of action to strengthen universal service provision, coordinate multiagency professional practice, and embed early stage/age intervention and prevention within everyday working practices of all agencies and practitioners supporting children and young people, to ensure that children and families get the help when they need it.

GIRFEC has its roots in the 'Kilbrandon' philosophy and the Children's Hearing System (i.e., the idea that service provision should be based on needs rather than deeds), and the principle of 'universality' (i.e., that all children should have equal access to services) is a central element of the approach (Coles et al., 2016). The *Children and Young People (Scotland) Act 2014* placed GIRFEC on a statutory basis. One of the key innovations of GIRFEC is that every child in Scotland will have a 'Named Person' available to them within universal services of health or education. The 'Named Person' can be someone such as a health visitor or a school teacher, and they act as a single point of contact for the child and their family, and as a gatekeeper for services. Where children have more involvement with services (such as children referred to the Children's Hearing System), they will also have a 'Lead Professional' to coordinate and monitor multi-agency activity (Coles et al., 2016).

Getting It Right for Every Child (GIRFEC)

The key elements of the GIRFEC approach are described by the Scottish Government as follows:

- **Child-focused** – ensuring that the child or young person and their family is the centre of decision-making and the support available to them.
- **Based on an understanding of the well-being of a child in their current situation.**
- **Based on tackling needs early** – aims to ensure needs are identified as early as possible to avoid bigger concerns or problems developing.
- **Requires joined-up working** – services working together in a coordinated way to meet the specific needs of children and young people and improve their well-being.

Source: *Scottish Government: Getting It Right for Every Child – Principles and Values.* Available *at*: www.gov.scot/policies/girfec/principles-and-values/

The *Whole System Approach (WSA) for Children and Young People who Offend* aims to prevent the unnecessary use of custody and secure accommodation. The WSA comprises of three main strands:

1. Early and effective intervention – aimed at reducing referrals to the Children's Reporter through pre-referral screening;
2. Diversion from prosecution;
3. Reintegration and transition support for young people leaving custody or secure care.

The implementation of the WSA was informed by key findings from the *Edinburgh Study of Youth Transitions and Crime*, which researched the pathways into and out of offending for a cohort of approximately 4,300 young people (McAra and McVie, 2010a). One of the most significant findings from this study was that diversionary strategies which stop or reduce the impact of contact with the criminal justice system are typically most effective in preventing further offending (McAra and McVie, 2007, 2010a). Another significant finding from this study was that children who do become involved in persistent and serious offending are themselves likely to have experienced victimisation and a range of adversity (McAra and McVie, 2010a).

The WSA is informed by the principles of GIRFEC, and it involves multi-agency working across a range of services (e.g., police, social work, the Children's Reporter) (Robertson, 2017). As Robertson (2017: 17) observes:

> The WSA signalled a change in direction in youth justice from the formal system of compulsory measures through Children's Reporting to a more flexible multi-agency approach.

An evaluation of the implementation of the WSA in three local authority areas carried out in 2015 found that there had been an overall reduction in patterns of recorded crime since the 2000s, which coincided with the *Preventing Offending by Young People Framework* and the implementation of GIRFEC (Murray et al., 2015). Some commentators have therefore noted a marked shift towards early intervention and preventing young people becoming involved in the youth justice system where possible (CYJS, 2022). These shifts have in part been informed by insights from research such as the *Edinburgh Study* (McAra, 2017b). While, overall, the numbers entering into the youth justice system have declined (as they also have in the other UK jurisdictions), it is also important to note that another key finding of the *Edinburgh Study* (as well as research on the use of stop-and-search by the police), is that young people from deprived neighbourhoods, and/or who become characterised as the 'usual suspects' are those most likely to be processed through the system (Murray, 2015; McAra, 2017b).

Minimum age of criminal responsibility (MACR)

Scotland has recently raised its MACR from 8 years of age to 12 after decades of persistent criticism of the low age from children's rights organisations and a range of researchers (Lightowler et al., 2014). Although before this legislative change Scotland had set the age of criminal responsibility at 8 years, the age of prosecution was 12 years. In practical terms this meant that a child younger than 12 years could not face criminal prosecution, however, the differential ages in the law was confusing. *The Age of Criminal Responsibility (Scotland) Act 2019* raised the MACR in Scotland to 12 years. This means that children under the age of 12 can no longer be charged or arrested. While the Scottish MACR is still lower than the European average of 14 years, and below the minimum age recommended by the United Nations Committee on the Rights of the Child, which has advocated a minimum of 14 years and an optimum age of 16 years (see Chapter 5), it is still above that of the other UK jurisdictions, which remain at 10 years.

Northern Ireland – Legacy of Conflict and Restoration

The current youth justice system in Northern Ireland was formed in the context of the transition from a violent political conflict. From the 1960s up until the late 1990s, the violent conflict, referred to colloquially as 'The Troubles', resulted in more than 3,500 deaths and 40,000 casualties (McKittrick and McVea, 2012). In 1998 the *Belfast (Good Friday) Agreement* paved the way for a peace process, which involved paramilitary groups decommissioning their weapons and a process for the release of prisoners who had been convicted of conflict-related offences (Dwyer, 2007; McAlinden and Dwyer, 2015).

Following the peace agreement, the Northern Ireland Assembly in Stormont was re-established, and a First Minister from the Ulster Unionist Party (UUP) and a Deputy First Minister from the Social Democratic Labour Party (SDLP) took up these positions in 1998. Under the terms of the *Good Friday Agreement*, there is a mandated power-sharing arrangement between unionist political parties (who want to maintain the union with the United Kingdom) and republican/nationalist parties (who want Northern Ireland to become part of a united Ireland) (Tilley et al., 2008).

Reform of the criminal justice system was an integral part of the process of conflict transformation, as parts of the criminal justice system itself (e.g., the police and prisons) had been embroiled in the conflict (McAlinden and Dwyer, 2015). The *Criminal Justice Review (2000)* recommended the establishment of a separate agency for youth justice, and the implementation of a restorative justice approach as the main response for children who offend.

Restorative justice in Northern Ireland

Restorative justice approaches had been developed at the community level during the political conflict to address offending by young people in the absence of trust in policing and formal criminal justice institutions (Eriksson, 2009). In some communities young people had been subject to paramilitary violence (e.g., so-called 'punishment beatings'), in response to alleged offending or anti-social behaviour. Community-led restorative justice initiatives aimed to both address the behaviour that had caused harm in the first instance and prevent further harm through violent responses (McEvoy and Mika, 2001). The *Criminal Justice Review (2000)* noted the success of such initiatives and recommended that they should be brought under the ambit of the formal youth justice system (Doak and O'Mahony, 2011).

The *Justice Act (Northern Ireland) 2002* established the Youth Justice Agency on a statutory basis and put in place the legislative framework for restorative justice as the main approach to juvenile offending (Haydon and McAlister, 2015). Restorative justice conferences are facilitated by the Youth Justice Agency (YJA). A restorative justice conference involves a meeting between the young person who has offended, the victim or victims of the offence where possible (in many instances a representative of the victim – e.g., a member of an agency such as Victim Support attends instead), the parent or carer of the young person, a staff member from the YJA who facilitates the conference and a police officer. The purpose of the conference is for the young person to hear about the harm caused by the offence, to offer their explanation about the reason for offending and to agree a plan of action (this takes the form of a conference plan) to repair the harm caused by the offence.

There are two types of conference provided for in legislation – a 'diversionary' **youth justice conference** and a court-ordered conference. A diversionary conference is one directed by the Public Prosecution Service (PPS) while a court-ordered conference is directed by the court. The plan agreed by a conference must be agreed by the referring party (i.e., the PPS or the Court). Conference plans typically include activities such as undertaking voluntary work for a period, writing a letter of apology, engaging in education and/or undertaking programmes to address problem areas such as substance misuse.

One of the underlining premises of restorative justice approaches is that all parties who are involved in an offence should have a say in determining how the harm caused by offending should be repaired (Zehr, 1990). Restorative justice approaches are also influenced by the theory of 'reintegrative shaming' (Braithwaite, 1989). The central premise of this theory is that shame plays an important function in signalling society's disapproval and sanctioning socially unacceptable behaviour. However, the focus should be on communicating disapproval of the behaviour, rather than disrespecting the person. John Braithwaite, an Australian criminologist who developed the reintegrative shaming theory, explains it as follows:

> Reintegrative shaming communicates disapproval within a continuum of respect for the offender; the offender is treated as a good person who has done a bad deed. Stigmatization is disrespectful shaming; the offender is treated as a bad person. Stigmatization is unforgiving – the offender is left with the stigma permanently, whereas reintegrative shaming is forgiving – ceremonies to certify deviance are terminated by ceremonies to decertify deviance. (Braithwaite, 1989: 1)

However, the role of shame in the context of restorative justice, even when the focus is intended to be reintegrative is contested (Harris and Maruna, 2006). For instance, the communication of shame may be experienced as stigmatising by the young person, despite an intention towards reintegration (Maxwell and Morris, 2002; Morris, 2002). Research which has explored young people's experiences of **youth conferences** has perhaps unsurprisingly reported mixed impacts (McAlister and Carr, 2014; Marsh and Maruna, 2016).

Some young people describe experiencing shame and stigmatisation within the conference setting, while other young people (particularly those who were the subject of multiple conferences), often struggled to recall the nature and the purpose of the conferences in which they participated (McAlister and

Carr, 2014). On the other hand, research conducted by Marsh and Maruna (2016) with young people who had previously gone through youth justice conferences and who had successfully desisted reported some experiences of 'personal epiphanies', whereby young people were confronted by the impacts of their actions on others, and these remained important reminders for them in the present.

Devolution of policing and justice powers

At the time of the re-establishment of the Northern Ireland Assembly in 1998, justice and policing policy remained under the reserved power of the Westminster government. This was in recognition of the fact that the criminal justice system had been a highly contested space during the Troubles. Prisons and policing were particular sites of contestation (McAlinden and Dwyer, 2015). Following the *Good Friday Agreement,* the Royal Ulster Constabulary (RUC) was disbanded and a new policing body – the Police Service for Northern Ireland (PSNI) – was established. Policing and justice powers were eventually restored to Stormont in 2010, and a Minister for Justice was appointed. In 2010 the new Minister commissioned a review of the youth justice system. The review reported in 2011 and made a series of recommendations (YJRT, 2011).

One of the foremost recommendations of the review was that the MACR in Northern Ireland should be raised from 10 to 12 with immediate effect, and that consideration should be given to raising the age further to 14 within two years (YJRT, 2011). While the Minister for Justice supported this recommendation, it was not possible to reach political consensus to introduce legislation to raise the age, and the MACR in Northern Ireland (as in England and Wales) remains at 10 years. As noted in Chapter 5, this has been a source of criticism from children's rights groups and the UN Committee on the Rights of the Child, which published its last periodic report in 2016 and criticised the low MACR of the UK nations (UN Committee on the Rights of the Child, 2016).

The 2011 Youth Justice Review also raised concerns about the issue of delay within the system. At the time of the review, youth conferences and youth courts took on average 260 days to reach a decision from the date on which the young person was charged or summoned (YJRT, 2011). The review also noted the fact that there was insufficient diversion from the system taking place, and that so-called 'diversionary' youth conferences should be renamed as they were not in fact truly diversionary. While these conferences diverted young people from the courts, they did not divert them from the youth justice system, and young people who were the subject of 'diversionary' conferences could experience just as much contact with the system as young people whose conferences were ordered by the courts.

Following from the publication of the Youth Justice Review in 2011, Youth Engagement Clinics (YECs) were established both to tackle delay within the system and to enhance diversion (Carr and McAlister, 2021). Referrals to YECs are received from the Public Prosecution Service (PPS) after consideration of whether the case is suitable for diversion from prosecution. For their cases to be processed via YECs, young people must admit to the offence/s. The most common outcome for cases referred to YECs was a youth conference plan (40%). Informed warnings and restorative cautions were the next most common outcomes (20.6% and 17.0%, respectively). In 2019–20 the median time taken for cases to reach completion through the Youth Engagement process was 49 days (Graham and Liddicoat, 2020). While the YECs are described as diversionary, the outcomes for some young people still entail significant involvement with the youth justice system, and concerns have been raised by children's rights bodies regarding the application of due process (e.g., access to legal representation) for young people.

Overall, and in common with the other jurisdictions of the United Kingdom, the numbers of young people in custody have declined in Northern Ireland (NIAO, 2017, 2020). However, there are still concerns regarding the 'churn' of some young people into and out of custody. There is one custodial facility for young people in Northern Ireland, the Juvenile Justice Centre (JJC), which is operated by the Youth Justice Agency. (In practice the JJC accommodates all young people placed in custody in Northern Ireland and since 2012 no under-18s have been placed in the prison system. However, there is still legislative provision that allows for a child to be placed in prison if there are specific security concerns. The fact that this legislation has not been changed remains a source of concern (Carr and McAlister, 2021).) Young people can be placed into custody under the Police and Criminal Evidence (PACE) Act for a short period, by remand from the court, or via a sentence. The greatest proportion of admissions to the JJC are under PACE provisions, so typically young people stay for a short time. However, young people placed into custody on remand continue to face lengthy delays in their cases being processed. Moreover, most young people placed into custody on remand do not subsequently receive a custodial sentence (Brown, 2020). The over-representation of Looked After Children (LAC) in the youth justice system was a further concern raised by the Youth Justice Review (YJRT, 2011) and it remains a persistent issue of concern (Carr and McAlister, 2021). The most recent data shows that children who are looked after account for more than half (52%) of all admissions into custody (Brown, 2020).

Despite the formal cessation of violence amongst the main paramilitary groupings following the peace process there remain concerns regarding the continued activities of paramilitary groups in communities. In some communities paramilitary groupings still exert control, and are involved in both criminal activity (e.g., drug dealing) and the exploitation of children and young people, as well as informally 'policing' such communities (Northern Ireland Policing Board, 2020). This includes carrying out so-called 'paramilitary-style' attacks, including punishment beatings on young people (McAlister and Carr, 2014; McAlister et al., 2021).

In recent years there have been attempts to address the continued impacts of paramilitary violence in communities, including in a government programme aimed at tackling paramilitary activity and organised crime (Morrow and Byrne, 2020). However, Northern Ireland has been without a government since early 2022, when the government collapsed following the resignation of the Democratic Unionist Party (DUP) First Minister in protest against the Northern Ireland Protocol (the post-Brexit agreement between the United Kingdom and the European Union, which placed a trade border in the Irish Sea). There has since been a failure to form a government following Assembly elections in May 2022 as the DUP have refused to re-enter government until the Northern Ireland protocol issue is resolved to their satisfaction. Until such a time as a local government is formed (or unless direct rule from Westminster is re-imposed), there are unlikely to be any further changes to youth justice policy in the interim.

Conclusion

This chapter has shown that there are distinct differences between the youth justice systems in the different countries comprising the United Kingdom, as well as points of policy and practice convergence. Each country has different institutional and practice structures governing the sphere of youth justice, and claims have been made in various analyses regarding the distinct nature of different systems, whether that be regarding the 'dragonization' of Welsh youth justice (Haines, 2009), or the 'detartanization' and 'retartanization' of the Scottish criminal justice system (McAra, 2010; Mooney et al., 2015).However, some analyses of broader trends over both time and place caution against claims of difference and have even argued that some of the surface differences are 'illusory', in that broader trends such as a focus on risk and responsibilisation in the sphere of youth justice exercise have totalising effects.

Comparative analyses of within-jurisdiction differences in practice and ultimately in outcomes for young people, also show that there may be more divergence *within than between* countries. Goldson and Briggs' (2021) analysis of the differential rates of the use of custodial disposals across different Youth Offending Team areas in England and Wales, for instance, shows strikingly different patterns in diversionary approaches as well as in the use of custodial detention. Their analysis suggests that different leadership approaches and philosophical foundations (i.e., whether teams and practitioners adopted penal welfare or offender management approaches), or whether decisions and practices were evidence-informed and grounded in an understanding of children's rights principles, were important distinguishing variables. All of which suggests the need to pay closer attention to granular differences in practice, as well as to young people's experiences of these.

That said, devolution has encouraged the development of distinct national approaches to the structuring of youth justice systems, as well as with regard to areas of social policy that impact more broadly on the lives of children and young people (including education and social welfare services). Across the different countries of the United Kingdom the numbers of children and young people entering the justice system has been on a downward trajectory for several years. The reasons for this decline are not fully explained, but one of its effects is a greater focus on the 'complex needs' of children within the system (a topic which we cover in more detail in Chapter 8). It is also important to note that the area of youth justice and the arguments made about distinguishing features of different systems within the United Kingdom, also tell us something about how youth justice policy interacts with broader questions of politics and national identity as well as political economy.

Further Reading

McAra, L. (2017) 'Youth Justice.' In: A. Liebling, S. Maruna and L. McAra (Eds.), *The Oxford Handbook of Criminology (Sixth Edition)*. Oxford: Oxford University Press (pp. 938–966).

This chapter in the *Oxford Handbook of Criminology* provides a very good overview of the different youth justice systems in the United Kingdom. It also considers the key paradigms which have been influential across the different jurisdictions.

Muncie, J. (2011) 'Illusions of Difference: Comparative Youth Justice in the Devolved United Kingdom.' *British Journal of Criminology*, 51, 1: 40–57.

This article is now over a decade old, but its analysis, which suggests that despite differences in system structures across the countries in the United Kingdom, there are a number of common trends and themes in operation, retains a relevance.

7

Trends in Youth Justice

Objectives

- This chapter will consider what we understand as 'the facts' of youth crime.
- The reader will be introduced to the different ways young people come to be identified as offenders.
- The chapter will discuss trends and patterns of offending by young people.
- The reader will also be provided with an overview of sentencing and the outcomes of the youth justice process.

How Do We Establish the 'Facts' About Youth Crime?

We do know that youth crime is the focus of considerable attention, from criminologists, policy-makers, politicians, social welfare and criminal justice agencies, the media and the general public. Each of these constituencies, along with young people themselves, of course, has an interest in establishing 'the facts' of youth crime, both about its extent and about how to respond to it effectively. There is a widespread consensus that these are important issues, deserving of the effort required to obtain credible answers.

In effect, there are several key questions associated with these concerns:

1. Who become classified as young offenders?
2. What crimes do they commit?
3. How are their offences dealt with by the criminal justice system?
4. What are the effects and outcomes of criminal justice interventions with young people?
5. What are their experiences of criminal justice?

As we shall see, merely seeking to determine how to tackle these questions will pose significant problems of definition and calculation; and this is an extremely important point. Whilst making every effort to achieve clarity and certainty, we must equally avoid the temptation to over-simplify or make definitive claims about an area of human activity where these aims are likely to be highly problematic. If we consider drug-taking, for example, we know that it is widespread, with about 20–25% of school students in England reporting that they have ever used drugs according to government estimates (NHS Digital, 2019). In some countries, though, drug use is not treated as a criminal matter. So, is simple drug use by young people a crime? And, if so, who are the criminals: drug users, addicts, suppliers? Should we differentiate between those who sell to their friends and those involved in organised drug distribution, such as '**county lines**'? Is it just those who are caught who are criminals, or all those involved? Should we treat those who are caught as offenders, or as a health risk? And, what about legal drugs – why should alcohol and cigarettes be treated differently? And so on...

This example is cited to illustrate the many and complex issues facing us when seeking to identify and then quantify the level of offending within the youth population; and then to consider how to respond to crime. We must proceed with caution, and perhaps recognise that in place of simple facts, we must very often rely on assumptions and inferences, drawing on our own powers of judgement.

Who become classified as young offenders?

As we can see from the example of drug use, relying on 'official' figures about youth crime and young offenders would only tell us part of the story. Most offending does not come to the attention of the authorities; and most of that which is reported is not detected. Several systemic factors account for this shortfall, including under-reporting and the limited capacities of crime enforcement agencies (MacDonald, 2002). It might therefore be helpful to start not with the official records, but with what young people themselves have to tell us about their involvement in crime and anti-social behaviour.

Self-report studies

According to Farrington (2001), self-report studies of young offenders can be traced back to the 1940s in the United States and the 1960s in the United Kingdom. Self-report studies adopt the quite logical approach of trying to identify the level and nature of youth offending by asking young people about their involvement. In one sense, this might well be an obvious step, but it does not entirely resolve the problem of trying to establish an accurate picture. For example, depending on the context (surveys are often school based), some potential respondents may be excluded from taking part, whilst others might be discouraged from answering with complete honesty. There are also problems, of course, of recollection, and of knowing what counts as a 'crime'. Nonetheless, self-report studies have proliferated, and now represent a substantial contribution to criminological knowledge, although they have tended to concentrate their focus on certain types of crime, perhaps more commonly associated with young people.

Short and Nye's (1957) survey of 2,358 14–17-year-olds in Wisconsin and Illinois is believed to have 'triggered' much of the subsequent work in this area of inquiry (Farrington, 2001: 5). Notably, amongst its major findings was the observation that there was no identifiable relationship between social class and offending, with the implication that the formal structures and processes of the justice system might be generating a distorted picture of the distribution of youth crime. The apparent concentration of offending by young people amongst particular – poorer, minority ethnic – communities thus appears to be an artefact of discriminatory criminal justice mechanisms and processes.

Similarly, other disparities between the official picture and self-reported crime began to emerge with subsequent studies. Gold and Reimer's (1975) longitudinal study found a decline of self-reported offending by young people of 20% between 1967 and 1972, whilst the same period saw a 29% increase in the number of cases coming to the juvenile court (Farrington, 2001: 6). Importantly, these early studies demonstrated the value of obtaining estimates of criminal behaviour which were not dependent simply on the highly selective nature of official statistics. It became possible to establish a clearer sense of patterns and trends than might be shown simply as a result of changes in recording practices or staffing levels. Maguire and Pastore (1999), for example, established a significant level of continuity over time, reporting very similar levels of car theft and shoplifting amongst American youth in 1996–98 as ten years previously.

In the United Kingdom, early self-report studies were carried out by Willcock (1974) and Belson (1975). Interestingly, these two studies, one national and the other based in London, showed considerable variations in offending levels, with around 3% of respondents stating that they had committed a burglary in Willock's study covering England and Wales; whilst the comparable figure for London reported by Belson was 18%. Other European countries, too, began to adopt the self-report survey as a means of determining the extent and distribution of crime amongst young people, in an attempt to discover the true extent of criminal activity lying beyond the official figures. These countries included Sweden, Denmark, Germany and the Netherlands (Junger-Tas and Marshall, 1999).

As Junger-Tas and Marshall have pointed out, however, the conduct of this kind of exercise also tended to illustrate the wide range and lack of precision in the types of behaviour deemed to be 'criminal'; and in particular, self-reporting relies on a huge variety of localised, cultural and individual-level definitions of what actually constitutes an offence. In addition, the choice of samples, response rates, location of the survey (often school-based), and the actual method used (interviews or questionnaires) might all impact substantially on the findings generated. Despite these concerns, Junger-Tas and Marshall, writing in 1999, concluded that the quality and reliability of self-report studies had improved significantly over previous decades.

Major UK studies of the 1990s began to offer more depth to our knowledge of patterns of youth crime (Graham and Bowling, 1995; Flood-Page et al., 2000). Graham and Bowling found that, according to their own accounts, a very small proportion of young people were identified as being responsible for more than a quarter of all offences committed amongst their peers. This particular survey, of 1,721 young people aged 14–25, supplemented with an additional 'purposive sample' of 808 participants from ethnic minorities (to ensure a sufficiently large representative sample size), identified that a much larger number, a quarter of males and one in eight females, admitted offending during the previous year. The survey was also able to determine that 15 was the peak age of offending for girls/young women, compared to 18 for boys/young men.

This survey (the Youth Lifestyle Survey) was subsequently repeated, and largely confirmed the initial findings (Flood-Page et al., 2000), and this time went on to provide an insight into the so-called 'risk factors' associated with patterns of serious or persistent offending behaviour. Young people more likely to report more substantial involvement of this kind were also more likely to report involvement with drugs, experience of 'poor' parental supervision, or having friends who were also involved in criminal activity.

In the early 2000s the Youth Justice Board commissioned a series of annual Youth Crime Surveys, later discontinued, which were helpful in demonstrating a fairly consistent picture of the distribution of offending amongst young people. Around a quarter of young people surveyed acknowledged that they had offended within the previous 12 months, and around 60 per cent consistently stated that they had 'ever' offended. Somewhat frustratingly, the final report on these surveys suggested the beginnings of a change in the overall pattern, with only 19% stating that they had committed a crime within the previous year (Anderson et al., 2010). Possibly this might have indicated the early signs of a downward trend, mirroring a similar decline in the number of official reports of youth crime.

In Scotland, the *Edinburgh Study of Youth Transitions and Crime* has also generated a wealth of material on the experiences and perceptions of young people, and the longitudinal nature of this study has been particularly helpful, as well as its scale, involving over 4,000 young people from that city. In particular, the Edinburgh study has informed our understanding of pathways into and out of crime, and distinctive offending patterns and profiles attributable to young people. The study shows, for example, a peak age of offending somewhat younger than other studies (age 14); and at the same time, it shows that this 'peak age' actually varies according to the type of offence (McVie, 2005: 9). Fare-dodging, for example, increases in frequency at least up to the age of 16, whilst carrying weapons tends to peak at around 14, once total offending is disaggregated.

Having been carried out in a series of data sweeps, the Edinburgh study is also able to identify distinctive offending patterns. Ten per cent of those surveyed over the series had never reported carrying out an offence of any kind; whilst, on the other hand, around a third had offended in the period prior to each repeat of the survey (McVie, 2005: 11). And, similarly to the analysis provided by Flood-Page et al. (2000), the Edinburgh study was able to identify factors associated with the likelihood of offending. In particular, persistent or serious offenders were found to be more likely themselves to have been the victims of harmful or abusive behaviour by their own accounts (McAra and McVie, 2010a: 185); patterns and pathways into and out of offending could depend on 'critical' moments or incidents in young people's lives, such as school exclusion in the early teens (p. 190); and, being identified as 'at risk' by way of contact with statutory services might result in young people being 'labelled', and thus more likely to become officially identified as offenders (p. 189).

As well as gaining some insight into the extent of offending amongst young people, and the factors which might be associated with them getting involved in crime, or becoming criminalised, we are also able to glean important insights into the distribution of offending, notably by ethnic group, or gender. The analysis of previous American studies carried out by Elliott and Ageton (1980) identified that little difference had been identified in self-report studies between respondents according to their ethnic origin. By contrast, official reports and records showed 'significant differences by both class and race' (p. 95). However, closer and more recent analysis, particularly of more serious offences, has suggested a more complex picture, with self-reported arrests (rather than offences) showing consistency with official arrest rates irrespective of ethnic background (Piquero et al., 2014).

In the UK, the study by Graham and Bowling (1995) found little difference between White and African-Caribbean respondents in their reported rates of involvement in violence, property offences or damage. However, subsequent surveys generated mixed findings (May et al., 2010), with only those of Asian origin reporting a consistently lower rate of offending than those from other ethnic groups. When other relevant factors are taken into account, ethnicity is not viewed as 'independently predictive of offending' (May et al., 2010: 20).

However, as May et al. (2010: 21) go on to argue:

> In summary, existing evidence suggests that while the lower prevalence of offending among Asian/Asian British young people might account for the under-representation of that group in the figures for detected youth crime, overall patterns of delinquency are unlikely to explain the over-representation of Black/Black British young people.

Official records and statistics

The picture provided by official statistics does not appear to reflect young people's own accounts of their involvement in crime, then, particularly in relation to ethnicity. It is likely to be the case that what we might term 'official records' represent more serious offences and more sustained involvement of particular young people; so, in this respect, they will certainly differ. Much relatively minor offending (petty shoplifting, for example) is likely not to be followed up, or simply remains undetected, whereas more serious crimes (of violence, say) are more likely to attract closer attention and the concerted efforts of criminal justice agencies to ensure that they are dealt with satisfactorily.

In England and Wales, this pattern has almost certainly become more apparent as the numbers of children and young people processed by the justice system has declined steeply over an extended period of time. By 2018/19, when 21,700 young offenders were dealt with formally and received a caution or a court sentence, this number represented an 82% decline over a 10-year period (Youth Justice Board/Ministry of Justice, 2021: 2). This illustrates very well the suggestion that statutory processes and the ways in which they are organised and implemented will inevitably play a very substantial part in defining the population formally classified as offenders.

A decline of this scale is unlikely to be accounted for simply by changing patterns of behaviour, or personal characteristics, but we can also safely assume that changes in the practices of criminal justice agencies and recording methods must play a part. This conclusion can also be drawn from the disparity between the findings of self-report studies of the early 2000s (see above), which showed a fairly constant level of offending by young people's own accounts, on the one hand, and on the other, the rapid rise in the numbers formally processed, largely because of a change in the policing targets set by government: 'in 2007, the number of substantive youth justice disposals imposed was 20% higher than in 2003' (Bateman, 2015: 9) (see Chapter 8 for further discussion).

The official statistics do suggest certain patterns in the distribution of the population of young offenders. According to the youth justice statistics for England and Wales in 2018/19: 'boys made up 51% of the general 10–17 population in England and Wales but accounted for 85% of the total number of children who received a caution or sentence in the latest year. This proportion has been steadily increasing over the past ten years' (Youth Justice Board/Ministry of Justice, 2021: 18).

Similarly, the age distribution of young offenders according to these figures indicates that criminal activity is associated with age, with 77% of all young offenders being 15–17, compared to only 23% being between 10 and 14. As with gender, this is largely consistent with self-report studies which indicate that young males make up the greater proportion of offenders; in addition, the peak age of offending is in the mid to late teens, for both males and females, as we have seen.

In relation to ethnicity, there appears to be an identifiable trend towards increased over-representation of certain ethnic groups among the young offender population. The proportions of both Black children and those from a mixed ethnic background cautioned or sentenced increased substantially from 2010 to 2019 – from 6% to 11% and from 4% to 8% respectively. By 2018/19, this meant that the proportion of Black children or young people identified as offenders was three times what would be expected from the general population figures. This figure is clearly not consistent with the evidence reported above of the prevalence of offending amongst different ethnic groups suggested by self-report studies. Once again, it suggests that we must consider the contribution to these disparities of 'system' effects, especially in the light of repeated evidence of institutional racism revealed by major inquiries (MacPherson, 1999; Lammy, 2017).

These observations certainly suggest that we should treat the official figures with some scepticism. Their relationship to the underlying behaviours and self-attributed criminal activities of young people is not straightforward, and the processes they represent may, themselves, contribute to the criminalisation (or not) of certain groups of young people. Nonetheless, however problematic they are, these figures do represent the processes which determine how young people, and their crimes, are dealt with by the justice system, and they are therefore a key focus of critical interest in terms of understanding these outcomes (see Chapter 8 for a further discussion).

What crimes do young people commit?

Of course, alongside our attempts to understand who the young offenders are, it is important to gain some idea of the types of criminal (and anti-social) behaviour for which they are believed to be responsible. For various reasons, it is likely that the nature of youth crime will look rather different to the profile of criminal activity across the population, and it will be helpful to explore this distinctive pattern of behaviour.

Thus, in 2018/19, across England and Wales, the official figures showed a changing pattern of youth offending, largely because of an increasing likelihood that what are seen as more minor offences would be disposed of informally, usually by way of a police warning. Offences of 'violence against the person' comprised 30% of all 'proven offences' by children and young people (aged 10–17) in 2018–19, and theft and handling stolen goods accounted for a further 11%, slightly more than criminal damage. Other offences, including burglary, robbery, 'motoring' offences and sexual offences made up smaller proportions of the overall total.

Even within these global figures, though, the seriousness of offences may not be represented simply by the category to which they are assigned, especially if falling under a catch-all heading such as 'violence'. When recorded formally, each offence is assigned a 'gravity score', a form of categorisation devised for the Police National Legal Database, in order to provide a finer gradation of offence gravity. Accordingly, only a small proportion of 'violent' offences committed by children/young people in 2018/9 were categorised with a gravity score of five to eight (Youth Justice Board, 2021: 23), whereas for burglary, robbery or sexual offences over half of these were rated at this level. As the Youth Justice Board (2021: 24) reports, very few crimes committed by young people fall into the most serious (gravity score eight) category (140 – 0.3% in 2019/20).

Significantly, the annual statistics had begun to incorporate a specific reference to 'knife crime' at this point. The pattern of knife crimes committed and dealt with over time differed somewhat from the continuing decline in youth crime in general. From 2009 until 2013, the number of knife crimes committed by young people fell from over 6,000 to fewer than 3,000, according to the official figures. From that point on, though, there was a steady increase to 2018/2019, although by 2019/20, the number had stabilised at around 4,400. Of these, though, 97% were identified as 'possession offences' and 3% as 'threatening with a knife or deadly weapon' (Youth Justice Board, 2021: 26). This type of offence might be viewed as inherently 'serious', but only 12% led to an immediate custodial sentence, whilst 29% were dealt with by way of a caution.

As Bateman observes, however, there is something of a paradox here, as far as the official figures are concerned:

> [Whilst] official statistics understate the extent of youth crime, they also, and for similar reasons, tend to exaggerate its seriousness. Minor incidents are more likely to remain undetected because victims are less inclined to report them and, where the police are notified, they may not merit the allocation of resources necessary for detection and processing. Where children engaged in such activities are apprehended, the authorities frequently use their discretion to avoid a formal outcome. (Bateman, 2017: 18)

As a result, then, the profile of offending by young people might be somewhat misleading if we rely solely on official figures. As Bateman also points out, self-report studies tend to show that incidents of theft are the most common offences carried out by children and young people, whilst: 'Discussion of youth criminality tends to focus on high profile, more serious incidents, such as gang-related activities, robbery, violence against the person and, particularly in the recent period, knife-crime' (Bateman, 2017: 18).

It might nonetheless be argued that the apparent imbalance in our knowledge of youth crime may, indeed, misrepresent the whole picture whilst at the same time actually helping to keep the focus on those crimes which are of greatest significance and lead to the greatest harm. In this sense, then, we might draw the conclusion that official statistics are helpful because they do focus attention on matters of greatest concern. However, there is a risk, too, that this leads to excessive fear and blame being directed towards young people, disproportionately. Knife crimes involving young people under the age of 18, for example, represented only about a tenth of the overall knife crime figure for the year ending March 2019 (Office for National Statistics, 2019).

At the same time, official figures, and the formal interventions they represent, may not capture well the complexity of the issues surrounding some offences, such as 'county lines' drug distribution, which is widely believed to involve young people extensively (Turner et al., 2019). According to a report commissioned by The Children's Society, as many as 46,000 children may be involved in 'county lines' networks, whereby they are recruited to travel to deliver drugs on behalf of suppliers. Whilst this is reported often to involve coercion and the exploitation of children, crime figures seem to show that this phenomenon is also associated with an increase in their criminalisation, with notable increases in those arrested for possession with intent to supply Class A drugs between 2015/16 and 2017/18. This example highlights another distinctive feature of the crimes committed by or attributed to young people, and this is to do with the interplay between their behaviour and their circumstances.

This may partly be to do with certain features of 'growing up', such as neurological changes, the importance of peer relationships or a relative absence of adult commitments and responsibilities, or it may be to do with specific circumstances and pressures to which young people are distinctively subjected. Young people are more 'visible', for example, to the extent that they may spend a large part of their time in public places, so they are perhaps more likely to be associated with various forms of anti-social behaviour and disorder offences. On the other hand, as just noted, there are certain vulnerabilities to which certain young people are exposed, which might also be viewed as criminogenic. Here, though, the link appears to exist between prior experience, or current circumstances and particular types of offence, rather than a more generalised sense of 'criminality'. For example, Batchelor's (2005) study of young women's involvement in crime in Scotland documented the close association between prior experiences of violence and abuse as victims, and their own violent behaviour:

> If you let people walk all over you, people will and people do [...] See if you stand back and let them hit you, they will keep hitting you. If you hit them back, then they usually stop. You have to be violent in here because I would say 70 percent of the lassies *are* violent, so if you're not then you won't get nowhere. You get bullied and you don't get any respect. It's simple. (Karen, quoted in Batchelor, 2005: 369)

Importantly, here we can see that patterns of youth crime are contextual, and very likely to be shaped by past experiences, as well as perhaps more contingent factors such as influence and opportunity. Thus, perhaps, there is an argument for disaggregating crime figures and adopting a more focused and nuanced approach to the task of identifying patterns and trends in young people's offending behaviour.

How are young people's offences dealt with by the criminal justice system?

Given that young people's crimes vary significantly in nature and impact, with very few demonstrating the highest levels of gravity, we could certainly expect the justice system to respond in very different ways according to the nature of the offence. Indeed, this does appear to be the case, with much low-level youth crime dealt with informally, or by way of some form of 'diversionary' measure, whilst custodial or other secure options are available, and used relatively infrequently, for those whose offences are deemed to be the most serious or to represent the most substantial continuing risk to others.

Firstly, though, it is important to acknowledge that there is considerable international variation in the way in which the crimes of the young are dealt with; and this is clearly reflected from the outset in different approaches to attributing criminal responsibility (see Chapter 5). In fact, there are substantial variations in law and policy on the question of whether or not and at what age children should be held (criminally) responsible for their actions. Of course, these legislative provisions are subject to change, but the following link provided by Child Rights International (CRIN) provides some idea of the kind of variations to be found: https://home.crin.org/issues/deprivation-of-liberty/minimum-age-of-criminal-responsibility.

Even though most countries do provide for children to be held criminally responsible for their actions at a specified age, there is also a wide consensus that they should be diverted from the formal justice system where possible. As a result, it is frequently found to be the case that a very substantial proportion of those coming to the attention of criminal justice agencies are then dealt with in ways which are intended to minimise their impact, and to enable them to avoid the possible stigma associated with a criminal record. In England and Wales, much offending by young people is dealt with informally. Even though the number and proportion of those formally processed who were cautioned showed a rapid decline during the 2010s, this tended to mask the extent to which police and Youth Offending Teams (YOTs) were dealing with many reported offences without recourse to such processes.

Dealing with Offences Informally: Community Resolution

Community resolution (CR) – is an alternative way of dealing with less serious crimes that allows the police to use their professional judgement when dealing with a child who has committed an offence. This approach would normally seek to resolve the offence in an informal way that brings closure for the victim, where one has been identified, in a timely manner. It may involve the young person doing something that 'puts right' the offending to the satisfaction of the victim and should take account of their views. Initial CRs may often be delivered directly by the investigating police officer, without the child having been arrested. This is sometimes referred to as 'Street RJ (restorative justice)'. A CR may also be given where, following consideration of the options available, it is more suitable than a caution. Receipt of a CR is recorded in local police systems but is not recorded on the Police National Computer (PNC) and does not form part of a formal criminal record. (HMIP/HMICFRS, 2018: 6)

Informal disposals of this kind constitute a significant proportion of the overall 'outcomes' delivered to children and young people who are identified as offenders, with cautions representing between 30% and 80% of the overall 'throughput' of YOTs (HMIP/HMICFRS, 2018: 14), although they are largely unacknowledged in official statistics (p. 12).

Although we must be cautious about comparability, New Zealand/Aotearoa, which shares a relatively low age of criminal responsibility with England and Wales, also makes extensive use of 'out of court' disposals (Spier and Wilkinson, 2016: 2). In that country, in 2013: '39% of child offenders were warned and 53% of cases were resolved by Alternative Action', that is, informal resolution by way of reparation to victims or community work, outside the formal court process. A relatively small percentage were dealt with by way of Family Group Conferences or prosecution. New Zealand's use of Family Group Conferences to seek positive resolutions for youth crime is distinctive, and closely linked with its overarching commitment to restorative practices. It does bear some resemblance, however, to the Scottish Children's Hearing System (see Chapter 6 for a fuller discussion), which also presides over all but the most serious offences, and which is geared as much towards promoting child welfare as to the attribution of guilt and punishment.

Trends in youth justice, then, suggest both a widespread decline in the numbers of offences by children and young people, and, in parallel, an increasing commitment to responses which bypass the court system and an associated reliance on non-penal measures. The emergence of restorative disposals as a significant feature of youth justice systems has been noteworthy. As restorative justice more generally has become widely accepted as a legitimate objective of the criminal justice process, it has begun to feature across the range of disposals available for offences attributed to young people. Significantly, the principles of restorative justice are applicable at any point in the process; and so its growing influence and presence can be observed across the spectrum from informal disposals through to custodial sentences. Speaking in 2017, the Chief Executive of the Youth Justice Agency in Northern Ireland said:

> Restorative practice is at the heart of the work of the Youth Justice Agency in Northern Ireland. It provides young people with an opportunity to play an active part in the resolution and repair of the harm caused by their actions. But importantly, it also gives victims a much needed voice that is sometimes absent from the traditional justice process. Communities too can benefit from the reparation work undertaken which can often help restore broken relationships. (Declan McGeown, 20 November 2017, launch of Restorative Justice Week: www.justice-ni.gov.uk/news/restorative-practice-heart-youth-justice-system)

In Northern Ireland, restorative interventions are promoted both as alternatives to the court process, and through the court process itself, whereby an order can be made for young people and their families to attend a 'youth conference', to address and resolve the issues associated with an offence by a young person (see Chapter 6 for a fuller discussion). Over the period 2008–2013, between 1,600 and 2,100 conferences were instituted each year, with a 76–78% completion rate (Marder, 2020). These conferences are similar in nature and purpose to the Family Group Conference model in New Zealand and the Referral Order process in England and Wales, and, according to Marder, similar approaches have been widely adopted throughout Europe, in Georgia, Albania, Belgium and Finland, for example.

As offences become more serious, or young people are deemed to be persistent offenders, though, more formal procedures and more punitive outcomes appear more prevalent, with sentences progressing through community disposals, usually with an element of compulsion, to forms of custodial detention. In England and Wales, the courts have available the Youth Rehabilitation Order (YRO), introduced in 2009, a composite sentence which enables them to combine elements of punishment, welfare and, indeed, restoration (from a 'menu' of 18 available requirements) and thus, potentially integrating the varied objectives of youth justice under a common framework. Bateman's (2017: 45) analysis of the YRO is somewhat sceptical. He points out that its many elements were often available under previous legislation under different names, and there was already the option of combining these in many cases.

Perhaps as a result, the YRO did not have any substantial effect in displacing other disposals available to the court, particularly in terms of reducing the proportion of custodial sentences imposed (Youth Justice Board, 2021: 28). In 2015/16: 'the YRO accounted for one quarter of all disposals compared with an equivalent figure of 30% in the year ending March 2009' (Bateman, 2017: 45), and by 2019/20 this figure was still around 22%. Notably, though, there does seem to have been a tendency for the intensity of YRO requirements to increase over time:

> the proportion of orders that contain five or more requirements [increased] from 2% in 2010/11 to 6% in 2013/14, and 11% in 2015/16. While this might, for some cases, reflect the use of higher-end community sentencing as an alternative to a custodial disposal, thereby contributing to the reduction in child imprisonment, it may also be an indication that community disposals, in at least some instances, are becoming more intrusive. (Bateman, 2017: 46)

Two of the most commonly used requirements of the YRO, according to Bateman, consist of 'supervision' (33%), and the imposition of a 'curfew' (14%), which seems to epitomise the underlying intention, at least, of combining a welfare element with a punitive sanction.

Norway's approach to community sentencing of young people incorporates similar principles and components, despite its very different framework for the delivery of youth justice. In that country, the minimum age of criminal responsibility is 15, but for those children aged 15–18 who are prosecuted, there has been no special provision in terms of judicial proceedings, and they are dealt with by adult courts (Winterdyk et al., 2016). However, within this framework, courts do have specific sentences available to them for young people in this age range, notably 'Youth Punishment', which incorporates a number of elements to be found in other jurisdictions, including an initial 'conference', reparation to offence victims, and a combination of elements of support and punishment, comparable to those found in the YRO. Despite this apparent consistency in practice across national boundaries, and despite some criticism of its practices by international observers, there is also a widely held view that Norway's model of youth justice is, overall, considerably less punitive than most other countries. However, concerns are raised about its treatment of marginalised or minority communities, as elsewhere (Winterdyk et al., 2016: 116). (For a discussion of comparative youth justice see Chapter 4.)

At the apex of the youth justice system stands penal custody, alongside other forms of secure institution provided specifically for children and young people. Current trends suggest that, in parallel with a falling crime rate, there has been a similar decline in the use of custody for young people. In England and Wales, there has been a substantial fall from the peak figure in the early 2000s of over 3,000 children in custody (Bateman, 2017) to substantially below

1,000 by 2020. Similar dramatic progress is reported elsewhere, as in Canada, for example:

> On an average day in 1997, 3,825 young people (ages 12 to 17) were serving sentences in Canadian youth prisons. By 2015, that number had decreased to 527, an 86 percent reduction. This is a drop from 157 per 100,000 12- to 17-year-olds to 23. (Doob et al., 2018)

Importantly, these figures represent the *rate* of incarceration rather than the number, thus taking account of any changes in overall population figures. As in the case of England and Wales, the decline in the use of youth custody in Canada did not seem to be mirrored in substantial changes in the imprisonment rate for adult offenders. Schiraldi (2020) also reports a halving in the use of youth incarceration in the United States from 2000 onwards. Certainly, within anglophone 'Western' nations, there appears to have been a common trend emerging (see Chapter 8 for a further discussion about the possible reasons for this decline in numbers and its effects).

Against what many would see as an encouraging backdrop of falling custody rates, some concerns remain, however. Firstly, it appears that the conditions for those young people experiencing custody are sometimes unacceptable. Willow (2015) and Simmonds (2016) have reported that custody is a disturbing experience for young people, where many (46%) feel 'unsafe' (Bateman, 2017: 53). Violence between residents is also reported to be at a significant and increasing level, compounded by the regular and often painful use of 'restraint' techniques (physical methods of control) by staff (Shenton and Smith, 2021). Between 2010 and 2016 in England and Wales, the number of assaults per 100 children in custody increased from 9 to 18.9 per month, and the monthly number of 'restraints' used by staff on children rose from 17.6 to 27.8 per 100 children (Bateman, 2017: 53), and by 2018–2019, this figure had risen significantly again, to 46.6 per 100. Custody for children appears to be becoming a more unpleasant and even dangerous place. Bateman (2017: 53) also reports that:

> minority ethnic children are less likely to think that staff treat them with respect than their white peers (58% against 68%) and more likely to consider that they have been victimised by staff (39% compared to 26%). This is no doubt reflected in the fact that more than half of BAME boys indicate that they have been physically restrained by comparison with just over one in three white boys.

This disproportionate treatment of ethnic minority children and young people within the custodial estate only serves to amplify the unequal treatment they experience throughout the operation of the justice system. Of particular concern have been the divergent trends for those subject to custodial sentences.

Whilst the overall number of young people has declined substantially, as noted previously, this has resulted in a strikingly disproportionate representation of Black children, in particular, in the secure estate (see Chapter 8 for more discussion of these trends). Cunneen and Tauri (2019) report, too, that Indigenous youth in Australia are 23 times more likely to experience custody than their non-Indigenous peers. So, once again, we can conclude that there is a broad pattern of discriminatory outcomes for minority (non-White) youths across many parts of the Anglophone world.

Youth justice outcomes

Looking beyond the pattern of agency practices and disposals, we might also ask the question of what do youth justice processes and systems achieve? How well do they succeed in delivering the objectives set for them, such as, in the English/Welsh context, the 'principal aim' of preventing offending by children. Typically, objectives are set for youth justice systems in terms of reducing levels of reoffending, and this is very often the default criterion against which interventions are judged. As Field (2007) has acknowledged, the shift of emphasis from promoting children's welfare (at least jointly) to an exclusive emphasis on reducing levels of crime is associated with the reform programme of the New Labour government (1997–2010), and in particular the major legislative initiative of the *Crime and Disorder Act 1998*. As Field (2007: 314) also acknowledges, these changes were not always welcomed, and practitioners certainly expressed the view that this represented a 'narrowing' of focus, with the potential dilution or loss of focus on a range of important objectives of intervention beyond merely preventing further offending. For many practitioners, indeed, the view was that (re-)offending and welfare were so closely linked that attending to children's needs was essential if the aim was to reduce the possibility of further offending:

> If you take the needs of the young person, if their basic needs aren't being met, their welfare needs, how on earth can they actually concentrate on not offending? If they are homeless, you are not going to address that offending behaviour because as far as they are concerned, they have got a priority need that they have to sort out before they are going to sit and listen to anything you have got to say. So I think it goes hand in hand ... (youth justice worker quoted in Field, 2007: 314)

Here, from the practitioner perspective we can see that there is an argument for considering a broader range of objectives and outcomes in youth justice than simply the issue of whether or not levels of offending are reduced. This viewpoint finds echoes in the emerging emphasis on 'desistance' and the ways in which pro-social outcomes for young people are bound up with positive changes across different aspects of their lives (McNeill and Weaver, 2010). Disposals and interventions in youth justice, then, are to be judged on a range of outcomes, of which levels of (re)offending is one, undoubtedly, but others, such as obtaining secure accommodation or employment, developing positive relationships or achieving improved health, are also to be considered, to the extent that they contribute to the achievement of 'good lives' (Ward and Brown, 2004).

Despite these caveats, we will firstly consider what is known about reoffending rates for young people, based principally on official figures. These figures are presented in terms of 'proven' reoffending, usually over a period of a year following conviction for an earlier offence (Ministry of Justice, 2020). Thus, for example, the reoffending rate for 'juvenile' offenders in England and Wales for the period January to March 2018 was 39.2%. This figure is reported to have fluctuated between 36.3% and 43.6% in the period from 2006 to 2018. Those with a higher number of previous offences are also reported to be considerably more likely to reoffend (Ministry of Justice, 2020: 9). There is also considerable variation depending on the offender's previous sentence or disposal, with 26.8% of those cautioned committing a further offence within a year, as compared to 67.6 % of those receiving an initial custodial sentence (Ministry of Justice, 2020: 12). This type of figure, of course, raises significant questions about the deterrent effect of punitive sentences on young people, and custody in particular.

More detailed analysis reveals a number of other patterns in reoffending by young people. Males, for example, reoffend at a consistently higher rate than females over time, and in 2017–2018, the respective figures were, for males, 40.5%, and for females, 27.4%. Official figures also suggest that reoffending rates for Black young people are higher than those for other ethnic groups (Youth Justice Board, 2021: 65). This disparity is perhaps also a sign of systemic effects which leave young Black people at more risk of being criminalised at all points of the justice process. Youth Justice Board figures also suggest that reoffending rates correlate with the severity of previous disposals, with a custodial sentence most likely to lead to a further offence, followed progressively by Youth Rehabilitation Orders, 'other' non-custodial sentences and cautions (Youth Justice Board, 2021).

Bateman's (2017) analysis of patterns of reoffending acknowledges that there is no straightforward correlation between type of disposal and its effect on the likelihood of further offending. He recognises that children who receive the most severe penalties are those whose pattern of offending is more deeply entrenched; they are thus perhaps more likely to reoffend irrespective of the sentence imposed. However, as Bateman (2017: 56) also observes:

> analysis by the Ministry of Justice suggests that, even when relevant factors … are controlled for, lower level community sentences are associated with significantly better reoffending outcomes than high intensity, community-based disposals. (Recidivism rates are 4% lower for the former type of order.) Moreover, children who receive custodial sentences of between

six and 12 months are significantly more likely to reoffend than a comparison group sentenced to a high level community penalty (again a four percentage point difference).

That is to say, there is some evidence that the severity of the sentence or other disposal is, itself, associated with a greater likelihood of a young person committing further crimes. This conclusion was also accepted by the government-commissioned *Taylor Review* of youth justice in England and Wales (Taylor, 2016).

Several possible reasons have been suggested for this. These include:

- The possibility that young people are subject to negative peer influences, through mixing with others who have similar or greater levels of involvement in crime;
- The effects of 'labelling' as young people are increasingly identified as serious or intractable offenders by criminal justice agencies and others;
- Exclusion from certain opportunities on the grounds of having a criminal record;
- The effects of 'dislocation' from the normal institutions of society – family, educational settings, non-delinquent peer groups;
- Loss of contact with 'pro-social' influences; or
- The inadequacy of post-sentence resettlement or rehabilitation provisions.

In combination, these factors are all believed to play a part in reinforcing the involvement of children and young people in offending and reducing their capacity to resume a valued law-abiding place in the community.

Hazel and Bateman (2020) draw attention to the persistently high levels of reoffending by children and young people on leaving custody in England and Wales; although they also acknowledge that this is an international problem. They note that effective resettlement of young people post-custody has been an explicit priority for policy-makers for a prolonged period, at least since the introduction of the *Detention and Training Order* in 1998. The aim was to provide a 'seamless intervention that offered a continuity of provision from the point of entry to the custodial institution, into the community' (Hazel and Bateman, 2020: 72); and this was further underlined with the publication of a Youth Justice Board resettlement framework in 2005. Again in 2010 and 2018, the YJB is reported to have re-emphasised this commitment, under governments of different political compositions.

The authors point out that resettlement models have been extensively evaluated, and there is evidence to suggest that certain approaches can be effective: 'reoffending was less likely when any organised activity – including education, training, employment or any constructive leisure – had been arranged for the child to occupy them on release' (Hazel and Bateman, 2020: 75). They are concerned, however, to note that repeated studies and investigations have found little progress has been made towards consistently implementing models of good practice. They suggest that this is partly so because of the limited, short-term, atomised and procedural focus of much resettlement planning and preparation.

Resettlement has only been considered instrumentally as a means to prevent reoffending and: 'there has been no attempt to identify a high-level aim for resettlement beyond preventing reoffending' (Hazel and Bateman, 2020: 80). Hazel and Bateman argue instead that the intrinsic value of resettlement should be recognised, and that it should be reconceptualised as an element in the young person's 'desistance journey' from a 'pro-offending' to a 'pro-social' way of life. Instead of applying a pathologising risk management model (Gray, 2011), services should invest in supporting the young person to develop their own sense of agency and capacity to make decisions to their own benefit.

Meanwhile Aizer and Doyle (2015) have carried out a substantial study of the effects of 'incarceration' in America, identifying similarly poor long-term consequences as seems to be the case in England and Wales:

> incarceration for this population could be very disruptive, greatly reducing the likelihood of ever returning to school and, for those who do return, significantly increasing the likelihood of being classified as having an emotional or behavioral disorder. (Aizer and Doyle, 2015: 759)

The evidence thus seems to suggest that longer-term adverse consequences for those young people receiving the more severe punishments for their offences go well beyond increased reoffending rates, and potentially lead to very longstanding problems across a range of aspects of their lives, including adverse health outcomes, for example (Schnittker and John, 2007).

Young people's experiences of youth justice

As is the case elsewhere in this book, we introduce the perspective and experiences of young people themselves at this point, because the subjective aspects of their youth journey provide an important dimension of our understanding of the subject; and also, as a matter of principle, and consistent with the argument that, in matters affecting them, children and young people's voices need to be heard and taken into account.

There has been a growing interest reflected in the youth justice literature in reporting the views of young people and understanding their experience of criminal justice interventions directly through personal accounts. As Sandøy (2020: 912) puts it, 'sociological approaches' have tended to highlight 'gaps' between the idealised expectations of criminal justice disposals and lived realities. Punishment effects can be distinguished, for example, between those which have 'concrete' effects, such as loss of liberty or other constraints, and those which have 'symbolic' effects, by which Sandøy means loss of autonomy or 'personhood'

(p. 913). As he comments: 'It follows from this that punishment experiences in custodial and non-custodial settings may take similar forms' (p. 913).

Sandøy's own study of young people involved in drug offences diverted from formal judicial processes in Norway indicates that some of the benefits to young people involved were offset by their feelings of being treated unreasonably and excessively through the imposition of programme conditions. The young people in this study had consented to a 'conditional waiver of prosecution', which meant that they had to undertake some form of alternative activity or additional requirement in order to qualify. These conditions usually involved drug testing, and sometimes additional requirements such as regular monitoring appointments (several times a week in some cases). Whilst young people did express a feeling of being 'pardoned' for their infractions, they also experienced the imposed conditions as restrictive:

> It's a bit tiresome. You must base your entire day on coming here [the drug testing centre], preferably as early as possible. If you come here when it opens, you get priority. But it's a bit like ... if I finish school late, you must come here right away, and if you don't make it, you have to wait in line. And you can't do anything else before you've been here, so it's a bit like your whole day is based on you coming here. (Tommy, 15, quoted in Sandøy, 2020: 916)

In another case, a young person had to attend an 'intensive supervisory programme' for six months, which had the effect of making him feel 'the whole thing cuts me off from other youth and from other people' (Anders, 16, quoted in Sandøy, 2020: 919). As Sandøy concludes, young people's experiences of punishment have often concentrated on the more obviously restrictive forms of penal sanction such as incarceration or community programmes involving extensive demands, but this may have overlooked the common grounds these experiences share with apparently less restrictive regimes, or even 'alternatives' to punishment.

McAlister and Carr (2014) discuss young people's experiences of restorative justice interventions, which, like, diversionary approaches, could be expected to feel rather different to young people than conventional forms of punishment: 'restorative justice is embedded in the language of inclusion, participation, and rights. Particularly suited to young people due to its "informal" and sometimes diversionary nature, it incorporates the rights and views of victims and young people' (McAlister and Carr, 2014: 244). And yet, as they acknowledge, restorative justice can be experienced as 'punitive, exclusionary and shaming'. In restorative youth justice conferences young people are expected to engage with others affected by their offences, including victims, and to achieve an agreed form of resolution.

However, from the perspective of young people the effects of restorative interventions are complex. Some young people found the challenge of accounting for their behaviour in front of the victim daunting, and 'punitive' (McAlister and Carr, 2014: 247). On the other hand, some appear to treat the conference as a kind of performance, where: 'you just have to sit down, and basically pretend, or not pretend, say you're sorry and look like you're sorry and that's it ...' (Garrett, 17, quoted in McAlister and Carr, 2014: 249). On the other hand, as the authors also found, young people's accounts of custodial regimes are also varied, with some, at least, finding them relatively less punitive than might be expected: 'Life is so easy in here [Woodlands Juvenile Justice Centre]. You have no worries about people looking for you, no worries about nothing. You have no worries about going hungry and getting food and things like that' (Robbie, 16, quoted in McAlister and Carr, 2014: 249).

In highlighting the complexities of young people's experiences of restorative justice or what might be seen as a conventionally punitive regime, McAlister and Carr draw attention to the difficulties of drawing straightforward conclusions about the treatment of young offenders and its relationship to policy demands or popular expectations. Apparent innovations such as restorative justice are, in fact, as encumbered with familiar demands and perceptions as forms of punishment which have been in place for very many years:

> Young people's accounts of their experiences of these two justice interventions – youth conferencing and custody – provide an illustration of the range of rationalities at play within the youth justice system. The mix of responsibilization, restoration, welfarism and punitiveness is evident. (McAlister and Carr, 2014: 251)

To provide further illustration of the variations in young people's perceptions, we can consider what happens at the far end of the scale, where young people are subjected to violence in custody, in the form of restraint by staff. For some, at least, this is a normal and even justifiable feature of the custodial regime: 'They [institutional staff] are trained to do it. At the end of the day they're just doing their job. Every time I've been restrained it's been my fault for fighting' (young person, quoted in Shenton and Smith, 2021: 168).

Clearly, for others, this is an unacceptable and harmful experience, associated in the past with the deaths of children in custody: 'One poor kid I saw him and he hadn't done a thing wrong. He got smacked onto the ground, had his glasses smashed .... You get restrained for anything inside, not sitting at the right seat at dinner, two screws get hold of you' (young person, quoted in Shenton and Smith, 2021: 168).

Conclusions: Making Sense of Patterns and Trends in Youth Justice

In this chapter, we have offered a relatively brief overview of the changing patterns of offending, interventions and outcomes in youth justice, concluding with some reflections on the experiences of young people themselves. We have been able to identify some common international trends, such as the widespread evidence of declining rates of offending amongst young people, both in terms of self-reported crimes and official records. (We discuss these trends further in Chapter 8.)

In parallel with declining crime rates, criminal justice interventions also appear to have changed in shape and intensity, moving towards a greater reliance on more informal, diversionary measures; and indeed, there has also been an increasing use of restorative models of practice. Nonetheless, use of custody remains the default position for the most serious or persistent offenders. Here, too, we see the sharpest evidence of the unequal and discriminatory treatment of young people from ethnic minorities. Young people's subjective accounts also offer us some insights, in the sense that the lived reality of the criminal justice process remains an essentially punitive and often discriminatory experience (Cox, 2013), with effects which are not only direct and material (loss of liberty, restricted movements), but also indirect and symbolic (feeling excluded, damaged sense of self). These complex and contradictory aspects of the experience are to be found at all points of the justice continuum, with significant implications for the ways in which we conceptualise youth justice and how we understand the deeper currents underlying apparently dramatic changes in patterns of offending and outcomes.

Further Reading

Bateman, T. (2020) *The State of Youth Justice 2020*. National Association for Youth Justice, https://thenayj.org.uk/cmsAdmin/uploads/state-of-youth-justice-2020-final-sept-(1).pdf

This is the most recent in a series of publications commissioned by the National Association for Youth Justice which provides a detailed and extensive overview of patterns and trends in youth justice, accompanied by an insightful in-depth commentary.

Hazel, N. (2008) *Cross-national Comparison of Youth Justice*. London: Youth Justice Board.

Although a little dated by now, this is one of very few attempts to provide detailed evidence of patterns and trends in youth justice internationally. It offers a useful template for similar work in future.

Youth Justice Board (2021) *Guide to Youth Justice Statistics*. Youth Justice Board, www.gov.uk/government/statistics/guide-to-youth-justice-statistics/guide-to-youth-justice-statistics

A helpful source to assist in navigating official publications on recorded trends in youth crime and sentencing.

8

Youth Justice Subjects

Objectives

- This chapter will consider the profile of young people who become the 'subjects' of youth justice systems.
- The chapter will discuss the evident decline in the numbers of young people being dealt with by youth justice systems across many countries.
- The reader will be introduced to some of the possible reasons for this decline as well as its effects.
- The reader will develop a critical understanding of some of the implications of 'concentration' effects in youth justice.

Introduction

This chapter discusses some recent patterns seen in youth justice systems in different countries. It highlights how in the context of overall declines in numbers we see some 'concentration effects', such as the over-representation of young people from racial and ethnic minorities in the youth justice system, as well as young people with cognitive and neuro-disabilities. Alongside the reduction in the numbers of young people in the youth justice system, there has also been an increased focus on the 'complexity' of the needs of young people. This has included attention towards experiences of adversity in childhood and developments in trauma-informed approaches.

A pattern of decline?

As outlined in Chapter 7, over recent years the numbers of young people coming into contact with the youth justice system has fallen markedly in many countries. For instance, in the United States official statistics show that the number of young people under the age of 18 being arrested has fallen to its lowest level in over four decades (Puzzanchera, 2021). Data produced by the Office of Juvenile Justice and Delinquency Prevention illustrates that in the United States the overall rates of juvenile arrests have declined since 1980, but that most of this decline has happened in the past ten years (between 2010 and 2019 the number of juvenile arrests fell by 58%). This pattern was seen across most offence categories, including violent crimes such as robbery and aggravated assault. There has been some fluctuation in juvenile arrests for murder over the past four years, but overall the numbers are significantly down since their highpoint in the mid-1990s (Puzzanchera, 2021). Similar trends are evident in Canada, where the population of young people in custodial facilities decreased by 73% between 1997 and 2015 (Webster et al., 2019).

These patterns are also seen across all of the jurisdictions of the United Kingdom (McAra, 2017a). In England and Wales the number of First Time Entrants (FTEs), meaning young people receiving their first reprimand, warning or conviction, has also declined. The most recent data published by the Youth Justice Board shows that the number of children arrested in England and Wales has fallen to its lowest level since the time series began, with 49,500 arrests of children (aged 10–17) for notifiable offences in 2020/21 (Youth Justice Board, 2022). With a 19% decrease in arrests compared to the previous year, this was the largest decrease in eight years; although some of the most recent decline can be partly attributed to the likely impacts of the COVID-19 pandemic on the youth justice system (Youth Justice Board, 2022).

In Scotland the numbers of offence referrals to the Children's Reporter (see Chapter 6 for an overview of the systems in place in the different UK jurisdictions), fell by 83% between 2005/06 and 2013/14. These reductions are also evident in the retraction of the numbers of young people in custody (McAra and McVie, 2019). In Northern Ireland the pattern is similar. The numbers of recorded offences committed by young people (aged 10–17) decreased by 23% between 2013–2014 and 2014–2015 (NIAO, 2017), and the numbers of young people at all stages of the system including the youth custodial population has declined markedly in recent years (Carr and McAlister, 2021). Similar trends regarding reduced numbers of young people in the justice system have been seen in European countries. In an overview of these patterns McAra and McVie (2019) report recorded reductions in Austria, Belgium, Denmark, Germany, Ireland, Poland, Slovenia, Spain, Sweden and Switzerland.

Explaining the fall in numbers

So what are the reasons for these declines in the numbers of young people coming into contact with the youth justice system across different countries? Broadly speaking, explanations can be divided into four categories. Firstly, there is some data to suggest that the decline in numbers of young people being processed through the youth justice system reflects the activity of the system. This explanation holds that potential changes in justice policies and practices, for example with regard to policing priorities, such as target arrest rates, impacts the numbers of young people being brought into the system. For example, Bateman (2012, 2014) describes the impact of the removal of 'Offences Brought to Justice' (OBTJ) targets for the police in England and Wales in 2008, which led to a reduction in young people being arrested and charged.

Offences Brought to Justice (OBTJ)

The OBTJ target was introduced in England and Wales in 2002 to close the 'justice' gap between the numbers of police-recorded crimes and the numbers of crimes for which there was a criminal justice outcome. The introduction of this police target resulted in a number of low-level offences (such as criminal damage) which are more commonly committed by young people being dealt with formally by the police. Some analysis suggests that young people were disproportionately affected by this target as they were easier to apprehend and prosecute (Bateman, 2015; Sutherland et al., 2017). The numbers of young people entering into the criminal justice system for the first time began to fall in 2007, and in 2008 the OBTJ target was revised to focus on more serious offences. One analysis of the relationship between the OBTJ target and the numbers of young people in the system found the following:

> The OBTJ target was revised shortly after the fall in FTEs was first observed during 2007, so it could not have directly caused the decrease. It is, however, possible that some police forces may have been aware of the forthcoming target revision and changed their practice in anticipation. Also, there is evidence to suggest that some practitioners felt the OBTJ target had resulted in too many people who had committed low-level crimes entering the youth justice system ... and it is possible that some police forces started to change their response to address this situation. (Sutherland et al., 2017: 11)

Secondly, some analysts have suggested that the decline can be explained by the efficacy of prevention and early intervention programmes as well as increased focus on diversion from the system. Research evidence from a wide range of studies in different contexts demonstrates that the further a child enters into the youth justice system the poorer their outcomes in terms of recidivism, educational attainment, and a wide range of other social measures (McAra and McVie, 2007; Motz et al., 2019). Examples of early intervention programmes include the Sure Start initiative, which was introduced across the United Kingdom in 1998 and which aimed to address intergenerational child poverty by the provision of supports for children aged under 4 years and their families in deprived areas (Glass, 1999). However, despite positive evaluations and evidence of benefits for children and families, funding for Sure Start provisions was eroded under the austerity measures introduced by the UK government in 2010, which led to an overall reduction in services and a diminution in positive impacts (Torjesen, 2016).

Diversionary approaches are those which aim to divert children from the criminal justice system and to minimise the negative impact of system contact. Part of the rationale for increased use of diversionary measures is a recognition of the fact that contact with the criminal justice system could itself be 'criminogenic' (i.e., it could be a contributory factor in further offending) and therefore it was more effective to divert children from the justice system when possible (McAra and McVie, 2019). The Whole System Approach (WSA) adopted in Scotland since 2011 (discussed in Chapter 6) is an example of diversionary approaches being adopted on a more systematic level.

Thirdly, some analyses point to the fact that the numbers of young people entering the youth justice system is a reflection of an actual decline in rates of offending. This has also been linked to changing behaviour patterns, such as reductions in drug and alcohol consumption among young people, as well as changes in how young people interact and socialise (Taylor, 2017). For example, there have been marked shifts in children and young people's use of leisure time, with more time spent online than in public spaces where they may previously have more readily come to police attention. This shift in patterns of behaviour does not necessarily mean that there has been a reduction in offending (although, as discussed in Chapter 7, the body of evidence such as crime survey data as well as data on recorded crimes indicate that this may be the case) but rather that the way in which young people offend has changed. In this vein, McAra and McVie (2019: 87) have suggested a 'potential displacement effect', pointing to the possibility that young people may have changed the locus of offending, moving from public spaces to online, which is less readily policed by authorities. They further observe:

> In sum, while there is still a lack of evidence about the changing profile of youth offending, we must allow for the strong possibility that the ease with which some forms of online crime can be carried out, and the lack of obvious surveillance or policing, opens up opportunities for those who have the propensity to engage in deviant acts to do so with minimal risk of sanction or exposure. (McAra and McVie, 2019: 89)

Fourth, and linked to some of these systemic changes, some commentary has suggested that this decline can at least in part be attributed to the 'de-politicisation' of youth crime. In other words, youth crime is not the hot political issue that it previously was, when commentators in some countries described a 'punitive turn' in relation to young people and offending (Muncie, 2008; Bateman, 2014).

However, there is no definitive explanation for the overall fall in young people coming into contact with the criminal justice system across different contexts (and indeed there may be differential explanations across time and places). However, in an analysis of these trends and drawing on data from education and health alongside findings from the *Edinburgh Study on Youth Transitions and Crime*, McAra and McVie (2019) observe what they describe as a 'cultural dissonance effect' and resultant 'concentration effect' within youth justice systems.

The Edinburgh Study of Youth Transitions and Crime

The *Edinburgh Study of Youth Transitions and Crime* is a longitudinal study that began in 1998 and which researched the pathways into and out of offending for a cohort of approximately 4,300 young people. The study has been conducted over a number of phases. The first six phases tracked the same group of young people who were aged between 12 and 17 years (i.e., they were eligible to attend secondary school), when the study first began. Two further phases of the study have involved updating criminal record information on the sample and further in-depth interviews with a sub-sample of the cohort when aged 23. An eighth phase has involved the further updating of criminal records and surveys and interviews with a sub-sample of the cohort (now aged 33).

The study involves multiple methods of data collection. The main method has involved self-completion of a questionnaire filled out by the same group of young people (the cohort) in the first six phases. Key themes covered in the questionnaire include self-reported offending; drug and alcohol use; experience of victimisation; friendship groups as well as friends' offending; leisure activities; family structure; neighbourhood dynamics; and contacts with police and youth justice agencies (McAra and McVie, 2007). As well as the self-completion questionnaires, information was sought regarding the cohort members from a variety of administrative records. This has included school records, social work records, police records, criminal records and Children's Hearing records (see Chapter 6 for information on the Children's Hearing System). This has enabled the study to explore the differences between young people's self-reports and information in official records. So for example, young people may report offending behaviour in the self-completion questionnaire, but never have come to the attention of authorities for this. This has enabled the researchers to explore differences between young people who have had contact with the criminal justice system and those who have not, as well as differences in young people's experiences of adversity and the impact of this on their lives to date.

This has led to a number of important findings. Firstly, that the early identification of children considered to be 'at-risk' is not a straightforward process and itself may be damaging. Many of the young people who reported involvement in serious and persistent offending in their self-report questionnaires at age 17 had been referred to services by age 15 (over two-thirds of young people), while most young people who were known to agencies had not come to the attention of social work services at an early age. Moreover, many young people who had had early system contact (i.e., those who had been in contact with services for behavioural problems by age 5), still had ongoing contact at age 13, and had further referrals at age 15. Significantly, almost half of the young people who had experienced very early system contact ended up with a criminal conviction by age 22 (McAra and McVie, 2013). McAra and McVie (2013: 5) summarise the significance of this findings:

> Taken together these findings highlight the difficulties faced by agencies in the early identification of at-risk children. Of those in our cohort who self-reported serious and persistent offending and who were known to agencies, most were first identified in the early teenage years. Importantly, this contact seems to have done little to stem involvement in offending. Moreover the poor criminal justice outcomes for those who were identified at a much earlier point (by age 5), are the first pointer to a labelling process which underpins agency decision-making, namely that these who are sucked into the juvenile justice system from an early age are not always the most serious and prolific offenders and, once in the system, this can result in repeated and amplified system contact.

The *Edinburgh Study* has also found that young people experience differential contact with police. With young males from deprived neighbourhoods and who had a free school meals entitlement (an indicator of disadvantage) more likely to be charged by the police than other young people in the cohort. The strongest predictor of being charged, however, was having been previously charged by the police, with the researchers finding that:

> Children who reported that they had been charged in previous years were *over seven times* more likely to be charged at age 15 than were children with no such history – a factor that is completely independent of their current involvement in serious offending and their more recent history of police adversarial contact. (McAra and McVie, 2007: 327)

Further analysis enabled by the longitudinal nature of the *Edinburgh Study* has also found that critical moments in the early teenage years are key to pathways out of offending. Comparisons of the different offending trajectories of young people shows in particular the importance of links between school exclusion and greater system contact (these themes are explored further in Chapter 9). Finally, and significantly, the findings of the study show that measures which divert young people from the criminal justice system are much more effective in facilitating desistance from offending.

Key findings from the *Edinburgh Youth Transitions Study*:

- Persistent serious offending is associated with victimisation and social adversity;
- Early identification of at-risk children can be problematic and lead to adverse effects;
- Critical moments in early teenage years are keys to pathways out of offending;
- Diversionary strategies which stop or reduce the impact of contact of children with the criminal justice system are most effective.

You can read more about the *Edinburgh Study* and explore some of the study's resources, including the questionnaires used for data collection with young people via this website: www.edinstudy.law.ed.ac.uk

Concentration effects

Despite more general trends regarding diversion and fewer young people coming into the system, McAra and McVie (2019) have identified that the 'usual suspects' continue to be drawn in. So, in the context of an overall decline in numbers, we still see disproportionate numbers of young people from lower income and deprived areas being stopped by the police (one of the gateways into the youth justice system). Analysis of Scottish police stop and search data shows for instance: 'that the rate of search increased according to level of area deprivation, with rates for 12–17 year olds in the 20% most deprived areas in Scotland being twice as high as for those in the least deprived quintile' (McAra and McVie, 2019: 90). Furthermore, data from the *Edinburgh Study* shows that when young people are brought into the system, they tend to be recycled through it. Meaning that earlier involvement with the criminal justice system predicts future decision-making by police and prosecutorial authorities.

Race and Ethnicty and Disproportionate Representation

While overall fewer young people are being drawn into the system, there is an over-representation of young people from racial and ethnic minorities in the youth justice system. These trends in relation to the disproportionate representation of young people from ethnic minorities are seen in youth (and adult) justice systems in many countries. In a comparative study between youth justice in England and Wales and four Australian states (see also Chapter 4 for a discussion), Goldson et al. (2021: 100) highlight the fact that Aboriginal and Torres Strait Islander children are over-represented in the Australian youth justice system, while similar patterns of 'criminalisation and racialisation' in relation to African-Caribbean children are evident in the English and Welsh systems. Goldson et al. (2021) also highlight the fact that young people from Muslim communities are also been increasingly drawn into the youth justice systems both in Australia and in England and Wales.

Drawing on the work of Phillips and Bowling (2017) and others, Goldson et al. (2021: 102) make the important point that the categories we use to describe and analyse difference in the criminal justice system 'rest upon both relative and arbitrary foundations' and risk essentialising race, as well as masking heterogeneity. They cite the example of the term BAME (Black Asian and Minority Ethnic), which has been used as an overarching category in criminal justice (and other) statistics in the United Kingdom and which has also been subject to criticism (Aspinall, 2020). While such shorthand categories can help identify patterns of disproportionality – for instance this term is used in an independent review into the treatment of, and outcomes for, Black, Asian and Minority Ethnic individuals in the criminal justice system in England and Wales (Lammy, 2017) – they also risk oversimplifying important differences in experiences.

The Lammy Review

The *Lammy Review* (2017) was an independent review into the treatment of, and outcomes for, Black, Asian and Minority Ethnic individuals in the criminal justice system in England and Wales. The Review was commissioned by the government and carried out by the Labour politician David Lammy. The Review explored all aspects of the criminal justice system (including the adult and youth systems). The report found evidence of disproportionality throughout the criminal justice system, but Lammy stated: 'My biggest concern is with the youth justice system' (2017: 3), the reason being that despite the overall decline in young people being processed in the youth justice system, the proportion of BAME young people as FTEs and reoffending had increased, as had the proportion of BAME young people in custody.

Moreover as Goldson et al. (2021: 103) argue:

> In obscuring complexity, broad categories and over-simplified fixed determinants serve only to attribute (implied if not explicitly stated) social meanings – connected to criminality – to diverse populations of children and young people whose only shared characteristic is not being white.

Similar issues regarding the over-representation of young people from minority ethnic groups, including migrants and gypsy and traveller populations, are seen in other youth justice systems in Europe, although, as Webster (2019) notes, this picture is somewhat partial because of the lack of systematic data. For instance, in some countries information on the race and ethnicity of young people in the justice system is not collected. Some recent studies, however, point to consistent patterns of over-representation. Petintseva's (2016, 2019) research on the processing of children from Roma Slovak and Czech backgrounds in the Belgian justice system shows how young people from these backgrounds are constructed in particular ways in the discourse of professionals. This includes patterns of 'responsibiliation' (i.e., treating young people and their families as rational actors making free choices) and pathologising accounts which characterise Roma youth 'as suspicious, untrustworthy and non-willing' (Petintseva, 2019: 18). Importantly, there was also evidence of what Petintseva (2019) describes as 'entextualisation', that is, a shared discourse in educational reports and youth justice reports which points to the inter-relationship between exclusionary patterns in the different institutions with which children and young people (and their families) come into contact. (This topic is discussed in further depth in Chapter 9.)

Terrio (2008) meanwhile has described the treatment of unaccompanied and undocumented minors in the Paris juvenile court who were prosecuted for non-violent offences in disproportionate numbers. Importantly, her work links the treatment of young people in the French juvenile justice system with widespread media coverage of the so-called 'urban menace created by the *petits Roumains*' (Terrio, 2008: 875). (*Petits Roumains* translates as 'small Roma'. However, Terrio (2008) makes the point that many of the children labelled as such were in fact from a diverse range of backgrounds, including Asian, South Asian, Chinese, North African and Eastern European migrants.) Such coverage points to the increased visibility of particular young people and which also has echoes with the manner in which the 'menace' of juvenile delinquency was characterised in the late 19th century. (This historical context is also discussed in Chapter 1.)

In the United States the term 'Disproportionate Minority Contact' (DMC) is used to refer to the over-representation of young people from ethnic minorities in the juvenile justice system (Kempf-Leonard, 2007). The US Department of Justice's Office of Juvenile Justice and Delinquency Prevention (OJJDP), collects and publishes data on DMC and there have been numerous national and state-led initiatives (including legislation requiring states to reduce minority over-representation) to address disproportionality in the juvenile justice system in the United States. (The OJJDP defines *minority* as youth who are American Indian and Alaska Native, Asian, Black or African American, Hispanic or Latino, or Native Hawaiian or other Pacific Islander.)

However, despite a policy focus and directed funding towards this issue, these efforts have been to limited and variable effect (Kempf-Leonard, 2007; Donnelly, 2015; Mallett, 2018).

In an historical overview of changes to the operation of the juvenile court in the United States, Feld (2017) notes the impact of the politicisation of crime and welfare policies from the 1980s onwards and its disproportionate impact on African Americans in particular. This is seen in the disproportionate numbers of African Americans imprisoned in the context of mass incarceration, as well as the wider effects on families and communities (Pettit and Western, 2004; Clear, 2009; Alexander, 2010). It is also evident in the impacts of so-called 'get tough' policies which exacerbated racial differences in the administration of juvenile justice (Feld, 2017). These have included legal reforms that have allowed for the transfer of young people into the adult criminal justice system, as well as the expansion of sentencing powers, including the controversial introduction of life sentences without the possibility of parole for young people in some states (Kokkalera and Singer, 2019).

In their comparative study, Goldson et al. (2021) identify some of the dynamics of criminalisation and racialisation in different youth justice systems. This includes the identification of particular social groups as threats or 'other', and subsequent dynamics that can occur at all points of the youth justice system. This includes racially targeted forms of policing, differential constructions of risk, less use of diversion for children from ethnic minorities and a disproportionate use of detention.

A broad range of research across time and place shows that the children and young people that are dealt with in youth justice systems tend to be overwhelmingly those who are poor and who have experienced a range of adversities in their lives. This is the case from the earliest days of youth justice system, with the emergence of juvenile courts (Platt, 2009), through to the present (Goldson et al., 2021). In many cases the adversities that children and young people experience are cumulative, meaning that if a child and their family are living in circumstances of poverty, they are more likely to experience additional strain in their families and less likely to be able to access good-quality schooling, and so on (Myers et al., 2021). Goldson (2006: 454) describes the intersecting challenges faced by young people in the youth justice system as follows:

> ... the fabric of life invariably stretches across: poverty; family discord; public care; drug and alcohol misuse; mental distress; ill-health; emotional, physical and sexual abuse; self-harm; homelessness; isolation; loneliness; circumscribed educational and employment opportunities and the most pressing sense of distress and alienation.

Mental Health, Disabilities and Neurodiversity

Recently attention has also focused on the over-representation of young people with mental health disorders and cognitive and neuro-disabilities in the criminal justice system.

Examples of mental health disorders include, but are not limited to, depression, anxiety and panic disorders, eating disorders, schizophrenia and trauma-related disorders such as PTSD. Cognitive disabilities include conditions such as attention deficit hyperactivity disorder (ADHD). Neuro-disability is an umbrella term and includes learning disabilities (mild to severe), foetal alcohol spectrum disorders (FASD) and autism spectrum disorders (ASDs). The term 'neurodiversity' is also increasingly used to refer to a range of these conditions (Kirby, 2021) (including: ADHD, autism spectrum disorders, dyspraxia, dyscalculia, dyslexia and developmental language disorders).

Research from different countries has shown that children with mental health disorders and cognitive and neuro-disabilities are over-represented in the youth justice system. For instance, a survey of the population in youth custody in New South Wales, Australia showed that 14% of young people had an intellectual disability, compared with approximately 4% of the general population (Indig et al., 2011). While data from the Republic of Ireland shows that over one-third of the population of children in detention have some form of learning disability (Oberstown Children's Detention Campus, 2017). Moreover, there is also evidence of co-morbidity, meaning that children who have neuro-disabilities may also have mental health disorders and/or other difficulties such as alcohol and substance misuse issues (Baldry et al., 2018; Kirby, 2021).

Baldry et al. (2018) use the term 'critical disability criminology' to move from 'individual constructions of impairment to the systemic disabling effects of youth justice and related institutional processes' (Goldson et al., 2021: 129). This approach places a focus on the interactions through which young people with mental health disorders and cognitive and neuro-disabilities and other complex and intersecting needs come to be over-represented in the youth justice system, and within adult criminal justice systems. As Goldson et al. (2021: 137) point out, young people with mental health disorders and cognitive and neuro-disabilities 'are both *inherently* and *systematically* more likely to be criminalized that other children and young people'. This may be a result of factors such as young people's difficulties with impulse control or managing frustration and problems with memory and recall. In some circumstances when young people are involved in offending in a group, the young person with mental health disorders and/or disabilities may be the one who is most likely to be apprehended or blamed. Young people with mental health disorders and cognitive and neuro-disabilities may be more likely to come to the attention of the police because of their behavioural characteristics, and they may struggle with understanding the context of interactions with the criminal justice system (Ellem and Richards, 2018).

In research conducted in Queensland, Australia with young people who had cognitive disabilities and with the staff working with these young people, Ellem and Richards (2018: 237) include the following quote from a youth lawyer which illustrates how the interaction between the police and a young person with cognitive disabilities quickly escalated:

> When he first saw the police he instinctively gets on the fence to leave ... the police pull him down ... the way he responds to the police, [was] probably inappropriate ... and he kept saying 'all I want to do is get up and play my basketball', because that's his coping mechanism ... and they wouldn't let him up. They push him harder down and he just responds accordingly and the whole thing escalates.

A further compounding issue is that a young person's disability and/or impairment may not be immediately evident and the young person themselves may be unable or reluctant to disclose their disability (Scior et al., 2013). Moreover, practitioners working in the youth justice system, ranging from police to people working with young people in the community, through to custodial settings, may have limited understanding of mental health disorders and cognitive and neuro-disabilities, and how best to communicate with young people (Kirby, 2021). This quote from a manager in a Youth Offending Team in England and Wales, who was a research participant in Baldry et al.'s (2018: 642) research, is illustrative:

> We did a bit of work with a couple of officers on the beat about a young man with autism. He was constantly being arrested ... so we organised a meeting, we got a psychiatrist who dealt with autism in and he talked about why he reacts the way he does ... We spent quite a long time with them explaining it ...things did improve after that. They were more tolerant and careful about how they dealt with him.

As Goldson et al. (2021) note in their comparative study of youth justice in England and Wales and Australia, the over-representation of young people with mental health disorders and cognitive and neuro-disabilities in the youth justice system, also intersects with their treatment in other systems, including the education and care systems (a topic discussed in detail in Chapter 9). This is in part due to a lack of early and adequate supports for children and young people and their families, and the poor provision of appropriate community-based services.

Girls and Young Women

There is a long tradition of research which has explored the differential experiences of women and girls in the criminal justice system. One of the key observations of research in this field is that because men and boys constitute the majority of the population in the criminal justice system and the youth justice system, the different experiences and needs of girls are often overlooked (Gelsthorpe and Worrall, 2009). Paradoxically, however, girls who have contact with the criminal justice system tend to be *hypervisible* (Sharpe, 2009). This is evident in some of the occasional moral panics about the extent of young women's offending and whether it is proliferating (Burman and Batchelor, 2009). Writing in the context of England and Wales in the late 2000s, Sharpe (2009: 254) noted:

> A profusion of media interest in young women's violence has contributed to, if not created perceptions that today's young women are increasingly appropriating (supposedly) traditional 'masculine' behaviours and turning into 'ladettes' in growing numbers ...

The above quote reveals the extent to which concerns regarding offending by girls is also often bound up with notions about gender. This echoes some of the earliest work within feminist criminology, which observed that women and girls who offend were often perceived as being 'doubly deviant', i.e., that their offending was seen to be a transgression of *both* legal and gender norms (Carlen, 1988; Gelsthorpe and Worrall, 2009).

The *Edinburgh Study* also reported gender differences in involvement in violence in the teenage years, with boys being significantly more likely to report involvement in violence in all stages of the study (McAra and McVie, 2016). This analysis highlights the extent to which girls' behaviour may be subject to different forms of social controls, including norms and expectations about the ways in which such girls should behave.

Some research has explored the different 'pathways' into offending for girls and women, and notes that girls' pathways into offending are often different from boys'. Research across a range of contexts shows that young women's experiences of victimisation and offending are often interlinked (Chesney-Lind and Irwin, 2008), and that girls and young women in the justice system will have experienced '**polyvictimisation**' (i.e., multiple forms of victimisation) (Kerig, 2018). Girls and young women involved in the justice system tend to report higher rates of interpersonal victimisation including sexual abuse and assault (Dierkhising et al., 2013). Vaswani's (2018) research exploring the extent of **Adverse Childhood Experiences** (ACEs) (see the section below for a discussion) amongst young people involved in serious offending in Scotland showed a higher prevalence of exposure to a multiple range of adversities for young women in the sample. This included experiences of all forms of abuse (sexual, physical, emotional) and neglect as well as exposure to domestic violence.

In the United States, where the overall number of juvenile arrests fell, the relative declines were greater for males than females, with females accounting for three of every ten juvenile arrests in 2019 (Puzzanchera, 2021). This means that the female share of juvenile arrests has grown (from 18% of all juvenile arrests in 1980, to 31% in 2019) (Puzzanchera, 2021).

In response to the greater proportion of girls and women in the criminal justice system, attention has been directed towards 'gender-specific programming' (GSP). This is particularly the case in the juvenile justice system in the United States, where, as Sharpe (2016: 4) notes:

> Although less well established elsewhere, GSP is now the dominant paradigm for juvenile justice intervention with girls in the United States, following an increase in federal funds dedicated to the identification of gender-specific risk factors for delinquency and offending and to the development of gender-specific juvenile justice services for girls.

Sharpe (2016: 4), however, is critical of the limitations of some of such 'gender-specific' approaches, arguing that they are based on a narrow and individualistic conceptualisation of risk that places both the problem and locus of intervention at the level of the individual and therefore fails to adequately account for structural issues, including 'the actions and omissions of state welfare and education agencies that over-determine young women's routes into crime and into the justice system'.

Concentration Effect and Complexity

As McAra and McVie (2019) observe, the overall decline in numbers of young people in the youth justice system across many countries has led to a 'concentration effect', whereby the young people in the system are often those with the most 'complex needs'. Or as Goldson et al. (2021: 130) put it:

> ... at times of relative penal parsimony there is mounting evidence that youth justice and penality is increasingly reserved for managing, regulating, controlling and ultimately punishing the very children and young people who are in greatest need.

There has been a growing recognition that many young people, especially those involved in serious offending, have often lived lives which have been affected by trauma, including abuse and neglect and disrupted attachments (McAra and McVie, 2010a; Myers et al., 2021). Findings from the *Edinburgh Study on Youth Transitions and Crime* has shown that violent behaviour is more prevalent amongst young people who experience the greatest level of adversities, including victimisation and abuse (McAra and McVie, 2010a); while research conducted in the United States has shown that a high proportion (90%) of 'justice-involved' young people reported exposure to some type of traumatic event and that many met the criteria of a mental health disorder or Post-traumatic Stress Disorder (PTSD) as a result (Dierkhising et al., 2013). As the authors of this research state:

> ... more severe forms of maltreatment (i.e., chronic or frequent maltreatment) have been found to be associated with more severe and chronic delinquent behavior and the relation between child maltreatment and justice involvement holds across gender and ethnicity. (Dierkhising et al., 2013: 2)

Relatedly, in many countries we see an over-representation of children who are in care and/or the recipients of child protection and welfare in youth justice systems. This is often because of complex inter-related factors (an issue discussed more fully in Chapter 9), but one of the identified reasons is because children in the care and child protection and welfare system will have, by definition, experienced a range of adversity (including maltreatment and abuse) which necessitated their involvement with these services in the first instance (Carr and McAlister, 2016).

An increased focus on the 'complexity' of the smaller number of young people in the youth justice system has also coincided with attention on many of these young people's experiences of trauma and adverse life events. A body of research focusing on adverse childhood experiences (ACEs) has linked such experiences in childhood with poorer outcomes in later life, in health and social domains (Felitti et al., 1998; Spratt, 2012). Research on the impact of ACEs derives from an original study conducted in the United States by Felitti and colleagues (1998). The original study involved a postal questionnaire administered to over 13,000 adults, who were asked questions about seven categories of adverse childhood experiences:

1. Psychological abuse;
2. Physical abuse;
3. Sexual abuse;
4. Substance misuse in the household;
5. Mental illness in the household;
6. Mother treated violently;
7. Criminal behaviour in the household.

ACE Questionnaire

In each of the ACE categories a few sub-questions were posed. So, for instance in the fields exploring childhood experiences of psychological abuse, or criminal behaviour in the household the following questions were asked:

Psychological

Did a parent or other adult in the household ....
Often or very often swear at, insult, or put you down?
Often or very often act in a way that made you afraid that you would be physically hurt?

Criminal behaviour in the household

Did a household member go to prison?

You can read more about ACE Scores and access the questionnaire via this link: https://developingchild.harvard.edu/media-coverage/take-the-ace-quiz-and-learn-what-it-does-and-doesnt-mean/

Using logistic regression analysis, this research found a relationship between the number of categories of exposure to ACEs and their cumulative effects on adult risk behaviours and diseases (which were the specific focus of this study) (Felitti et al., 1998). The authors concluded:

> We found a strong graded relationship between the breadth of exposure to abuse or household dysfunction during childhood and multiple risk factors for several of the leading causes of death in adults. (Felitti et al., 1998: 245)

Research on ACEs has been taken up in lots of fields internationally, including in public health programmes (Bellis et al., 2014) and in child protection and welfare services (Spratt et al., 2022). There have been multiple studies exploring the extent to which the preventing or ameliorating adverse childhood experiences would potentially lead to better outcomes in a range of areas (e.g., in relation to physical and mental health, substance misuse, criminal justice involvement, etc.).

Some studies have explored the prevalence of ACEs amongst young people in the justice system and have found a high prevalence of adverse childhood experiences amongst this population (Baglivio et al., 2014, 2015). For example, Baglivio et al.'s (2015) research explored the characteristics of 64,000 adjudicated juvenile offenders in the State of Florida and found that a higher number of ACEs influenced official offending trajectories. In this study a higher number of ACEs was associated with an earlier age at first arrest and was also associated with a greater likelihood of arrest from childhood through to late adolescence. This research also found that a higher number of ACEs was a significant predictor of more chronic offending (Baglivio et al., 2015).

However, there have been some substantial critiques of policy and service attention to ACEs. Some have argued that the focus on ACEs is overly determinative and potentially stigmatising (Lacey and Minnis, 2019), while others have critiqued the lack of focus on structural disadvantage. Many of the areas categorised as ACEs are strongly correlated with poverty (Wastell and White, 2017; White et al., 2019), yet interventions aimed at addressing ACEs are often silent on these broader structural issues (Spratt et al., 2022). There have also been criticisms of the overly simplistic and crude measurements of ACE scores as well as the methodologies adopted in different studies (Kelly-Irving and Delpierre, 2019; Devaney et al., 2021). For example, some studies are retrospective (based on people's recollections of their childhood experiences), with the attendant methodological difficulty of accurate recall, while other studies adopt a prospective longitudinal design (i.e., aiming to establish whether current ACEs will continue to have an impact in the future). White et al. (2019: 458) are therefore critical of what they characterise as a 'chaotic concept': 'an abstraction that both conflates issues and divides indivisible process with the consequence of hiding or ignoring the essential features shaping an outcome'.

These concerns find echoes in some of the earlier critiques of the 'Risk Factor Prevention Paradigm' (RFPP) in youth justice (O'Mahony, 2009; Haines and Case, 2015; Goddard and Myers, 2017), whereby assessment tools (such as the Asset tool developed by the Youth Justice Board in England and Wales), aimed to identify a range of risk factors for individual children to target interventions in these areas. One of the critiques of this approach was that the range of risk factors measured (which were drawn from work such as the Cambridge Delinquency Study) were too narrowly focused on the level of the individual child and failed to adequately account for wider structural factors such as poverty (O'Mahony, 2009).

Some have argued, however, that because it is a relatively easy to understand concept, ACEs have utility 'in bridging scientific and lay communities' (Devaney et al., 2021: 2247).

One counterpoint to the focus on ACEs is a recognition of the need to account more for the ameliorating effects of positive childhood experiences (PCEs), in recognition of the fact that many people who experience adverse experiences in childhood do not later experience negative life outcomes (Narayan et al., 2018). Moreover, not all children's experiences are uniform. Again, this focus finds echoes with attention to factors that promote resilience as a corrective to risk-focused approaches (Rutter, 2000; Boeck and Fleming, 2011). (In fact, the critique that the Asset assessment tool did not adequately account for strengths and resilience factors led to an update of this tool by the Youth Justice Board, when the Asset Plus Tool was introduced in 2014.)

Trauma-Informed Practice

Alongside an increased focus on adverse childhood experiences, the terms 'trauma-informed care' or 'trauma-informed practice' have gained greater currency within youth justice systems. Trauma-informed approaches are responses which aim to foster a sense of safety among users with histories of trauma exposure (Harris and Fallott, 2001). Young people can respond to trauma in many ways. Some common responses include hypervigilance (this means operating in an elevated state of constantly assessing potential threats); attachment difficulties, depression and anxiety; impulsivity and aggression; and problems with concentration and information-processing (Silvester, 2021). Moreover, involvement in the youth justice system itself may be a 'trigger' for further psychological distress. Practices such as police use of 'stop and search', which in some instances may involve body searches, or the use of restraint in a custodial environment, can trigger memories of prior experiences of trauma (Branson et al., 2017).

Trauma-informed approaches involve a recognition that children and young people's behaviours, such as withdrawal or engagement in risk activities, may in themselves be responses to trauma (Silvester, 2021). Such types of behaviour can be broadly classified as 'internalising' or 'externalising' (with withdrawal being an example of the former and engagement in risky activities being an example of the latter). Trauma-informed responses mean that practitioners should focus on underlying needs behind the behaviour, rather than merely reacting to the behaviours themselves. Silvester (2021: 342) explains this as follows:

> Trauma-informed interventions are often based on the principle that the concerning presentation is just a manifestation of hidden unmet needs and thus a symptom of the problem, rather than the target of the solution.

This also means that practitioners working in the youth justice system require training to recognise children's needs and respond effectively. While practitioners might find an intuitive appeal in working in ways which recognise children's past experiences and are responsive to their needs, they are also working in broader systems and contexts which often still place an emphasis on risk assessment and risk management. In recent research conducted with practitioners working in England and Wales, Day (2022) describes some of the challenges that staff experienced in working with and integrating various models of practice. These included approaches focused on risk, desistance from offending, 'Child First' and 'Trauma-Informed' practice. In this research Day (2022) reports that practitioners found some of these competing priorities to be confusing.

The *Youth Justice Blueprint for Wales (2019)* has committed to embedding trauma-informed approaches into community and custodial settings, which align with its 'Children First' approach (Evans et al., 2020) (see Chapter 6 for a fuller discussion of youth justice in Wales). This has included the development of an Enhanced Case Management (ECM) approach, which involves a multi-agency comprehensive assessment of the child's needs as well as specific training for Youth Offending Team (YOT) practitioners in ACE and trauma-informed approaches (Evans et al., 2020; Glendinning et al., 2021). As the authors of an evaluation of the ECM approach explain:

> In brief, ECM utilises psychology to understand what has happened to a child combined with their developmental needs, personal strengths and protective factors. ECM takes a trauma-informed perspective to help professionals identify where trauma may have shaped a child's development and to respond in a compassionate and empathic way. (Glendinning et al., 2021: 15)

The ECM is also informed by a Trauma Recovery Model (TRM), drawing on Maslow's Hierarchy of Needs (1943, 1954), which depicts human need on a hierarchical level. Its central principle is that a person's basic needs (such as physiological needs for food, shelter, clothing, etc.) must be met before other needs can be attended to. In Maslow's original conceptualisation 'self-actualisation' (i.e., a person's desires to become what they want to be) is at the top of this pyramid, and by implication cannot be achieved unless other needs below this level (physiological, safety, love and belonging, and esteem) are met (Maslow, 1954). In the TRM this framework is applied to understand how children who offend might respond best to interventions. At its simplest then if children's basic needs are not met, such as having adequate food and structure, or an adult whom they can trust to recognise and respond to their needs, then they cannot engage in cognitive work related to their offending (e.g., development of insights into the impact their offending may have had on victims).

Trauma-informed approaches have also been adopted in other contexts, including in Canada (Oudshoorn, 2015) and in the United States. A systematic review of the trauma-informed interventions for young people considered to be 'at risk' or involved with the justice system, found that that evidence regarding the effectiveness of such approaches (with effectiveness conceptualised both in terms of benefits to the young people themselves, and in relation to other desired outcomes, such as a reduction in reoffending), was modest and inconclusive, but nonetheless promising (Olaghere et al., 2021). Meanwhile an evaluation in Wales found that the adoption of a trauma-informed approach led to an increased recognition of the needs of children, more responsive engagement and better experiences for some young people (Glendinning et al., 2021).

Conclusion

This chapter has explored some of the patterns of the reduction in numbers of young people entering into the youth justice system in different countries in recent years. It has highlighted, however, that in the context of these declines, issues regarding the disproportionate numbers of young people from racial and ethnic minorities in the youth justice system are brought more sharply to the fore. Alongside the reduction in the numbers of young people and 'concentration effects' in the youth justice system, there has also been an increased focus on the 'complexity' of the needs of young people. This has included a focus on experiences of adversity in childhood and developments in trauma-informed approaches.

Further Reading

Sharpe, G. (2013) *Offending Girls: Young Women and Youth Justice.* London: Routledge.

This book draws on original research with young women involved in the youth justice system to explore the dynamics of their lives and how they experience contact with the justice system.

Myers, R. and Goddard, T. (2019) 'Editors' Introduction to the Special Issue: "Neoliberal Youth Carceralism and Alternative Visions of Justice".' *Critical Criminology*, 27: 521–525.

The editors' introduction to this special issue of *Critical Criminology* and the issue itself present a critical analysis of the manner in which youth justice systems in different countries, while ostensibly less punitive, continue to act as a significant mechanism of social control.

9

Youth Justice and Intersecting Systems

Objectives

- This chapter will explore the intersections between youth justice, education and the child protection and welfare systems.
- It will outline research which has documented the links between school disciplinary processes, including exclusions, and criminal justice system contact.
- Drawing on research, it will explore the reasons for the over-representation of children in care in the criminal justice system.
- The chapter will highlight the interconnectedness of children's lives and the cumulative impacts of disadvantage.

Introduction

> It's the usual stuff isn't it? Exclusion from school, early contact with children's social care, lots of welfare issues that have been unmet over a period of time. Difficulties at school, behavioural problems ... we are one of the poorest boroughs in England (E&W, Community Supervision Manager). (Baldry et al., 2018: 640)

The quote above from a manager working in a Youth Offending Team in England and Wales, taken from a study exploring youth justice and penality in comparative context (Baldry et al. 2018), provides a very good illustration of the way in which youth justice systems do not operate in isolation. It also underscores the fact that many of the young people involved in the youth justice system will have had experiences of other systems and services throughout their lives. All children and young people will have contact with the education system. However, in the case of children and young people in the youth justice system, there is lots of evidence that poor school experiences, and school exclusion, can lead to young people becoming further involved in offending and entrenched in the criminal justice system.

Many of the young people involved in the justice system will also have contact with other services such as the child protection and welfare system. However, there is evidence from a range of different countries that children who have interactions with the child protection and welfare system and/or who are placed in the care of the state are over-represented in the youth justice system. Furthermore, a range of research which has explored the demographics of people involved in the criminal justice system as adults has shown that many have had prior experiences of the care system as children and young people. This chapter therefore explores some of the intersections between young people in the justice system and other systems of state and welfare interventions. The chapter focuses on two specific intersections – education and youth justice, and the care system and youth justice. Of course, other services, such as health provision, are also important; however, we have chosen to focus on these particular intersections here because of the range of research evidence available on these topics, and in order to illustrate the interconnectedness of children's lives. The chapter presents research evidence from a range of different countries exploring some of the dynamics of children's involvement (and indeed exclusion) from these systems and their involvement with the youth justice system.

Schools and Youth Justice

Concerns regarding the links between school experiences and subsequent criminal justice involvement have been voiced in recent years across a range of contexts. The *Taylor Review of the Youth Justice System in England and Wales* (2016) placed a particular emphasis on the backgrounds of young people in the youth justice system and the failures of other systems, including education, health and social care, prior to young people's contact with the criminal justice system. The report author, Charlie Taylor (who has since become the Chair of the Youth Justice Board in England and Wales), stated the following:

> Many of the children in the system come from some of the most dysfunctional and chaotic families where drug and alcohol misuse, physical and emotional abuse and offending is common. Often they are victims of crime themselves. Though children's backgrounds should not be used as an excuse for their behaviour, it is clear that the failure of education, health, social care and other agencies to tackle these problems have contributed to their presence in the system. (Taylor, 2016: 2)

The *Taylor Review* (2016) commented specifically on the inter-relationship between school truancy, poor educational outcomes and school exclusions, and involvement in the youth justice system:

> Many of the children in the youth justice system have had little or no engagement in education. It is common for children in trouble with the law to have had poor school attendance from an early age, and to have begun to play truant as they got older. Many have learning difficulties and lack the basic skills in literacy and numeracy to succeed at school, while many have been permanently or temporarily excluded. I have often heard about children who are sent to low-quality alternative provision or placed (illegally) on a reduced timetable for extended periods of time. There are also a number of children whose parents have been persuaded to take their child off the school roll and, nominally, educate them at home. (Taylor, 2016: 10)

The links between school exclusions and involvement in the youth justice system have been further documented in a range of research. In the United States, the relationship between responses to students' behaviour in schools and subsequent involvement in the criminal justice system have led to the descriptor 'the **school-to-prison pipeline**'. These authors elaborate further:

> In what has come to be known as the 'school-to-prison pipeline', scholars have suggested that changes in school and justice policy have created a funnel structure in which negative school outcomes are linked to involvement in the criminal justice system. (Rocque and Snellings, 2018: 3)

Moreover, experiences of school exclusion can also impact on involvement in the criminal justice system later in life. Research conducted in New Zealand drawing on longitudinal data (a study of youth transitions to adulthood), showed a significant relationship between school exclusion, increased delinquency and later contact with the criminal justice system (Sanders et al., 2020). Interestingly, this research also found that girls who were excluded from school faced particularly poor outcomes.

However, as Arnez and Condry (2021: 87) note in an overview of the research literature on this topic – 'Despite a correlation between school exclusion and crime, the relationship is complex, and the different factors involved require unpacking'. One of the obvious areas of overlap between school exclusions and criminal justice involvement is that the behaviours that lead to school exclusion may also bring children to the attention of police in the first instance (e.g., possession of drugs, involvement in violence) (Berridge et al., 2001). The most common reason for school exclusions reported in data from England is 'persistent disruptive behaviour' and the second most common reason is physical assault against an adult or a pupil (DfE, 2012). Research has also observed that some children's involvement in offending occurs prior to their experiences of school disciplinary measures, including exclusions (Hodgson and Webb, 2005). While there is clearly some debate regarding causality or correlation, Arnez and Condry (2021) explore a range of criminological theories that may provide some explanations for the relationship between school exclusions and offending. These are summarised in the Box below.

Criminological Theories That May Explain the Relationship Between School Exclusions and Youth Offending

General theory of crime (Gottfredson and Hirschi, 1990)

This theory places a strong emphasis on self-control, with the proponents arguing that individuals with lower capacities for self-control are more likely to be impulsive, risk-taking and engage in criminal and 'analogous' behaviours (meaning those behaviours that may be associated with crime, such as substance misuse). They argue that the cause of poor self-control can be found in parenting. But also that other systems, such as schooling, play an important role in promoting self-control and conformity.

Age-graded theory of informal social control (Sampson and Laub, 1993)

This theory was developed from a longitudinal study exploring differential patterns of offending across the life-course amongst a sample of men in Boston, Massachusetts. The original data on 1,000 boys was collected as part of a study conducted by Eleanor and Sheldon Glueck and published in their book *Unravelling Juvenile Delinquency* (Glueck and Glueck, 1950). Subsequent follow-ups with this sample in adulthood conducted by Robert Sampson and John Laub sought to explore the different paths these men's lives took. Sampson and Laub were particularly interested in the processes of desistance (i.e. how and why people stopped offending). Their findings regarding the different pathways of these men led them to develop their age-graded theory of informal social control, a central tenet of which is that different social institutions (and people's attachments to these institutions) can have an impact on the propensity to offend. The age-graded element of the theory refers to the fact that different institutions are likely to be more relevant at different ages and stages of people's lives. Hence the role of the school as an institution of social control is particularly important for children and young people.

Routine activities theory (Cohen and Felson, 1979)

This theory draws on 'rational choice theories' (i.e., offending is based on the rational choice of an offender) and is premised on an understanding that there are three elements necessary for an offence to occur:

A potential offender;

A suitable target;

An absence of a capable guardian.

Children's exclusion from school may mean that they do not have the oversight of a capable guardian, and, moreover, depending on where they spend their time outside of school, there may be more 'suitable targets' for offending (e.g., opportunities for shoplifting).

Labelling and social reaction theories (Lemert, 1967; Becker, 1963; Cohen, 1955)

These theories place a strong emphasis on the way in which social reactions to offending and labelling can lead to people identifying with these labels and therefore increase their likelihood of further offending. Edwin Lemert (1967) distinguished between 'primary' and 'secondary' deviance. Whereby the primary deviance was a transgressive act, and the secondary deviance was where the person involved in the transgression (and labelled as such) took on this master identity. Becker's (1963) work on the social responses to labelling and their effects also offers important insights. Meanwhile Albert Cohen's (1955) work explored the manner in which young people may experience 'status frustration', whereby they are unable to meet the demands of parental or societal standards, and respond to this through 'reaction formation' (i.e., rebelling against these norms). These theories may explain why young people who are perceived to be 'failing' in school react against the system, and also how being labelled a 'troublemaker' in school may impact on children's sense of self and how young people may respond to this identity through offending.

A further important dimension of labelling theories is that systems and professionals can also respond to such 'labels' by targeting the 'usual suspects', thereby creating a circular effect (McAra and McVie, 2013). Findings from the *Edinburgh Study on Youth Transitions and Crime* provides some evidence of these interactive effects:

> The same children are continuously labelled 'troublemakers' by teachers and often find it impossible to shrug off these labels, even in cases of subsequent appropriate and conforming behaviour or high academic performance.

Also, these labelling processes seem to be based on the reputation and socioeconomic status of certain families, rather than on the gravity of the pupil's challenging behaviour, and often result in school exclusion (McAra and McVie, 2012: 356–357) (cited in Arnez and Condry, 2021: 90)

Further reading

Arnez, J. and Condry, R. (2021) 'Criminological Perspectives on School Exclusion and Youth Offending.' *Emotional and Behavioural Difficulties*, 26, 1: 87–100.

The relationship between labelling in the context of the education system and the way in which these labels can become 'sticky' in other settings has been explored in some research. In a study conducted in Belgium, Petintseva (2019) has documented the inter-relationship between school-based assessments of Roma young people and subsequent assessments in the criminal justice system. This research explored the case files of Slovak and Czech Roma young people who had been referred to the youth courts in Belgium, and it also involved interviews with practitioners. It found that some of the characterisations of the perceived attitudes towards education of the Roma community found in the school case files (e.g., that education was not valued, or that young people from these backgrounds were more likely to truant), subsequently shaped judicial assessments and impacted on how young people were then treated within the criminal justice system:

> ... school discourses (i.e. input from schools and other accounts of the educational situation) had a key role to play in shaping judicial decision-making. Indeed such discourses were not only informative but also performative, affecting the ways in which young people were positioned in this institutional context. (Petintseva, 2019: 4)

Petintseva (2019) also notes that in the context of reports provided to the court, school-based assessments are considered 'authoritative'. This can contrast for example with the views of parents. This research therefore illustrates how labels in one setting (the school) can be transmitted into another setting (the youth court). This research also highlights the intersection of racialised discourses and attitudes and prejudices about particular groups with assessments regarding behaviour and proposals on what should be done to address 'deviant' behaviour.

Data on school exclusions shows that young people from certain racial and ethnic minorities, young men, those with Special Educational Needs (SEN), children in local authority care, and those from lower socio-economic backgrounds are all more likely to be excluded from school (Timpson, 2019). This points to intersections with discrimination and other aspects of structural disadvantage (as also discussed in the previous chapter, Chapter 8). These patterns are evident in different countries. Research from the United States repeatedly demonstrates that young people from racial and ethnic minorities are more likely to experience school exclusions (Skiba et al., 2006; Welch and Payne, 2012). In Australia Torres Strait Islander and Aboriginal children experience higher school exclusion rates (Goldson et al., 2021). While in England young people from Black Caribbean backgrounds are disproportionately excluded from school. Recent data from England and Wales shows that Black Caribbean young people were nearly four times more likely to receive a permanent exclusion than the rest of the school population, and were more than twice as likely to receive a fixed term exclusion (Demie, 2021). The only ethnic group with a higher exclusion rate were Gypsy/Roma young people.

Research on the reasons for the over-representations of Black Caribbean youth amongst students excluded from schools in England identifies a number of interrelated causal factors for these trends, including teachers' low expectations and institutional racism, as well as the labelling of young people, insufficient training for teachers and other educational staff and an overall lack of diversity in the school workforce (Demie, 2021). The quote below is from a parent interviewed as part of Demie's (2021) research which explored Black Caribbean pupils' experience of school exclusion in England:

> When we talk about behaviour issues, there are a lot of youngsters Black and White who misbehave. Because of stereotyping and the media, as far as teachers are concerned, we are talking about a system that has taught them that the Black male has a problem, or is difficult, so as soon as a young Black boy picks up something and throws it, he is regarded as being a difficult child. If a White boy does it, they say he is having a bad day. It's the branding. (Parent cited in Demie, 2021: 59)

More recently the term '**adultification**' has been used to describe the differential treatment of Black girls in schools and in other settings (Epstein et al., 2017). As Drew et al. (2022: 244) explain:

> Adultification means that adults regard Black girls as older than they are and therefore as less innocent and as needing less nurturing, protecting and comforting. This increases their likelihood or being disciplined as early as age five.

This means that for Black girls their behaviour may be more likely to be judged according to a differential standard, that their behaviour is less likely to be considered as 'childlike', and therefore they are seen as being more culpable. This issue of 'adultification' has been brought sharply to the fore in a recent case regarding a Black girl who was subject to a strip search by the police in her school in London.

Child Q: Police Strip Search in School

In June 2022, the media reported that four Metropolitan police officers were facing an investigation for gross misconduct following the strip search of a 15-year-old Black girl, referred to as 'Child Q' in reports, in her school. The girl was strip searched by police officers, while she was on her period, after she was wrongly suspected of carrying cannabis at her London school. The search of Child Q took place without another adult present. In media reports of the incident, which came to light in 2022, Child Q, who is taking legal action against the Metropolitan Police, is reported as saying:

> 'Someone walked into the school, where I was supposed to feel safe, took me away from the people who were supposed to protect me and stripped me naked, while on my period.'

Revelations about this incident prompted a public outcry and an investigation by the Local Authority, the Independent Police Complaints Commission, and the Children's Commissioner in England. The racial dimensions of the case, including the 'adultification' of Child Q by the police, have been highlighted. Following this case, the Children's Commissioner in England carried out a review of the police practice of strip searching children, and reported the following:

> I am deeply concerned by the information that I have received. I am not reassured that what happened to Child Q was an isolated issue, though it was certainly rare and the context unique. Instead, I believe it indicates more systemic problems around child protection. I remain unconvinced that the Metropolitan Police is consistently considering children's welfare and wellbeing. (Dame Rachel de Souza, Children's Commissioner for England: Children's Commissioner, 2022: 3).

This review by the Children's Commissioner found that a significant number of children are subjected to the intrusive and traumatising practice of strip searching. In London between 2018 and 2020, 650 children were strip searched, 25% of whom were between 10 and 15 years old. Despite guidance that an **Appropriate Adult** (AA) should be present when a child is strip searched, an AA was not present on almost a quarter (23%) of all occasions when the Metropolitan Police strip searched children. Furthermore, there was significant evidence of over-representation of Black youth in the strip searches carried out by the Metropolitan Police – 58% of all boys searched were Black. The Children's Commissioner has identified this as an area requiring immediate scrutiny and is now looking into the practices across all police forces in England.

You can read more about the media reporting of the case of Child Q and the practice of police strip searches here:

Guardian: 'Child Q: Four Met Police Officers Facing Investigation Over Strip Search': www.theguardian.com/uk-news/2022/jun/15/child-q-four-met-police-officers-facing-investigation-over-strip-search

Washington Post: 'London Police's Strip-search of Hundreds of Children Sparks National Probe': www.washingtonpost.com/world/2022/08/09/london-met-police-children-strip-searches/

The 'fortification' of schools (e.g., using CCTV and metal detectors) and the involvement of the criminal justice system (e.g., calling the police to deal with disciplinary issues) have also been identified as reasons for the interrelationship between poor school outcomes and the criminal justice system. This has also included the criminalisation of student behaviour and schools adopting zero tolerance approaches to school discipline (Kupchik et al., 2015). Some researchers have observed the links between risk management approaches and 'new penology' in the criminal justice system (Rocque and Snellings, 2018). 'New penology' was a thesis put forward by Malcolm Feeley and Jonathan Simon (1992) to describe a shift from a focus on rehabilitating the individual, towards a focus on the assessment and management of risk. Writing in the context of the United States, Rocque and Snellings (2018: 6) have coined the phrase the 'new disciplinology' to describe the perceived overlap between school and criminal justice responses. They identify the following characteristics of 'new disciplinology':

- New discourses in education in relation to punishment (which mirror discourses in criminal justice);
- New objectives which are secondary to education (e.g., increased focus on safety in schools);
- New techniques of risk management (e.g., increased security measures such as searches, metal detectors, etc.).

Of course, the focus on safety in schools has a particular salience in the United States where many school shootings have occurred with tragic repercussions. However, as some commentators have observed, the implementation of gun control measures at a wider societal level would have a much more general public safety effect than more targeted securitisation of schools.

In a comparative study of school punishment in England and the United States, Kupchik et al. (2015) explore differences in the framing of the problems of behaviour and school punishment, and school punishment and security policies. They found that American schools adopted a narrow focus on punishment, where rules were more rigidly enforced and the involvement of the criminal justice authorities was more routine, for example through the placement of police officers or security guards in school premises. In England meanwhile, they found more of a focus on children's needs; however, there were some questions about how this rhetoric translated into practice. Moreover, despite differences at policy level, this research reported similar rates of school exclusions in the American and English systems:

> In short, the policy discourse about punishment practices within each country diverges extensively, but the rates of the most common punishment – suspensions/exclusions – are fairly similar. Socially disadvantaged youth, racial minorities, and males are severely overrepresented in exclusion rates in both countries. (Kupchik et al., 2015: 16)

This research concluded that school discipline and punishment is shaped by broader cultural contexts, so that general cultural attitudes towards crime and punishment also shape school responses to transgressions.

Impacts of School Exclusions

Although offending by children and young people has generally declined, and serious offending by children is rare (see Chapter 8 for a full discussion), the UK Government's Serious Violence Strategy, published in 2018, identified a relationship between school exclusion and children's involvement in the most serious forms of offending. It is also noted that children who were subject to school exclusions were also more likely to be victims of serious offending (HM Government, 2018). One of the possible explanations for the inter-relationship between school exclusion and experiences of serious violence is that children who are excluded from school tend to face a range of other disadvantages and that when excluded they face higher risks of being exploited. A particular concern is young people's exploitation in drug markets and through involvement in 'county lines'. The term county lines refers to the transportation of drugs for one area to another, often across police and local authority boundaries, usually by children and vulnerable people. The 'county line' is the mobile phone used to take the orders for drugs.

A review of school exclusions in England carried out in 2019 highlighted the need to develop more positive school cultures and to further train and equip school staff with the skills to identify children's needs and to support them. It also recommended greater collaboration between schools and Local Authorities to advocate for and support vulnerable children (Timpson, 2019).

More evidence of the interactive effects of school experiences and contact with the criminal justice system is provided by recent findings from the *Edinburgh Study on Youth Transitions and Crime*. Across the United Kingdom in recent years there has been a policy focus on young people who are referred to as NEET (Not in Education, Employment or Training). This is based on the concern that young people in this situation can become entrenched in situations of poverty and social exclusion (Brynner and Parsons, 2002). Analysis from the *Edinburgh Study* shows that by age 18 approximately 6% of the study cohort (of around 4,300 young people) could be characterised as NEET, and 'that contacts with the juvenile justice system were significantly linked to later NEET status' (McAra, 2017b: 782). Furthermore:

> ... core dimensions of the school experience shaped the odds of being NEET including relationships with teachers, lack of attachment to school and low aspirations. (McAra, 2017b: 782)

A further significant finding is that children in care also faced much higher likelihood (four times more likely) of being NEET. These findings point to potential interactive effects for children involved in different systems, and to the nature of cumulative disadvantage. The experiences of young people in care and their contacts with the youth justice system are explored further in the next section.

Looked After Children and the Youth Justice System

Children are referred to child protection and welfare services and/or placed in care for a range of reasons, most commonly because of experiences of child abuse and neglect.

Data on referrals to child protection and welfare services and placement of children in care across the four jurisdictions of the United Kingdom shows that the majority of referrals are for reasons of abuse or neglect. When a report is made to Social Services, or when a child is identified as being in need, a range of interventions can take place. This can include the provision of support services to families and young people, the development of a **Child Protection Plan** with a set of actions to keep a young person safe, or in some instances the placement of a young person in care.

Overall, the number and rate of children in care in the UK are increasing but the trends vary between the four nations (NSPCC, 2021). The most recent data on the number and profile of children in need of child protection and welfare services and Looked After Children (LAC) in the different jurisdictions of the United Kingdom shows variations across time and place. In England in 2021, there were 80,850 children who were looked after (an increase of 1% from the previous year) which follows an overall trend of rising numbers since the mid-1990s, when the number of looked after children was fewer than 50,000 per annum (GOV.UK, 2022). The numbers of children considered to be 'in need' (i.e., referred to child protection and welfare services) has also risen in this period.

Although the way in which the classification of being a 'child in care' is legally defined varies across jurisdictions, for example in Scotland a child may be in care while living at home under a 'compulsory supervision order', when looking at the overall rates of children in care (that is the number of children in care per 10,000 of the population under 18 years), we see upward trends across the UK jurisdictions and in the Republic of Ireland in recent years (Figure 9.1) (NISRA, 2021).

However, as Table 9.1 shows, the rate of looked after children varies markedly across the four jurisdictions.

These differences in rates are partly (but not fully) explained by different definitions regarding the status of a child in care. For instance, as described above, in Scotland children living at home under the supervision of Social Services are counted in the numbers of children in care. However, research exploring the differentials in rates of care across the United Kingdom also shows that the threshold for interventions and the level of support provided to children and families vary across and within regions.

Research by Bywaters and colleagues (2016) shows that there are wide variations in the intervention rates of child protection and welfare services across the various jurisdictions of the United Kingdom. This research showed variation in child protection rates across the four jurisdictions of the United Kingdom from 24.7 per 10,000 children to 46.8 per 10,000 children in 2013 (Bywaters et al., 2016). These differences have led Bywaters et al. (2016) to identify an 'inverse intervention law' which they describe as follows:

> Overall a child's chances of a child welfare intervention increased significantly with deprivation but, comparing equivalent levels of neighbourhood deprivation, a child in a more affluent LA [Local Authority] overall was more likely to be on a CPP [Child Protection Plan] or to be LAC [Looked After Child]. (Bywaters et al., 2016: 454)

These patterns of inequality in relation to the provision of child protection and welfare services were similar to patterns regarding the provision of healthcare services and provide evidence of differential access to these services across England. Further research has shown that following the impact of austerity measures in England, local authorities reduced their expenditure on children and young

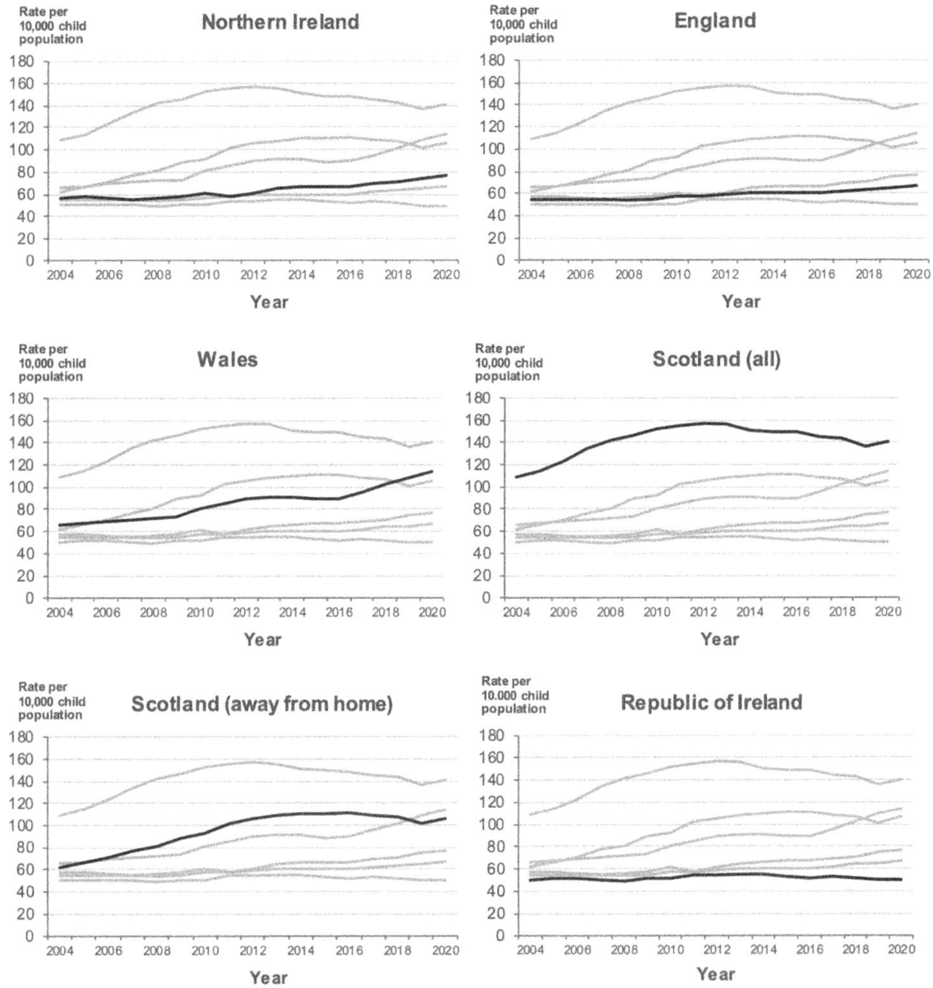

Figure 9.1 United Kingdom and Ireland Comparison of Rate of Children in Care per 10,000 Children (2004–2020)

Source: NISRA (2021: 41).

Table 9.1 Rates of Looked After Children in England, Scotland, Wales and Northern Ireland.

	England	Northern Ireland	Scotland	Wales
Rate of looked after children per 10,000 of the under-18 population (31 March 2019)	65.4	74.8	136.2	108.7

Source: NSPCC (2021).

people's services, and that paradoxically these reductions were most severe in areas with the highest levels of deprivation (Bywaters et al., 2018). Overall, this has meant less investment in broader family services that support children and families below the threshold of care (i.e., at a stage when children and their families can be supported at home and not at the point of immediate crisis).

The vast majority of children in care do not have contact with the criminal justice system. However, there is substantial evidence from a range of countries of the over-representation of young people in care (or who have had care experience) in the youth justice system (Cusick et al., 2012; Barn and Tan, 2012; Mendes et al., 2014; Goldson et al., 2021). Various research has explored the reasons for this over-representation and has identified what can broadly be divided into two main themes. Firstly, that young people in care will often have faced a range of adversities in their lives that may place them at higher risk of offending, and secondly that the care experience may itself be 'criminogenic' (which means that it may contribute to the reason young people offend and come to the attention of the criminal justice system) (Carr and McAlister, 2016).

Reasons for Over-Representation of Children in Care in the Justice System – Views From Service Providers

These are some extracts of submissions made from service providers to a 'call for evidence' in a research project conducted in Ireland exploring the reasons for the over-representation of children in care in the youth justice system (Carr and Mayock, 2019). They highlight some of the challenges faced by children and young people in care at an individual and structural level that lead some young people to have an increased risk of contact with the criminal justice system.

> It has troubled us greatly to note that many of the charges that young people will accumulate relate directly to their behaviour while in care settings themselves – young people often face charges for destruction of property, assault of care staff and other issues such as drug possession in the care placement. While not condoning the behaviour of young people who act out and understanding the consequences for behaviour are important it has been difficult to note in many situations we have encountered that the Gardaí [police] are involved in issues that if happening in a family home they would not be involved with. (Cork Life Centre Submission)
>
> Another pattern which we have observed is that young people from backgrounds in care have often been before the Courts for what might be called 'domestic incidents' such as damage to property or assault of staff in residential settings. This may be linked to poor relationships between young people and staff, anger issues on the part of young people, and residential centre policies which require all incidents to be reported to the Gardai. (Le Chéile submission)

Source: Carr and Mayock (2019: 17).

The first set of explanations, that children in care may have experienced life events that place them at higher risk of involvement in the criminal justice system, is influenced by risk factor research which has sought to identify characteristics that contribute to children's 'risk' of offending. This broad body of research, sometimes referred to as the 'Risk Factor Prevention Paradigm' (RFPP) (Haines and Case, 2008) is premised on identifying precursors to personal and socially harmful behaviours in order to intervene to reduce risk and harm (Haines and Case, 2008; O'Mahony, 2009) (see Chapter 8 also for a wider discussion). Some of the risk factors which this research identifies as being associated with offending, such as familial disruption, experiences of adversity etc., may also be experienced by young people involved in the child protection and welfare and care systems (Malvaso and Delfabbro, 2015), although it is also important to note that the majority of young people in care do not have any involvement with the criminal justice system (Carr and Mayock, 2019).

Other explanations focus on the fact that aspects of the care system itself may be 'criminogenic' (Hayden, 2010). Writing in the context of children in care in New South Wales, Australia, McFarlane (2018) for instance notes that 'care-criminalisation' can occur in residential care, when staff call police to help manage children's behaviour. This can happen in the context of lack of staff training, and in the absence of proper policies. A similar finding was observed in relation to the criminalisation of young people in care in Ireland (Carr and Mayock, 2019).

The Howard League in England and Wales has also outlined concerns regarding the criminalisation of young people in care, identifying important issues from the perspectives of young people such as how responses to trauma are dealt with (Howard League, 2016, 2018). In one account a young person describes how their care placement's response to their self-harming was to call the police, resulting in them spending the night in a police cell. In another account, Jodie, a young person in care, described that the policy of reporting young people who were 'missing' from their care placements again resulted in contact with the police:

> I went missing from care quite a few times when I was there. And then the police started to charge me with wasting police time. I would literally walk out the house and the police would be called, literally the second I walked out the house, which isn't in the missing from care plan. There is no prevention there. There is no explanation there. (Jodie, cited in Howard League for Penal Reform, 2018)

Part of the issue identified in Jodie's quote above is that children in care may be more likely to come into contact with the police because of their circumstances, and that this contact with the police may result in further contact with the criminal justice system. This echoes McAra and McVie's (2010a) finding from the *Edinburgh Youth Transitions Study* regarding the 'usual suspects' being processed by the criminal justice system (see also Chapter 8).

A further important dimension regarding the over-representation of children in care in the criminal justice system relates to the supports available for young people as they transition from care. In many contexts young people from care must make the transition from care in the absence of adequate supports. Numerous empirical studies in a range of countries attest to the challenges faced by young people transitioning from care, particularly when these transitions are fractured, accelerated and poorly supported (Courtney et al., 2010; Mendes and Moslehuddin, 2006). In some instances, young people 'age out' of the care system, that is, they reach adulthood and are no longer in the care of the state. While leaving care supports are available in different contexts, these are often conditional. For example, young people may be required to engage in education to access leaving care supports including accommodation and certain benefits (as is the case in the Republic of Ireland) (Carr, 2014).

Girls and Women With Experience of Care and the Criminal Justice System

Research conducted in England and Wales has looked specifically at the routes between care and custody for girls and women (Fitzpatrick et al., 2022). This research identified some of the causes for this over-representation, which included the impacts of trauma, unmet mental health needs and criminalisation in care. Some of the girls who participated in this research reported experiences of Child Criminal Exploitation (CCE) and Child Sexual Exploitation (CSE), and that the care system did not adequately respond to their experiences of trauma. This research identified that:

> Coping strategies, such as 'kicking off' or running away, were often met with criminal justice responses. (Fitzpatrick et al., 2022: 3)

Moreover, children who had mental health needs experienced inadequate service provision. This research made several policy recommendations to address the problem of girls and women with care experience becoming involved in the criminal justice system. These recommendations include:

- Ensure the availability of timely and meaningful mental health support where required.
- Renew the commitment to local protocols aimed at keeping children in care out of the justice system.
- Make the prevention of unnecessary criminalisation in care a statutory duty.
- Divert care experienced women from custody wherever possible.

- Confront the intergenerational harms that imprisonment creates.
- Improve support for care-experienced girls and women already involved with the justice system.
- Extend the age at which meaningful leaving care support is available.
- Raise the minimum age of criminal responsibility.

You can read more about this research, which is funded by the Nuffield Foundation, at this website: www.nuffieldfoundation.org/project/girls-and-women-with-experience-of-care-and-the-criminal-justice-system

An independent review exploring the interactions of children in care with the criminal justice system in England and Wales made a series of recommendations to ensure a more targeted approach to address the criminalisation of young people in care and to support young people from the care system if they become involved in the criminal justice system (Laming, 2016). The recommendations included the need for leadership to address this issue at the national level; more consistency in police practice; earlier supports for children and families at risk; better joint working between children's social services and criminal justice agencies and a recognition of the important role of good parenting by the state (Laming, 2016).

When a child is placed in care the state is essentially assuming parental responsibility for this child. Therefore, the onus should be on the state to provide good parenting, which would involve protecting children from criminalisation. Amongst other things, this would involve the provision of adequate services to meet children's needs, particularly in the context where they have experienced trauma, and the supports of positive role models (Laming, 2016). Attempts to address the over-representation of children in care in the youth justice system have included the introduction of protocols which have looked at areas such as the inter-relationships between care homes and the police, and the procedures that should be followed if a child is reported missing from care. While addressing these issues may have some impact, there is lots of evidence that wider systemic change is required (Fitzpatrick et al., 2022).

As well as concerns regarding the over-representation of children in care in the youth justice system, there is also a range of evidence that shows that people in the adult criminal justice system have had previous care experience as children. Data produced by the Ministry of Justice in England and Wales on prisoners' childhoods and family backgrounds shows that a significant minority of prisoners have lived in care. One study which looked at the past and present family circumstances of newly sentenced prisoners documented that almost a quarter of the sample (24%) had been in care at some point in their childhood (Williams et al., 2012). Moreover:

> Those who had been in care were younger when they were first arrested, and were more likely to be reconvicted in the year after release from custody than those who had never been in care. (Williams et al., 2012: ii)

Including prisoners with care experience, almost a third (29%) of the sample reported experiences of emotional, physical or sexual abuse as a child (with higher rates reported amongst the women prisoners). Similar findings are reported in the Scottish Prisoner Survey, where almost a quarter of prisoners reported being in care as children (Carnie and Broderick, 2019).

Meanwhile, a longitudinal study of people placed in foster care as children in the Mid-West (Illinois, Iowa and Wisconsin) of the United States, reported relatively high rates of criminal justice involvement into adulthood (when compared to the general population) (Courtney et al., 2011). In this study data was collected over several sweeps (at ages 17–18, 19, 21, 23–24 and 25–26). It showed that by age 26 a majority of young women and more than four-fifths of young men in the total sample (n = 732) reported ever having been arrested, while nearly one-third of young women and almost two-thirds of the young men reported spending at least one night in jail since they were 17 or 18 years old. Young people in this sample also reported higher levels of criminalisation than people in the general population (Courtney et al., 2011). This research has highlighted differentials in the supports available to young people as they transition from care, and also points to the cumulative effects of disadvantage over time.

Conclusion

This chapter has highlighted some of the intersections between the youth justice system and other systems of intervention in children and young people's lives through a discussion of some of the research which explores the links between experiences of school disciplinary measures (including school exclusions) and involvement in the criminal justice system, and by looking at some of the intersections between the child protection and welfare system and the youth justice system.

The evidence of the interactions between school exclusion and criminal justice involvement and the over-representation of children in care in the criminal justice system points to the impacts of cumulative disadvantage. Children who are excluded from school, are more likely to have criminal justice involvement, and children who are excluded from school are more likely to be from backgrounds of socio-economic disadvantage. The over-representation of children in care in the youth and (subsequently) adult criminal justice system has been a source of concern in many countries, and the target of policy and practice interventions. However, the continued relevance of this as an issue points to the need for wider systemic changes, including the need to provide supports to children and their families that might prevent their entry into care in the first instance.

Further Reading

The Child Welfare Inequalities Project: This is a comparative research project funded by the Nuffield Foundation that has explored differential patterns of child welfare interventions across the four jurisdictions of the United Kingdom. This website provides further information about the project and access to the project reports and other publications: www.nuffieldfoundation.org/project/inequalities-in-child-welfare-intervention-rates

School-to-prison pipeline: You can read more about the school-to-prison pipeline in the context of the United States, including about a campaign to end police presence in schools, via the American Civil Liberties Union (ACLU) website. This site also includes a podcast on exploring this topic: www.aclu.org/issues/juvenile-justice/juvenile-justice-school-prison-pipeline

10

Taking Account of the Views of Children and Young People

Objectives

- This chapter introduces the voice and perceptions of young people themselves, and particularly those who are involved with the justice system in some way.
- This chapter will introduce the reader to autobiographical accounts of young people's involvement with crime and the justice system.
- Readers will be able to explore the findings of researchers who have lived alongside young people who have been involved in offending, in order to explore their experiences and the meaning they attach to their activities.
- The chapter will follow the journeys taken by young people through the justice system and their subjective accounts of its impact.
- Recent attempts to introduce participatory principles into youth justice service delivery and practices will also be discussed towards the conclusion of the chapter.

Introduction

A very great deal of what is written about young people and youth justice relies on interpretations of young people's behaviour, on the one hand, and critical examination of the systems and practices designed to deal with their offending, on the other. Often missing from these accounts are attempts to gain a proper understanding of what crime, criminality and justice mean from young people's own perspective. Perhaps unsurprisingly, this could well be said to mirror the ways in which practitioners and organisations have conventionally sought to account for and respond to the problematic behaviour of children and young people, without providing space to listen to their views or experiences or taking steps to incorporate these into formal interventions. As time passes, though, there is a growing body of thought which argues that we cannot work effectively with young people without understanding the world as it is for them, and taking account of how their own lived experiences help to shape their beliefs, attitudes and actions.

As we have seen previously (see Chapter 5), for some time there has been a developing framework of international instruments and standards which has sought to give substance to a globally defined body of rights for children experiencing criminal justice interventions. These are closely aligned with wider provisions, such as the United Nations Convention on the Rights of the Child (UNCRC), which sets out minimum standards of entitlement and participation for all children. Notably, for instance, Article 12 of the Convention provides for children to have the right to be heard and taken seriously, and Article 39 provides for all children to receive help in response to harmful or distressing events which happen to them. These Articles are universal, meaning that they do not differentiate between children (that is, those who offend or are institutionalised, and children in general). Accordingly, it is important to hear the views of children involved in the criminal justice system and to respond to their needs appropriately.

In light of this observation, this final chapter will attempt to foreground the perceptions and experiences of children and young people, and it will consider the implications for our wider understanding of youth crime, as well as the actions taken by state institutions and others in response.

The young person's perspective

We will firstly reflect on what are described as 'self-report' studies, that is, surveys and other investigations into young people's own accounts of their involvement in crime. It will be helpful to consider both the extent of such involvement and whether it shows youth offending in a different light to that offered by crime statistics or victim studies.

The chapter will then move on to review a number of ethnographic studies which explore children's lives and experiences in context, and which therefore provide in-depth and detailed insights into their own perspectives on crime and criminality.

Following this, we will consider the evidence emerging from young people's accounts of their journeys into and through the justice system, its impact on them, and how they have sought to negotiate the challenges it has presented to them. Extending this discussion further, we will then consider the relationship between harmful experiences within and beyond the justice system, and criminal victimisation, as this is understood by children and young people. And, finally, drawing on a body of work which is currently emerging, we will consider the growing evidence of efforts to improve young people directly as participants, in terms of shaping youth justice systems and intervention, and in this way in fact taking direct responsibility for dealing with crime and its impacts.

Personal Narratives: Autobiographical Accounts of Young People's Involvement in Crime

As we saw in Chapter 2, self-report studies have been a feature of the criminal justice landscape for some time now; and they tend to show that youth crime is more widespread and perhaps commonly accepted than official statistics and formal processes would lead us to believe. Whilst we must be equally careful not to over-generalise on this basis, it is certainly helpful, too, to think about first-hand accounts, and what they can tell us about the experience of offending. These may offer the additional value of being unedited, representing direct evidence.

One example of this kind of narrative is the 'My Story' collection produced by the Centre for Crime and Justice Studies (Grimshaw, 2011), which brought together personal accounts from three young people who had been sentenced for serious crimes. Although these accounts were based on interviews with a researcher and subsequently edited, the attempt was made to ensure that the words used and the stories presented remained true to their experiences.

'Story 1' is that of a young woman, in prison at the time of interview. For her, the death of her father was associated with losing interest in school, and being excluded from mainstream education: '[A]fter that I was always late for school, I couldn't really be bothered going in ... I got put into a [Pupil Referral] unit. ... I hated it. Because I wasn't with any of my mates anymore. I just stopped going' (quoted in Grimshaw, 2011: 19). After this, it seems that she began to 'drift' (Matza, 1964) towards crime:

> I started hanging round with my cousins ... I was just doing nothing. ... I'd probably just stay out at my cousin's ... and probably come home late when everyone was home from school. So, I think that's when I started going off the rails a bit. I started drinking ... staying out all night. ... Just getting into trouble all the time. (Quoted in Grimshaw, 2011: 20)

She describes her mum trying to manage her behaviour, and her refusal to cooperate, then running away with another relative to the city. She also describes being controlled by her relative's older boyfriend, and 'just following what he told us to do really. And it probably just got from bad to worse' (Grimshaw, 2011: 20). As far as the offence which led to her imprisonment was concerned, she says that it is 'hard when I try and talk about [it] because I think people might think I'm lying that I'm saying I can't remember but I really can't remember' (Grimshaw, 2011: 20). She then goes on to describe her attempted return to a 'normal' life, her feelings of guilt and regret for the offence ('I wouldn't want someone to do that to me ... I know ... right from wrong so I knew that was wrong'), but also the sense that it was something which happened more or less beyond her control: 'I was just in a situation that I couldn't get out of and was just going along. But probably I could have got out of it, but you just feel like you can't' (Grimshaw, 2011: 22).

Story 2 is the account of a young man serving an indeterminate custodial sentence for serious crimes. Like the narrator of Story 1, his description of his early life includes episodes of violence perpetrated by his father against his mother: 'He hit her over the head with a broom. ... And then there were other times' (Grimshaw, 2011: 23). From early in life, too, he mentions having had 'behaviour problems ... just started being naughty, staying out late, arguing with my mum, smashing up the house and things like that. ... For my safety and for mum's safety ... I went into a boarding school for behavioural and emotional problems' (Grimshaw, 2011: 23). The account continues with a description of his parents' abusive behaviour (being locked in a cupboard by his father, and 'my mum hanged me over a balcony'), but 'it's something you've got to get on with, there's no point holding grudges' (Grimshaw, 2011: 28).

As far as his offending went, his account attributes its origin to a lack of guidance or control: 'I never had no boundaries. ... That was my thinking when I was young that I can do these things and I don't get in trouble for it. ... I just thought that it was okay' (Grimshaw, 2011: 29). His offences were sexual, and his story puts them in a context where sexual norms were either not recognised, or not enforced. At boarding school: 'there was a number of times that I'd been caught in bed with girls and I never got in trouble for it. ... I was never suspended, I never got kicked out of school'. In this sense, we can locate his offending within a conceptual frame of 'neutralisation' (Sykes and Matza, 1957) or 'normalisation' (Young, 1997). Even though the behaviour may not conform to socially accepted standards of behaviour, the absence of constraints or regulation appears to provide justification for it.

Story 3 in this collection is provided by another young man, who had been detained indefinitely for murder at the time he was interviewed. His early recollections are of constant arguments between his parents, his father spending time in custody, and his parents' eventual separation. Police involvement seems to have been a regular occurrence, and it clearly had an adverse effect on him: 'I cried all the way to soccer school because ... I'd seen the police arrest my dad before, but this time I'd never seen that many police' (Grimshaw, 2011: 42). Violence appears to have been a central feature of family life, much of it associated with his grandfather: 'he beats my nan up regularly. He put her in hospital the other month, but what can you do?' He goes on to say: 'The rest of my family messed my life up and they're pretty much the reason that I'm in jail'. Unsurprisingly, perhaps, his narrative links his problematic family life to beginning to get into trouble: 'I was quite well behaved when I was in primary school, but when I hit junior school, the older I've got, the problems with my mum and dad. ... I suppose I had my mum and dad's temper' (Grimshaw, 2011: 43).

He goes on to describe his father's alcoholism, their joint visits to the pub and his own increasing involvement with drink and drugs, and the associated crimes of theft and burglary carried out in order to finance this. He recounts becoming part of a 'gang' hanging out 'on the estate' and getting involved in more or less spontaneous acts of violence. For him, crime had simply become a feature of everyday life by the age of 13: 'Basically, I was thinking I could go on for the rest of my life thieving, turning over a tiny little bit of profit when I do ... deals on the drugs, and drinking, and that's how I thought I would spend my life' (Grimshaw, 2011: 50). In the event, he became involved in a murder, leading to his current period of indefinite detention. This he attributed to the example set by his father, whose routine use of violence, and the reputation associated with it, had come to form a central part of his life.

We should be wary of generalising too widely based on three accounts of young people's pathways towards the commission of serious crimes, although Grimshaw (2011: 4) does identify common themes, such as challenging relationships with parents, and episodes of loss and enduring trauma. The advantages of this approach to personal accounts are that they are documented consistently and presented without much embellishment. Editing is intended to provide safeguards such as anonymity, and to clarify and make the material as accessible as possible.

By contrast, there are a considerable number of autobiographies published in book form by, or in collaboration with, offenders or former offenders, which incorporate reminiscences of early involvement in crime and the part it played in their lives as children and young people. Some of these are well known, such as *The Jack-Roller* by Clifford Shaw (1966), *Down These Mean Streets* by Piri Thomas (1997), *Diary of a Juvenile Delinquent* by Steven Berkoff (2010), and *Riding in Cars with Boys* by Beverly Donofrio (1992). These accounts are predictably dramatised at times, but they may still provide important insights into the early stages of criminal careers, the contexts and influences which are important to young people, and the factors which seem to be associated with continued involvement in crime, on the one hand, or desistance, on the other. In several cases, they draw particular attention to issues such as gender, or the problematic relationship between criminalisation and racism.

Racism and social exclusion are central to the narratives of Thomas (1997) writing about growing up as a Puerto Rican in New York, and Smith (2004), from an Irish background and growing up in South London during the 1970s. In both these cases, the backdrop to their involvement in criminal behaviour is one of everyday violence, and open conflict with a police force characterised by racism and brutality. In a criminological sense, these accounts perhaps suggest that the border line between right and wrong in any absolute sense may become quite blurred, and that, in these cases, crime becomes normalised. Berkoff's (2010) case is different, in that he escaped long-term involvement with the criminal justice system for a life in the theatre, but the same sense of early rejection, discrimination (anti-semitism in this instance) and a drift into lawbreaking because it was part of everyday life, is apparent.

There is certainly a great deal of interesting material to be found in these personal accounts, and they convey some powerful messages about the relationships between young people, their communities, and social institutions (such as schools) and the justice system. Reading them criminologically, though, as we must, we also need to bear in mind that they are narratives produced with a general readership in mind, so may appear as dramatised to some extent. We might wonder, for instance, whether conversations and events from a number of years previously can be recalled precisely, and we need to acknowledge that what is reported is presented from a particular point of view. Of course, it is also likely to be the case that such autobiographies are particularly marketable, and thus attract a disproportionate level of interest relative to patterns of crime in general; most youth crime is much more low-key and incidental. Nonetheless, these striking personal stories do prompt a number of significant questions, meriting further exploration, especially where these narratives coincide, or align with wider bodies of evidence. Smith (2004) and Berkoff (2010) both refer to the brutality of detention centre regimes, for example, which is certainly supported by subsequent evidence from a wide range of sources.

Ethnographies of Young People and Crime

Alongside personal accounts, we can gain important insights into the relationship between young people, crime and the criminal justice system through close and detailed reporting of their daily lives, in the form of **ethnographic** accounts undertaken by academic researchers. Of course, just as is the case with autobiography, the stories we read of this kind are the product of a process of recording and interpretation, but they certainly add another level of understanding in our search for effective explanations of young people's journeys, and especially the immediate social contexts within which they make choices which may shape their lives.

Mendoza-Denton (2008) provides a useful account of female (Latina) 'gangs' in a US city, based on a period of several years (1993–97) exploring the lives of students at a particular high school in Silicon Valley, California. Here, she overcame initial suspicion that she might be an undercover cop and drew on her own similar ethnic and cultural background to gain a close understanding of the daily experience of girls and young women who were gang members. As she points out, however, the very use of the term creates problems and tends to have a labelling effect: 'definitions of gangs by the police and by teachers expand in widening circles and throw a blanket of suspicion over minority youth who have very little to do with the criminality propelled concerns under the traditional definitions of gangs' (Mendoza-Denton, 2008: 79). As she observes, the process of identifying or becoming identified with different groups (Norteñas or Sureñas in this instance) was much more central to the lives of the young people concerned than involvement in criminal activity, although this might be incidental of course, in terms of confrontation and fighting: 'I grew up with – where a lot of Mexicans used to be and that's the only color I knew about and so I started hanging around with them ... just looking at who I am and what I claim sometimes I got into fights ... they were calling me scrap and stuff ...' (15-year-old of South Asian origin, identifying with the Sureñas, quoted in Mendoza-Denton, 2008: 136).

When it came to the police, however, members of rival groups would show a united front: 'me and a Sureño were both trying to jump the same fence ... the cops was coming, so he [Sureño] helped me up and I [Norteña] helped him up ... when it comes down to the cops we both would cover up for each other' (T-Rex, quoted in Mendoza-Denton, 2008: 143).

Mendoza-Denton (2008: 295) emphasises that she wants to treat gang involvement as being about a group 'dynamic other than violence, the control of territory or the traffic of drugs, factors routinely considered as paramount in both police intervention and gang research'. This, she explains, helps us to understand gang allegiances within a wider social-structural context, within which criminality and the interventions of the criminal justice system may best be seen as features of a more extensive and more complex picture.

Howard Parker's (1974) influential study *View from the Boys* captures the same sense of a community of boys and young men, from a particular neighbourhood in Liverpool, with both a strong sense of identity and belonging, and a history of civic neglect and marginalisation. Parker's initial role as a youth worker enabled him to gain access to this community in order to pursue an in-depth research study at close hand. He became a regular companion of the group, becoming very familiar with their unlawful behaviour, particularly the theft and disposal of car radios (at a time in the early 1970s when these were easily detachable from car dashboards). In a context of limited opportunities and disaffection with mainstream education, the subjects of his study became involved in offending for very instrumental reasons, it seems, as a route to quick cash, and the sort of lifestyle (fashion, drinking) to which they aspired:

> The Boys were concerned, all in all they were skint. They made a fairly conscious effort to plan a couple of 'robberies'. ... There was no question of worrying about the morality of planning property thefts, which seemed like crimes without real victims, The Boys' main concern was how much they could sell the gear for, and how likely they were to get caught. (Parker, 1974: 75)

So, the move into stealing and selling on car radios seemed like a reasonable 'business' decision, with the impact of victimisation helpfully 'neutralised' in Matza's (1964) terms. At this time, car radios had become quite common accessories in newer and more 'luxurious' cars, and there was a ready market for them amongst other car owners. Certain makes and models of car, notably the Rover 2000, were easy and profitable targets. As some of the Boys began to make what seemed like good money, so others joined in, and soon 'at least twenty of the network were screwing cars, some regularly, others occasionally' (Parker, 1974: 77). Elaborate operating methods were established, involving the scrutiny of likely locations and target vehicles ('pipe-ing'), developing improved techniques and establishing specialised roles amongst the teams of thieves taking part.

Interestingly, though, this activity was not devoid of moral reasoning, or self-imposed rules as to acceptable and unacceptable behaviour: 'Screwing cars is wrong if they can't afford it. But ... [i]f they've got money to pay for Rovers they're all right' (Joey, quoted in Parker, 1974: 85). This form of conditional moralising extends, in particular, to other forms of crime, too, especially those against friends, family or neighbours, as described by Fosser, who had once stolen a purse 'from the flat next door ... when they found out ... I got called all sorts at home. ... I really learned my lesson there' (quoted in Parker, 1974: 84).

Inevitably, too, the Boys' expanding operation brought their activities to the attention of the police, and so they began to experience criminalisation, as some were caught, taken to court, and even incarcerated in a few cases. For some, this clearly resulted in a recalibration of their earlier choices, and a desire to opt out of anything illegal. Others, though, sustained their commitment, reasoning that 'if you rob properly, you've got a good chance of getting away with it' (Colly, quoted in Parker, 1974: 91). Their differential commitment to 'robbing' began to take effect, and some of those on the fringes of the action began to opt out. Some were deterred by the experience of going to court or custody, others were not. Some formed relationships and began to disengage from the wider group and their crimes, whilst others continued despite having girlfriends and an apparently conventional route towards adult life.

Importantly, Parker's work enables us to explore crime, criminality and the trajectories of those involved in the light of a range of criminological theories, and therefore to interpret and modify these as they offer us partial and intersecting explanations. We see the decision to get involved in offending, where and how, and whether or not to continue, as essentially governed by a series of what could be interpreted as 'rational choices'. We see that the decision to stop stealing may be the consequence of deterrence, or of socialisation. For some, delinquency is 'just a phase'; whilst for others, the experience of criminalisation and the justice system may have the opposite effect, and, for them: 'Crime will become a business' (Parker, 1974: 206). As Parker points out, context is important, and these individual trajectories, decisions and influences should be viewed in that light: 'Since, the Boys have rarely encountered good legitimate opportunities with people who are willing to form attachments and nurture commitments in them, they tend to 'mess up' the occasional good chances. Their problem is thus related to the scarcity of good chances and practice, not pathology' (Parker, 1974: 205).

Yates' (2012) ethnographic study, carried out in a poorer area of Liverpool like Parker's, albeit some thirty years later, draws similar conclusions: 'environment, shaped by structural disadvantage, impacted not only on their [young people's] experiences, and likelihood, of becoming involved in crime but also their routes to desistance' (Yates, 2012: 434). In the same way as Parker had previously identified, Yates' study (2006) enables us to gain a close sense of what the community and its embedded relationships mean to young people:

> A lot of people who aren't from the Estate think that this is a dump, they think we're all tramps, scroungers, you know – skivers robbing off each other and stuff. They think the Estate is just full of TWOCkers [Taking a Vehicle Without Consent] and thieves. I just think fuck 'em, I'm from here and I don't care what they think. (quoted in Yates, 2006: 196)

Here, the rules and obligations of the community are clearly at odds with those of the mainstream and the conventional justice system; although, as Parker had found previously, this does not mean that there is no sense of mutual responsibility or right and wrong, as in the case of domestic burglary, for example (Yates, 2006: 205). Even though there is considerable hostility towards the police, and an established rule that you should not 'grass' on anyone you know, breaking into someone's house is still unacceptable.

It is a matter of learning the informal structures and codes of behaviour within which you must live, if you are a young person on 'the Estate': 'crime's been a big part of growing up round here ... it's part of living here – you just have to learn to deal with it' (YR, quoted in Yates, 2006: 203).

So, there may be widespread acceptance of receiving stolen goods, so long as they are not personal possessions (i.e., they are still in their original packaging), for example:

> Like that's what you need in the run up to Christmas, you're watching your pennies so you think yeah so and so, or me Nonna, would love that for Christmas in her stocking, normally I wouldn't be able to afford that, I don't ask any questions, but I know it's not from someone's house – it's in the box. (quoted in Yates, 2006: 202)

The community nonetheless applies its own behavioural norms and enforces them rigorously: '... you know there's people you don't fuck with, houses and cars that you wouldn't go near' (quoted in Yates, 2006: 207).

Ethnographic accounts such as this provide a valuable insight into the detail of young people's lives, their daily interactions with peers, and with others including authority figures, and the extent to which 'crime' is both an essentially normal feature of their lives, and yet does not play a big part in them. It is just something that happens; it may provide a talking point for a while, but it is largely unexceptional.

Journeys Through the System

For those young people who do come into contact with the justice system, the nature of the experience from their perspective is also of considerable interest, for several reasons. Clearly, the insights offered provide a particular angle on how and why they may come to the attention of criminal justice agencies, plus they also shed light on the impact of criminal justice on them. These subjective accounts, for example, act as a counterpoint to the assumptions embedded in the operation of the justice system about the administration of justice, and its intended effect on young people's lives and behaviour. Bevan's study (2016, 2019) of young people's experiences on first contact with the justice system provides an interesting starting point, in that it illustrates the young people's general lack of understanding about criminal justice and how the 'system' works. Her initial investigation into the views and understandings of secondary school students is informative, in that young people in the general population appear to know remarkably little about the workings of the police, the courts and other criminal justice agencies.

Using a number of pre-prepared scenarios (providing cannabis to a friend, 'sexting'), Bevan explored with a number of focus groups (male and female, and from varying ethnic backgrounds) young people's perceptions of the nature of the behaviour, looking at questions such as the seriousness of the offence, and what would happen should it come to official notice. She noted a number of variations between schools in different locations, with a greater awareness and sensitivity to crime-related issues amongst the students from 'higher crime areas' (Bevan, 2016: 13). So, in the eyes of one young person: 'when police prosecute like youngsters it does interest me because like it, it involves us as well in a way because we're youngsters so it reflects on us ...'.

When it came to the examples of offences used in the scenarios, Bevan (2016: 17) identified only a limited understanding amongst young people about their nature and seriousness, as well as the likelihood of the formal justice system taking an interest. Thus, as Bevan (2016: 18) observed, one young person thought that 'sexting' was 'too frequent' for it to be the subject of effective prosecution. Similarly, cannabis use was described as 'normal' in one area, and most respondents were not aware of the current classification of the drug, while a considerable number did not realise that passing a quantity on to a friend would be viewed as a more serious offence than possession should it become the subject of formal action.

Beyond offending, Bevan also found very limited understanding on young people's part either of their rights, or of the processes and outcomes of the justice system: 'The participants' understanding of their rights surrounding contact with the police was patchy and this prompts concerns on various levels' (Bevan, 2016: 24). Nor did they appear to have much idea about the likely sentence to be incurred for the scenario offences, with a wide divergence of opinion in evidence, and if anything, a perception that the likely sentence for an offence would be rather more punitive than is actually the case.

Bevan's (2019) subsequent work built on these findings to explore young people's experiences at the point where the police become involved; that is, when they become suspects and are arrested. In this context, her findings appear to raise substantial concerns. Once taken into police custody,

> [m]any young research participants struggled to cope with a detention experience which is punitive, unnecessarily lengthy and very minimally adjusted to account for their youth. Their accounts are dominated by feelings of uncertainty, helplessness and desperation to 'get out' of the cell. (Bevan, 2019: 7)

As Bevan recounts, young people display a consistent lack of awareness of how the early stages of the justice process operate, in the context of arrest and detention, and this has a significant impact on their ability to participate in an informed way which preserves their self-interest:

> Lack of understanding of the various aspects of the process emerges repeatedly ... Failures of comprehension occurred across the process, starting with a total lack of awareness of the authorisation of detention process,

> lack of appreciation of the purpose of the RA [risk assessment], and misunderstanding of the scope and operation of their rights and entitlements. Critically, many young suspects failed to appreciate the role and benefits of the solicitor, and the nature of their right of silence. (Bevan, 2019: 300)

These findings are largely supported by those of earlier studies (Hazel, 2006; Botley et al., 2010). Young people appear to be confused and uncertain of what is going on, and they frequently report an unsympathetic response from police officers following arrest. Young people are concerned about being treated without proper respect:

> They tell us what to do, and we got to do it. There's no reason or asking, because they're in authority they can make us, so they do.
>
> They've got the authority, just abuse the power they've got, so they know they can do it, they know they can get away with it, there's nothing no one can do about it. (Young people quoted in Botley et al., 2010: 8)

Despite some positive comments about their contacts with police officers, Hazel's (2006) findings appear to mirror these largely negative experiences:

> Just the way they spoke to you like with no respect at all. It's like well I'm a human being as well, do you know what I mean? (15-year-old male, quoted in Hazel, 2006: 11)

Botley et al.'s study also considered other aspects of the criminal justice system, although the emerging themes seem rather similar. Thus, for example, young people's experience of court hearings appears to be confusing and alienating. As the authors observe, it is understandable that a court appearance is inevitably an uncomfortable and difficult experience, but at the same time, young people's discomfort appears to be exacerbated by the lack of information and support during the process (Botley et al., 2010: 13). Hunter et al. (2020) make similar observations on the court experience. Whilst in some cases judges, magistrates, or court officials made great efforts to make young people comfortable and ensure they understood the process, for many defendants the experience was one of confusion and anxiety. As one young person put it, it felt as if the outcome had already been decided: 'You're supposed to be innocent until proven guilty, but it was the complete opposite way around … They're there to sentence, not think you're innocent' (quoted in Centre for Justice Innovation, 2019: 4). Nonetheless, some young people spoke quite highly of Youth Offending Service staff who showed their willingness to offer continuing support and guidance through the court process.

Similarly, a study carried out by Phoenix and Kelly (2013) presents a mixed picture of young people's experiences at later stages of the youth justice experience, when they are subject to court orders following sentence. The backdrop for the young people in this particular study (Phoenix and Kelly, 2013: 427) is one of social deprivation, and a sense of criminal involvement being part, albeit just one part, of a lifestyle, whereby friendship, 'something to do', excitement and sometimes physical rewards (money, alcohol or cigarettes, perhaps) were all associated with some form of lawbreaking.

These young people were likely to have been identified as 'persistent' offenders, and thus to have considerable experience of the justice system, too. For these young people, the question of whether or not their supervisor (Youth Offending Team worker) 'cared' about them was of considerable importance: 'You can tell when someone cares because, like, they ring you up, like, before your interview, like say you had a job interview, they'd ring you up and wish you good luck. Stupid things like that' (quoted in Phoenix and Kelly, 2013: 428). On the other hand, for the majority, it seemed that there was little evidence that youth justice practitioners actually did care: 'They write whatever they think down. Like I say this is what's going on in my life and they may or may not write it down. They write what they want to see and what fits their forms' (quoted in Phoenix and Kelly, 2013: 429). Similarly, a number of the young people in the study complained of not being listened to, and that their supervisors appeared preoccupied with making their job as easy as possible.

Not only was the apparent lack of interest frustrating for young people, but they were also concerned that they were not being helped, despite the requirements of their court orders. According to Phoenix and Kelly (2013: 431), this was not because they disputed the legitimacy of the order itself, with all agreeing that it was right for people who committed offences to be punished. Instead, it was because they felt that formal compliance rather than substantive intervention seemed to be practitioners' principal objective: 'Action plan and supervision orders, they are all the same thing. There was nothing different in there. They might write up on a bit of paper a bit different, but what's actually happening is no different. It's all the same thing and its nothing' (quoted in Phoenix and Kelly, 2013: 431). Phoenix and Kelly draw the rather unsettling conclusion that much of the work undertaken with young people by professional practitioners is unhelpful and may even 'further alienate and isolate them' (Phoenix and Kelly, 2013: 434). From this, the young people seemed to assume that the kind of changes that would make a difference to their lives lie predominantly outside the control of those who work within the youth justice system.

McAlister and Carr's (2014) study of the experiences of some young people undergoing youth justice interventions in Northern Ireland is in some senses rather more positive. Noting that youth justice in Northern Ireland is strongly based on restorative principles, they observe that restorative conferencing may have an impact. Some of those interviewed spoke in depth about conferences and their immediate effect in terms of accepting responsibility for their offences. Their longer-term impact seems less clear, however, with some young people continuing to offend: 'I'd say if you asked ... the conference worker well I wouldn't really say it hit home much with where I am sitting (in custody) at the moment. It's up to me to change it like' (quoted in McAlister and Carr, 2014: 249).

Ironically, perhaps, these young people spoke of their custodial experiences as a time of 'respite', where they were able to step away from the stresses and challenges of their everyday lives, and make changes, such as coming off drugs: 'I like it in here, it's good .... Cos it's kinda a detox centre, you just come in and get off all the drugs and all and get fit again' (quoted in McAlister and Carr, 2014: 250). As the authors note, this is paradoxical in two senses: firstly, that an ostensible punitive measure is seen as beneficial and a positive experience by young people; and, secondly, that their welfare needs appear to be better met in custody than in the community, at least from their own perspective.

The System and Its Impact

An increasing amount of evidence has been generated on the effect on young people of their youth justice experiences, as expressed in their own words, and it must be observed that this, too, paints a largely negative picture. Some might argue that, as offenders, those subject to court-imposed penalties or constraints should expect to experience some form of punishment, whether in the form of restrictions on their movements in the community, mandatory restitution, or even the loss of liberty. However, it might also be argued that this should not involve additional harm or hardship over and above the specific requirements of the court order, and that it is important in view of this to understand the nature of the experience from the young person's own point of view.

Gyateng and colleagues' (2013) study included an extensive survey of 1,245 young people in various secure settings (Secure Children's Homes (SCHs), Secure Training Centres (STCs) and Young Offender Institutions (YOIs)). The survey formed part of a larger study and was intended to obtain a representative view of the experiences of young people coming towards the end of their sentences, across different institutional environments. The survey obtained some reasonably encouraging findings, with 70% of respondents reporting their relationships with institutional staff as 'positive', for example, although this did vary according to the institution. Most young people thought that they were treated with respect, although '26% felt that most staff did not treat them with respect' (Gyateng et al., 2013: 21).

In terms of general living conditions, the quality of food was considered to be good by 64% of those in SCHs, compared with only 32% in STCs and 22% in YOIs (Gyateng et al., 2013: 23). Most reported that they were able to have regular visits from friends and family, although as many as 16% of those in YOIs reported having no recent visits. The educational experiences reported by young people surveyed were broadly positive, although here Black young people were markedly less satisfied with the provision than those from other ethnic groups (57%, as opposed to 75% of their White peers, for example: Gyateng et al., 2013: 47).

In terms of possible mistreatment, a number of young people did report concerns about the behaviour of staff: 'While most young people reported a positive relationship with staff, a minority (9% in YOIs, 7% in STCs and 8% in SCHs)' said that they had been bullied by a member of staff (Gyateng et al., 2013: 25). The researchers also found that 15% of those in STCs and SCHs, and 12% of those in YOIs reported being bullied by other young people in the institution (Gyateng et al., 2013: 3); and other file-based information suggested that a considerable number were also self-harming whilst in custody. Across all types of institution, there was also considerable evidence of young people reporting that they had been physically 'restrained' by staff at some point (39% in YOIs, 44% in STCs and 53% in SCHs; Gyateng et al., 2013: 32). Restraint techniques are supposedly employed by staff only in circumstances where they are necessary to prevent harm (either to the young person or to someone else), but their use has proved to be controversial, and they have been associated with seriously harmful outcomes themselves (Shenton and Smith, 2021).

More broadly, a substantial number of respondents reported feeling 'low' or 'upset', or needing someone to talk to during their time in custody (29% of those in YOIs, 38% of those in STCs and 41% of SCH residents; Gyateng et al., 2013: 27). This particular study reported this range of survey findings factually, without going on to make detailed recommendations about addressing points of particular concern, and concentrating instead on broad proposals to enhance the quality of custodial regimes. It may be partly because of the nature of the survey method and the context in which it was deployed that serious questions about the negative aspects of custody were not explored in more detail.

Following this early work, further surveys of young people in custody have been undertaken by the prisons inspectorate in England. These, if anything, have revealed a substantially more worrying picture than that of Gyateng and colleagues:

> Children's perceptions of their day-to-day life were particularly concerning. Most did not feel cared for by staff and many spent long hours locked up in their cells, particularly at the weekend. Less than half reported being able to sleep easily, and even fewer felt they were getting enough food. In YOIs, though the proportion had improved from 2018–19, only 68% were able to shower every day. (HM Inspectorate of Prisons, 2021: 4)

Violence, too, seemed to be a prevalent feature of the experience, with 44% of young people surveyed reporting that they had been bullied or victimised whilst in custody (HM Inspectorate of Prisons, 2021: 4).

From the point of arrival, young people seem to have faced challenges with the custodial regime, according to the inspectorate. Whilst 71% reported being treated well at this point, many also referred to problems which had gone unaddressed and a lack of help from staff – only 23% at Feltham YOI reported receiving such help, for example. In YOIs, again, nearly a third of young people reported that they did not have access to sufficient clean, suitable clothing. For a significant number of young people, time out of their cells was severely limited at weekends, according to the report, and in most institutions the quality of the food was rated as less than good by most young people; and in most cases it was also rated as insufficient (HM Inspectorate of Prisons, 2021: 25).

In terms of healthcare, young people consistently reported that it was difficult to get to see a medical professional (doctor, dentist or nurse), and less than two-thirds of those who said they had health problems had received help for these. The Inspectorate also drew attention to the safety of young people in secure settings, identifying that: 'Overall, over a third (35%) of children said that they had, at some point, felt unsafe in their establishment. At the time of the survey 10% said that they were feeling unsafe' (HM Inspectorate of Prisons, 2021: 34). At the same time, only just over half of those surveyed were able to say that they had not been 'victimised' by other children whilst in custody. A similar proportion reported that they had not experienced victimisation by staff, although this still means that nearly half of those responding may have experienced oppressive behaviour or bullying by those responsible for caring for them. Around two-thirds of respondents reported that they had been physically 'restrained' at some point by staff, and a similar number had been subject to some form of punishment in the form of being isolated from other children. Perhaps partly as a result:

> Overall, only around two in five (41%) of children reported that they felt cared for by most staff in their establishment. Children from black and minority ethnic backgrounds were significantly less likely than children from white backgrounds to report this (36% compared to 48%). (HM Inspectorate of Prisons, 2021: 42)

Other studies of young people's experiences of secure settings within the justice system have employed different methods; as a result they have been able to gain more substantial insights into young people's experiences, as expressed in their own words. Lyon and Wilson (2000), for example, were provided with the opportunity by the Home Office to carry out focus groups with 84 young people in custody (aged 15–21), across a number of prison establishments.

For these young people, the custodial establishment was an extension of a system which was hostile and demeaning. They spoke of 'hassle', violence and racism on the part of police (Lyon and Wilson, 2000: 21), and this formed the backdrop to their experiences of custody. Whilst some spoke of staff who were 'straightforward' or 'safe', most were critical of the way they were treated: 'they come here and suddenly they're working with a load of kids that they can shout at and they talk down to you ...' (quoted in Lyon and Wilson, 2000: x). Here, the sense of a pervasive lack of respect on the part of staff also feels much more similar to the findings of the prisons inspectorate than those of Gyateng and colleagues.

Some aspects of the custodial experience were viewed quite positively, including the educational provision: 'they treat you like you're in college' rather than as a prisoner, according to one young woman (Lyon and Wilson, 2000: 38). Here, some at least valued being treated as learners and the opportunities provided to gain qualifications. On the other hand, they spoke in very negative terms about other aspects of the regime. They spoke about the lack of someone to talk to about their problems, and the indifference of staff to bullying: 'I've seen people get bullied bad and nothing happens about it, when the screws blatantly know about it' (quoted in Lyon and Wilson, 2000: 47). Indeed, for one young person, it was the staff who were the bullies: 'It's the screws that are bullying you, that's what I think' (quoted in Lyon and Wilson, 2000: 47). Further still, a number of young Black people spoke of their experiences of racism from staff.

These aspects of custody appear to reflect a broader ethos of disrespect and mistrust: 'Some of them just have bad attitudes and you're asking them things and they ... just speak down to you' (quoted in Lyon and Wilson, 2000: 34). The overuse of staff power also seems to be a matter of concern in specific contexts, such as the use of 'restraint'; that is, the exercise of physical power to restrict a young person's movements, supposedly in situations where someone (the young person, another young person or a member of staff) is at risk of being harmed (Shenton and Smith, 2021). Young people comment on the 'normality' of staff use of force to exercise control, and of situations where the staff reaction to young people's behaviour is seen as excessive:

> You can get restrained for fighting, shouting at staff, swearing, breaking stuff, getting in their face. It happens a few times a day somewhere like *** YOI, maybe 10 times a day is normal. (Ian, quoted in Shenton and Smith, 2021: 167)

The rather pessimistic conclusion to be drawn from this array of evidence is that young people's experience of youth justice processes, disposals and institutions is predominantly negative; and there are serious concerns about the standard of their treatment across the range of settings they experience. As is the case in other contexts, this pattern is skewed, with young people from ethnic minorities, and young Black people in particular, often being reported as experiencing worse treatment in one way or another.

Young people, participation, co-production and youth justice

> Traditional youth justice interventions and support have been described as something that is done to a child or young person, rather than with them .... Participation, on the other hand, seeks to put the child at the centre of structures that support them to express their opinion, to articulate beliefs and – should they wish – influence decisions. (CYCJ, 2021; www.cycj.org.uk/wp-content/uploads/2021/06/Section-15.pdf)

The consistent messages about young people's negative experiences of youth justice systems may be partly responsible for an emerging interest in hearing more from the perspective of children and young people, and encouraging a much more participatory approach. This development perhaps also reflects a wider interest in promoting children's **participation**, and active engagement in shaping key aspects of their own lives. Jans (2004), for example, has described the impact of changing notions of citizenship on our understanding of children's rights: 'The late modern condition allows children increasingly to present themselves as social actors, within as well as outside the family' (Jans, 2004: 40). Thus, children should not just be viewed as the objects of care or protection, or as passive recipients of knowledge or instruction, but rather as active players in the project of making sense of the social world and influencing its design and construction. As this kind of idea has taken hold, it has of course prompted us to consider the place children should play in this process. How should they be involved in designing education programmes, for example? How should they be informed and enabled to take part in decisions about healthcare and treatment? What part should they play in local and national democratic processes? And of course, what is their role in shaping criminal justice interventions and practices?

Exploration of these questions has resulted in a degree of frustration from the perspective of those who believe that progress in implementing children's rights has not been fast enough (for example, Larsson et al., 2018), and that adult 'systems' have persistently resisted change (Percy-Smith and Thomas, 2010). Nonetheless, a number of recent developments within youth justice appear to suggest that there has been increasing recognition of the value of participatory approaches. Several studies and reports have focused more directly on young people's expectations and hopes for what youth justice interventions might offer to them. In an overview of what children wanted in respect of participation in youth justice, Hart and Thompson (2009) have summarised these as follows, for example:

- 'Give me more opportunities to choose what I do rather than just talking about my week.'
- 'Choose what days and times I come in.'
- 'Have more of a say in the activities I do.' ...
- 'I'd like them to come to my house sometimes, rather than me going to them all the time.'
- 'I'd like some optional activities that won't result in me being breached if I don't come.'.... (Hart and Thompson, 2009: 24)

Although each of these requests may seem relatively straightforward in isolation, overall we gain a sense of young people's frustrations at being unable to influence agencies or practitioners; or to achieve what to them would be more meaningful engagement with the supervision process.

In Greater Manchester, an extensive programme of work has explored the potential for innovation in involving children and young people more extensively in service design and delivery. The Greater Manchester Youth Justice University Partnership was established in 2014 – its membership comprising Manchester Metropolitan University, the Youth Justice Board and the region's ten youth justice services – and its work has led to the establishment of 'a new framework for youth justice called Participatory Youth Practice'. Its core principles are outlined in the Box below:

Participatory Youth Practice

Participatory Youth Practice (PYP) is based on a set of *eight theoretically framed principles* for youth justice practice that were co-created with young people.

These are...

1. Let them participate;
2. Always unpick why;
3. Acknowledge limited life chances;
4. Try to avoid threats and sanctions;
5. Help problem solve;
6. Help them find better options;
7. Develop their ambitions;
8. Remember that ultimately, it's their choice.

For further information on these principles and their application in practice see: www.mmu.ac.uk/mcys/gmyjup/

Importantly, the Greater Manchester Partnership has gone beyond stating principles prescriptively from the outside, and instead bases them on an extended participatory project with young people already involved with the youth justice system. These principles are thus based on their experiences and aspirations. The criminogenic nature of the social context and the justice process itself thus becomes a focal point for intervention, for example. Although changes are relatively limited in scope, the collaborative nature of the partnership has led to practice developments:

> [W]e are seeing some concrete examples of PYP being embedded into practice. For example, when overseeing young people's cases, one team has replaced a set of questions addressing risk with the PYP principles, while another has integrated the principles into their supervision sessions with young people. Through the creation of 'working groups' with young people, one of the teams has even facilitated the participation of young people in decision-making about the development and delivery of new initiatives and programmes. (Smithson et al., 2020: 14)

This approach is said to have become central to local policy and practice:

> PYP has been embedded into the strategic plans of the majority of the Greater Manchester YOTs, resulting in it becoming 'hard-wired' into youth justice service provision. (Smithson and Gray, 2021: 10)

Participatory approaches in youth justice have also been documented in Wales, with young people being actively involved in service design, recruitment of staff, advising local youth justice partnerships and providing views and feedback through the use of online tools (Nacro Cymru, 2009). In this context, the importance of a broad-based approach is emphasised, so that both individual and collective views can be integrated into the design and delivery of services (Nacro Cymru, 2009: 8). In Scotland, participation in youth justice has been encouraged through a number of routes, including the establishment of the Youth Justice Voices Newsletter (see, for example, www.staf.scot/youth-justice-voices-newsletter-issue-one), which provides a platform for young people to air their views and seek to influence service delivery. Thus, a request for better provision on release from custody can be aired directly; 'I think the staff at the homeless place I got out could have helped me better. Told me I would have a house in couple a months and was in there six months then not got one offer' (quoted in Issue 1 of the newsletter).

The Howard League's UR Boss project was a similar initiative, which enabled a group of young people with experience of the criminal justice system to represent their own and other young people's views publicly. The establishment of an effective group of young advisors familiar with the realities of youth justice and its institutions meant that a series of campaigns were able to have an effective impact, contributing, for example, to the ending of strip searching on arrival at Young Offender Institutions (Fleming et al., 2014: 66). By enabling young people to speak directly with professionals about practice, UR Boss also appeared to be influential in helping to change the prevailing culture and reinforcing recognition of the value of the young person's voice (Fleming et al., 2014: 67).

On a wider scale, Defence for Children International (2016) has articulated the importance of children's participation in youth justice, particularly in light of Article 12 of the UN Convention on the Rights of the Child (the right to be heard). Here, too, young people's views reflect the lack of choice and their feelings that they are treated without respect:

> I would like them to listen to us more when we propose ideas, e.g. do sports outside and not inside the building when it is hot. (Child in a Belgian detention centre, Defence for Children International, 2016: 42)

In fact, there does seem to be a degree of tension between the increasingly common references to children and young people's participation in youth justice processes affecting them and the extent to which this is reflected in any meaningful sense in everyday practice. Rap (2016), for example, highlights the very limited opportunities for young people to participate effectively in formal hearings, citing only the Scottish children's hearings and Swiss juvenile justice models as affording such opportunities. By contrast, Rap (2016: 108) suggests, the youth courts in Spain and in England and Wales provide very little room for young people to be heard.

So, it seems, where there is scope for young people to have a say in relation to the youth justice system, this tends to apply more to consultative mechanisms and discussions taking place at strategic and policy levels. Here, there has been some movement towards facilitating participatory activities, whether through the work of non-governmental organisations (Defence for Children International, the Howard League), or partnership activities (Greater Manchester). More emphasis has been placed on promoting participation, too, as a result of academic debate and research (for example, Smithson et al., 2020). It is less clear, however, that these moves have achieved a consistent or sustainable measure of change in practice settings, where young people experience youth justice interventions, and where they have consistently provided evidence of negative and sometimes harmful treatment (HM Inspectorate of Prisons, 2021). There seems to be something of a disconnect between *hearing* children's voices on the one hand, and *acting* on what they say, on the other.

Conclusion: Are We Listening to Children and Young People in the Youth Justice System?

In this final chapter, we have tried to present a picture of youth crime and youth justice from the point of view of children and young people themselves. To do so, we have included autobiographical accounts, and young people's voices, alongside more formal academic studies, and inquiries by agencies such as the various justice inspectorates. These studies have often involved researchers 'immersing' themselves in the world of the young people concerned, undertaking ethnographic investigations to try to capture a sense of what it is like to live and act in settings which bring them into contact with the justice system. Other approaches have used interviews and similar methods to explore the lives and experiences of young people in particular contexts, such as custodial institutions.

Whilst it is perhaps unhelpful to over-generalise, we might be able to offer some impressions at least of what these accounts seem to tell us. Firstly, there is a sense in which casual involvement in unlawful activities appears to be a relatively 'normal' feature of many young people's lives; although at the same time, they probably do not see themselves as criminals, or significantly different from the rest of society. In addition, conflict with the law may be viewed as an unwelcome, but not entirely unexpected, feature of one's lifestyle; and something that just has to be borne as a hazard of adolescence. In this context, young people appear to understand and accept the 'rules of the game', whilst also taking exception to agencies and criminal justice personnel who act unfairly or oppressively.

For those who do become much more closely embroiled in the justice system and its processes, this issue becomes more acute. Young people have a distinct sense of what is acceptable and unacceptable behaviour on the part of police, courts and other staff; and, for many, their experience is predominantly of the misuse of power, alongside unreasonable conditions. This perception is supported by the evidence gathered through both academic studies, and inspection reports, so it is more than just a reflection of the pains of punishment.

This generally negative picture of young people's experience of the justice system appears to have prompted a growing interest in the preservation of their rights *within* the system, and, alongside this, the development of participatory approaches, grounded in the principle that children and young people should be heard and taken seriously, whatever their current circumstances, and whatever they may have done previously. Whilst it is the case that this kind of initiative has only had a limited effect on the way in which the youth justice system operates to this point, the emphasis on children's rights does seem to be assuming more prominence, even in the pronouncements of policy-makers and key agencies, such as the Youth Justice Board.

Further Reading

Parker, H. (1980) *A View From the Boys*. Newton Abbott: David & Charles.

An important and ground-breaking study (at the time), based on a concentrated period of research, undertaken alongside a group of young people who were involved in a variety of criminal activities, and giving a direct account of their experiences and attitudes towards offending.

Smithson, H., Gray, P. and Jones, A. (2021) 'They Really Should Start Listening to You': The Benefits and Challenges of Co-Producing a Participatory Framework of Youth Justice Practice.' *Youth Justice*, 21, 3: 321–337.

A significant article which summarises the 'benefits and challenges' of seeking to introduce participatory principles and children's voices in a youth justice context.

References

Abdullahi, A., Khan, M. and Abdulrahman, A. (2016) 'A Review of Youth Violence Theories: Developing Interventions to Promote Sustainable Peace in Ilorin, Nigeria.' *African Sociological Review*, 20, 2: 40–60.

Abrams, L.S., Jordan, S.P. and Montero, L.A. (2018) 'What is a Juvenile? A Cross-National Comparison of Youth Justice Systems.' *Youth Justice*, 18, 2: 111–130.

Adshead, G., Brodrick, P., Preston, J. and Mayura, D. (2012) 'Personality Disorder in Adolescence.' *Advances in Psychiatric Treatment*, 18: 109–118.

Agnew, R. (1985) 'A Revised Strain Theory of Delinquency'. *Social Forces*, 64, 1: 151–167.

Agnew, R. (2016) 'Race and Youth Crime: Why Isn't the Relationship Stronger?' *Race and Justice*, 6, 3: 195–221.

Aizer, A. and Doyle, J. (2015) 'Juvenile Incarceration, Human Capital, and Future Crime: Evidence from Randomly Assigned Judges.' *Quarterly Journal of Economics*, 130, 2: 759–803.

Albrecht, A. (1910) 'Cesare Lombroso.' *Journal of Criminal Law and Criminology*, 1, 2: 71–83.

Alexander, M. (2010) *The New Jim Crow: Mass Incarceration in the Age of Colorblindness*. New York: New Press.

Almond, T. (2012) 'Asset: An Assessment Tool that Safeguards or Stigmatizes Young Offenders?' *Probation Journal*, 59, 2: 138–150.

Anderson, E. (1999) *Code of the Street*. New York: Norton.

Anderson, F., Worsley, R., Nunney, F., Maybanks, N. and Dawes, W. (2010) *Youth Survey 2009*. London: Youth Justice Board.

Ariès, P. (1962) *Centuries of Childhood*. New York: Vintage.

Armitage, V., Kelly, L. and Phoenix, J. (2016) 'Janus-faced Youth Justice Work and the Transformation of Accountability.' *Howard Journal of Crime and Justice*, 55, 4: 478–495.

Arncz, J. and Condry, R. (2021) 'Criminological Perspectives on School Exclusion and Youth Offending.' *Emotional and Behavioural Difficulties*, 26, 1: 87–100.

Aspinall, P.J. (2020) 'Ethnic/Racial Terminology as a Form of Representation: A Critical Review of the Lexicon of Collective and Specific Use of the Terms in Use in Britain.' *Genealogy*, 4, 3: 87, https://doi.org/10.3390/genealogy4030087

Baglivio, M., Epps, N., Swartz, K., Sayedul Huq, M., Sheer, A. and Hardt, N. (2014) 'The Prevalence of Adverse Childhood Experiences (ACE) in the Lives of Juvenile Offenders.' *Journal of Juvenile Justice*, 3, 2: 1–23.

Baglivio, M., Woolf, K.T., Piquero, A.R. and Epps, N. (2015) 'The Relationship between Adverse Childhood Experiences (ACE) and Juvenile Offending Trajectories in a Juvenile Offender Sample.' *Journal of Criminal Justice*, 43: 229–241.

Baier, D., Hanslmaier, M. and Kemme, S. (2016) 'Public Perceptions of Crime.' In D. Baier and C. Pfeiffer (Eds.), *Representative Studies on Victimisation*. Baden-Baden: Nomos (pp. 39–64).

Baker, K., Jones, S., Roberts, C. and Merrington, S. (2003) *Validity and Reliability of Asset*. London: Youth Justice Board.

Baldry, E., Briggs, D.E., Goldson, B. and Russell, S. (2018) '"Cruel and Unusual Punishment": An Inter-jurisdictional Study of the Criminalisation of Young People with Complex Support Needs.' *Journal of Youth Studies*, 21, 5: 636–652.

Bandura, A. (1969) 'Social Learning of Moral Judgments.' *Journal of Personality and Social Psychology*, 11, 3: 275–279.

Barkan, S. and Rocque, M. (2018) 'Socioeconomic Status and Racism as Fundamental Causes of Street Criminality.' *Critical Criminology*, 26: 211–231.

Barker, V. (2013) 'Nordic Exceptionalism Revisited: Explaining the Paradox of a Janus-faced Penal Regime.' *Theoretical Criminology*, 17, 1: 5–25.

Barn, R. and Tan, J.P. (2012) 'Foster Youth and Crime: Employing General Strain Theory to Promote Understanding.' *Journal of Criminal Justice*, 40, 3: 212–220.

Batchelor, S. (2005) '"Prove Me the Bam!": Victimization and Agency in the Lives of Young Women Who Commit Violent Offences.' *Probation Journal*, 52, 4: 358–375

Bateman, T. (2011a) '"We Now Breach More Kids in a Week than We Used to in a Whole Year": The Punitive Turn, Enforcement and Custody.' *Youth Justice*, 11, 2: 115–133.

Bateman, T. (2011b) 'Punishing Poverty: The "Scaled Approach" and Youth Justice Practice.' *The Howard Journal of Criminal Justice*, 50, 2: 171–183.

Bateman, T. (2012) 'Who Pulled the Plug? Towards an Explanation of the Fall in Child Imprisonment in England and Wales.' *Youth Justice*, 12: 36–52.

Bateman, T. (2014) 'Where Has All the Youth Crime Gone? Youth Justice in an Age of Austerity.' *Children and Society*, 28, 5: 416–424.

Bateman, T. (2015) *The State of Youth Justice 2015: An Overview of Trends and Developments*. https://thenayj.org.uk/wp-content/uploads/2015/10/State-of-Youth-Justice-Oct15.pdf

Bateman, T. (2017) *The State of Youth Justice 2017: An Overview of Trends and Developments*. https://core.ac.uk/download/pdf/130975212.pdf

Bateman, T. (2020) *The State of Youth Justice 2020: An Overview of Trends and Developments*. National Association for Youth Justice. https://thenayj.org.uk/cmsAdmin/uploads/state-of-youth-justice-2020-final-sep20.pdf

Bazemore, G. and Schiff, M. (Eds.) (2001) *Restorative Community Justice: Repairing Harm and Transforming Communities*. Cincinatti, OH: Anderson Publishing Co.

Beck, U. (2002) 'The Terrorist Threat: World Risk Society Revisited.' *Theory, Culture and Society*, 19, 4: 39–55.

Becker, H. (1963) *Outsiders: Studies in the Sociology of Deviance*. New York: Free Press.

Bellis, M.A., Lowey, H., Leckenby, N., Hughes, K. and Harrison, D. (2014) 'Adverse Childhood Experiences: Retrospective Study to Determine their Impact on Adult Health Behaviors and Health Outcomes in a UK Population.' *Journal of Public Health*, 36: 81–91.

Belson, W.A. (1975) *Juvenile Theft: The Causal Factors*. London: Harper and Row.

Benekos, P. and Merlo, A. (2015) 'Juvenile Justice in the United States.' In J. Winterdyk (Ed.), *Juvenile Justice: International Perspectives, Models, and Trends*. Boca Raton, FL: CRC Press (pp. 369–394).

Berkoff, S. (2010) *Diary of a Juvenile Delinquent*. London: JR Books.

Berridge, D., Brodie, I., Pitts, J., Porteous, D. and Tarling, R. (2001) *The Independent Effects of Permanent Exclusion from School on the Offending Careers of Young People*. London: Home Office.

Bevan, M. (2016) 'Investigating Young People's Awareness and Understanding of the Criminal Justice System: An Exploratory Study'. https://howardleague.org/wp-content/uploads/2016/06/Investigating-young-people%E2%80%99s-awareness-and-understanding-of-the-criminal-justice-system.pdf

Bevan, M. (2019) 'Children and Young People in Police Custody.' PhD thesis, London School of Economics.

Beyleveld, D. and Wiles, P. (1975) 'Man and Method in David Matza's "Becoming Deviant".' *British Journal of Criminology*, 15, 2: 111–127.

Blakemore, S-J. (2018) *Inventing Ourselves: The Secret Life of the Teenage Brain*. London: Doubleday.

Blakemore, S-J. and Robbins, T. (2012) 'Decision-making in the Adolescent Brain.' *Nature Neuroscience*, 15, 9: 1184–1191.

Boeck, T. and Fleming, J. (2011) 'The Role of Social Capital and Resources in Resilience to Risk.' In H. Kemshall and B. Wilkinson (Eds.), *Good Practice in Assessing Risk: Current Knowledge, Issues and Approaches*. London: Jessica Kingsley (pp. 48–65).

Bogdanor, V. (2019) *Beyond Brexit: Britain's Unprotected Constitution*. London: Bloomsbury Publishing Company.

Botley, M., Jinks, B. and Metson, C. (2010) *Young People's Views and Experiences of the Youth Justice System*. Leeds: Children's Workforce Development Council.

Bourdieu, P. (1990) *The Logic of Practice*. Stanford: Stanford University Press.

Braithwaite, J. (1989) *Crime, Shame and Reintegration*. Cambridge: Cambridge University Press.

Braithwaite, J. (2000) 'Shame and criminal justice.' *Canadian Journal of Criminology*, 42, 3: 281–298.

Branson, C.E., Baetz, C.L., McCue Horwitz, S. and Hoagwood, E. (2017) 'Trauma-Informed Juvenile Justice Systems: A Systematic Review of Definitions and Core Components.' *Psychological Trauma: Theory, Research, Practice and Policy*, 9, 6: 635–646.

Brewster, D. and Jones, R. (2019) 'Distinctly Divergent or Hanging onto English Coat-tails? Drug Policy in Post-devolution Wales.' *Criminology and Criminal Justice*, 19, 3: 364–381.

Brown, A. and Charles, A. (2021) 'The Minimum Age of Criminal Responsibility: The Need for a Holistic Approach.' *Youth Justice*, 21, 2: 153–171.

Brown, S.A. (2012) *Trends in Juvenile Justice State Legislation 2001–2011*. Washington, DC: US Department of Justice. Available at: www.ojp.gov/ncjrs/virtual-library/abstracts/trends-juvenile-justice-state-legislation-2001-2011

Brown, S. and Stillington, A. (2017) 'Childhood adversity and the risk of substance use and delinquency: The role of protective adult relationships.' *Child Abuse and Neglect*, 63: 211–221.

Brown, T. (2020) *Northern Ireland Youth Justice Agency Annual Workload Statistics 2019/20*. Belfast: NISRA/DoJ.

Bruce, S. and Yearley, S. (2006) *The Sage Dictionary of Sociology*. London: Sage Publications.

Brynner, J. and Parsons, S. (2002) 'Social Exclusion and the Transition from School to Work: The Case of Young People Not in Education, Employment, or Training (NEET).' *Journal of Vocational Behavior*, 60, 2: 289–309.

Burman, M. and Batchelor, S.A. (2009) 'Between Two Stools? Responding to Young Women Who Offend.' *Youth Justice*, 9, 3: 270–285.

Bywaters, P., Brady, G., Sparks, T. and Bos, E. (2014) 'Child Welfare Inequalities: New Evidence, Further Questions.' *Child & Family Social Work*, 21, 3: 369–380.

Bywaters, P., Brady, G., Sparks, T. and Bos, E. (2016) 'Inequalities in Child Welfare Intervention Rates: The Intersection of Deprivation and Identity.' *Child & Family Social Work*, 21, 4: 452–463.

Bywaters, P., Brady, G., Bunting, L., Daniel, B., Featherstone, B., Jones, C., Morris, K., Scourfield, J., Sparks, T. and Webb, C. (2018) 'Inequalities in English Child Protection Practice under Austerity. A Universal Challenge?' *Child & Family Social Work*, 23, 1: 53–61.

Cavalcanti, R. (2020) *A Southern Criminology of Violence, Youth and Policing: Governing Insecurity in Urban Brazil*. London: Routledge.

Caplan, N. (1965) 'Intellectual Functioning.' In H. Quay (Ed.), *Juvenile Delinquency*. Princeton, NJ: Van Nostrand (pp. 100–138).

Carlen, P. (1998) *Women, Crime and Poverty*. Milton Keynes: Open University Press.

Carnie, J. and Broderick, R. (2019) *Prison Survey*. Scottish Prison Service. Available at: www.sps.gov.uk/Corporate/Publications/Publication-7196.aspx

Carr, N. (2014) 'Invisible From View: Leaving and Aftercare Provision in the Republic of Ireland.' *Australian Social Work*, 67, 1: 88–101.

Carr, N. and Mayock, P. (2019) *Care and Justice – Children and Young People in Care and Contact with the Criminal Justice System*. Dublin: IPRT.

Carr, N. and McAlister, S. (2016) 'The Double-Bind – Looked After Children, Care Leavers and Criminal Justice.' In P. Mendes and P. Snow (Eds.), *Young People Transitioning from Care: International Research, Policy and Practice*. Basingstoke: Palgrave.

Carr, N. and McAlister, S. (2021) *Tracing the Review: Developments in Youth Justice in Northern Ireland 2011–2021*. Belfast: Children's Law Centre, Include Youth, NIACRO, VOYPIC.

Carrington, K., and Hogg, R. (2017). 'Deconstructing Criminology's Origin Stories: A View from the Global South.' *Asian Journal of Criminology*, 12: 181–197.

Carrington, K., Hogg, R. and Sozzo, M. (2016) 'Southern Criminology.' *British Journal of Criminology*, 56, 1: 1–20.

Case, S. (2007) 'Questioning the "Evidence" of Risk that Underpins Evidence-led Youth Justice Interventions.' *Youth Justice*, 7, 2: 91–105.

Case, S. and Browning, A. (2021) *Child First Justice: The Research Evidence-Base*. Available at: https://repository.lboro.ac.uk/articles/report/Child_First_Justice_the_research_evidence-base_Full_report_/14152040

Case, S. and Haines, K. (2015) '*Children First, Offenders Second* Positive Promotion: Reframing the Prevention Debate.' *Youth Justice*, 15, 3: 226–239.

Case, S. and Smith, R. (2021) 'The Life Course of Delinquency: Reflections on the Meaning of Trajectories, Transitions and Turning Points in Youth Justice.' *International Journal of Comparative and Applied Criminal Justice*, 45, 4: 391–404.

Case, S., Clutton, S. and Haines, K. (2005) 'Extending Entitlement: A Welsh Policy for Children.' *Wales Journal of Law and Policy*, 4, 2: 187–202.

Case, S., Drew, J., Hampson, K., Jones, G. and Kennedy, D. (2020) 'Professional Perspectives of Youth Justice Policy Implementation: Contextual and Coalface Challenges.' *The Howard Journal*, 59, 2: 214–232.

Case, S., Johnson, P., Manlow, D., Smith, R. and Williams, K. (2017) *Criminology*. Oxford: Oxford University Press.

Catalano, R. and Hawkins, J. (1996) 'The Social Development Model: A Theory of Antisocial Behavior.' In J. Hawkins (Ed.), *Delinquency and Crime: Current Theories*. Cambridge: Cambridge University Press (pp. 149–197).

Cavadino, M. and Dignan, J. (2006a) *Penal Systems: A Comparative Approach*. London: Sage.

Cavadino, M. and Dignan, J. (2006b) 'Penal Policy and Political Economy.' *Criminology and Criminal Justice*, 6, 4: 435–456.

Centre for Justice Innovation (2019) 'Young People's Voices on Youth Court.' *Briefing Paper*. Available at: https://justiceinnovation.org/publications/young-peoples-voices-youth-court

Chadee, D. (2001) 'Fear of Crime and the Media: From Perceptions to Reality.' *Criminal Justice Matters*, 43, 1: 10–11.

Cheely, C., Carpenter, L., Letourneau, E., Nicholas, J., Charles, J. and King, L. (2012) 'The Prevalence of Youth with Autism Spectrum Disorders in the Criminal Justice System.' *Journal of Autism and Developmental Disorders*, 42: 1856–1862.

Chesney-Lind, M. and Irwin, K. (2008) *Beyond Bad Girls: Gender, Violence and Hype*. New York: Routledge.

Children's Commissioner (2022) *Strip Search of Children by the Metropolitan Police Service – New Analysis by the Children's Commissioner for England*. London: Children's Commissioner.

Christiansen, K. (1977) 'Preliminary Study of Criminality among Twins.' In S. Mednick and K. Christiansen (Eds.), *Biosocial Bases of Criminal Behaviour*. New York: Gardner Press (pp. 89–108).

Ciprani, D. (2009/2016) *Children's Rights and the Minimum Age of Criminal Responsibility: A Global Perspective*. London: Routledge.

Cleghorn, N., Kinsella, R. and Nicholls, C. (2011) *Engaging with the Views of Young People with Experience of the Youth Justice System*. London: National Centre for Social Research.

Clear, T.R. (2009) *Imprisoning Communities: How Mass Incarceration Makes Disadvantaged Neighborhoods Worse*. Oxford: Oxford University Press.

Cohen, A.C. (1955) *Delinquent Boys: The Culture of the Gang*. London: Routledge & Kegan Paul.

Cohen, L.E. and Felson, M. (1979) 'Social Change and Crime Rate Trends: A Routine Activity Approach.' *American Sociological Review*, 44, 4: 588–608.

Coles, E., Cheyne, H., Rankin, J. and Daniel, B. (2016) 'Getting it Right for Every Child: A National Policy Framework to Promote Children's Well-being in Scotland, United Kingdom.' *The Millbank Quarterly*, 94, 2: 334–365.

Commission on Justice in Wales (2019) *Justice in Wales for the People of Wales, October 2019*. Cardiff: The Commission on Justice in Wales.

Committee on the Rights of the Child (2007) *General Comment No. 10: Children's Rights in Juvenile Justice*. CRC/C/GC/10 25 April 2007. Geneva: UNCRC.

Committee on the Rights of the Child (2016) Concluding observations on the fifth periodic report of the United Kingdom of Great Britain and Northern Ireland. Available at: https://crae.org.uk/publications-and-resources/un-crc-committees-concluding-observations-2016

Committee on the Rights of the Child (2018) *Draft Revised General Comment No. 10, 2007*. Available at: https://www.ohchr.org/EN/HRBodies/CRC/Pages/DraftGC10.aspx

Connell, R. (2007) *Southern Theory: The Global Dynamics of Knowledge in Social Science*. London: Wiley.

Cooper, A., Swartz, S. and Mahali, A. (2019) 'Disentangled, decentred and democratised: Youth Studies for the global South.' *Journal of Youth Studies*, 22, 1: 29–45.

Council of Europe (2015) *Guidelines of the Committee of Ministers of the Council of Europe on Child-Friendly Justice*. Strasbourg: Council of Europe.

Courtney, M.E., Dworsky, A., Brown, A., Cary, C., Love, K. and Vorhies, V. (2011) *Midwest Evaluation of the Adult Functioning of Former Foster Youth: Outcomes at Age 26*. Chicago: Chapin Hall, University of Chicago.

Courtney, M.E., Hook, J.L. and Lee, J.S. (2010) *Distinct Subgroups of Former Foster Youth During Young Adulthood: Implications for Policy and Practice*. Chicago, IL: Chapin Hall Center for Children at the University of Chicago.

Cox, A. (2013) 'New Visions of Social Control? Young People's Perceptions of Community Penalties.' *Journal of Youth Studies*, 16, 1: 135–150.

Cox, A. (2021) 'The New Economy and Youth Justice.' *Youth Justice*, 21, 1: 107–126.

Cox, A. and Abrams, L. (Eds.) (2021) *The Palgrave International Handbook of Youth Imprisonment*. London: Palgrave Macmillan.

Cox, P. and Shore, H. (Eds.) (2002) *Becoming Delinquent: British and European Youth, 1650-1950*. London: Routledge.

CPT (Committee for the Prevention of Torture and Inhuman and Degrading Treatment (2020) Report to the United Kingdom Government on the visit to the United Kingdom carried out by the European Committee for the Prevention of Torture and Inhuman or Degrading Treatment or Punishment (CPT) from 13 to 23 May 2019. CPT/Inf (2020) 18. Strasbourg: Council of Europe.

Craig, J., Piquero, A., Farringdon, D. and Ttofi, M. (2017) 'A Little Early Risk Goes a Long Bad Way: Adverse Childhood Experiences and Life-course Offending in the Cambridge Study.' *Journal of Criminal Justice*, 53: 34–45.

Criminal Justice Review Group (CRG) (2000) *Review of the Criminal Justice System in Northern Ireland*. Belfast: HMSO.

Croall, H. (2006) 'Criminal Justice in Post-Devolutionary Scotland.' *Critical Social Policy*, 26, 3: 587–607.

Cullen, F., Gendreau, P. and Wright, J. (1997) 'Crime and the Bell Curve: Lessons from Intelligent Criminology.' *Crime & Delinquency*, 43, 4: 387–411.

Cunneen, C. (2007) 'Crime, Justice and Indigenous People.' In E. Barclay, J. Donnermeyer, J. Scott and R. Hogg (Eds.), *Crime in Rural Australia*. Leichardt: Federation Press: 142–153.

Cunneen, C. and Tauri, J. (2019) 'Indigenous Peoples, Criminology, and Criminal Justice.' *Annual Review of Criminology*, 2: 359–381.

Cunneen, C., Goldson, B. and Russell, S. (2016) 'Juvenile Justice, Young People and Human Rights in Australia.' *Current Issues in Criminal Justice*, 28, 2: 173–189.

Cusick, G.R., Havlicek, J.R. and Courtney, M.E. (2012) 'Risk for Arrest: The Role of Social Bonds in Protecting Foster Youth Making the Transition to Adulthood.' *American Journal of Orthopsychiatry*, 82, 1: 19–31.

CYCJ (Children and Young People's Centre for Justice) (2021) 'A Guide to Youth Justice in Scotland: Policy, Practice and Legislation.' Strathclyde University. Available at: https://cycj.org.uk/wp-content/uploads/2021/06/Section-15.pdf

CYCJ (Children and Young People's Centre for Justice) (2022) *Children and Young People in Conflict with the Law: Policy, Practice and Legislation*. Available at: https://www.cycj.org.uk/wp-content/uploads/2022/06/Section-1.pdf

Davis, B. and Dossetor, K. (2010) '(Mis)perceptions of Crime in Australia.' *Trends & Issues in Crime and Criminal Justice*, 396: 1–6.

Day, A. (2022) '"It's a Hard Balance to Find": The Perspectives of Youth Justice Practitioners in England on the Place of "Risk" in an Emerging "Child-First" World.' *Youth Justice*, doi.org/10.1177/14732254221075205

Defence for Children International (2016) *Children's Right to Participation and the Juvenile Justice System*. Defence for Children International. Available at: https://defenceforchildren.org/wp-content/uploads/2016/03/DCI_-_Twelve_handbook_eng_web.pdf

Delmage, E. (2013) 'The Minimum Age of Criminal Responsibility: A Medico-legal Perspective.' *Youth Justice*, 13, 2: 102–110.

Demie, F. (2021) 'The Experience of Black Caribbean pupils in School Exclusion in England.' *Educational Review*, 73, 1: 55–70.

Devaney, J., Frederick, J. and Spratt, T. (2021) 'Opening the Time Capsule of ACEs: Reflections on How We Conceptualise Children's Experiences of Adversity and the Issue of Temporality.' *British Journal of Social Work*, 51, 6: 2247–2263.

DfE (2012) *A Profile of Pupil Exclusions in England*. London: Department for Education.

Dierkhising, C.B., Ko, S. and Goldman, J.H. (2013). *Trauma-informed Juvenile Justice Roundtable: Current Issues and New Directions in Creatng Trauma-informed Juvenile Justice Systems*. Los Angeles, CA: National Center for Child Traumatic Stress. Available at: www.nctsn.org/resources/topics/juvenile-justice-system

Dillard, D. (2013) 'Limited Disproportionate Minority Contact Discourse May Explain Limited Progress in Reducing Minority Over-representation in the US Juvenile Justice System.' *Youth Justice*, 13, 3: 207–217.

Doak, J. and O'Mahony, D. (2011) 'In Search of Legitimacy, Restorative Youth Conferencing in Northern Ireland.' *Legal Studies*, 31, 2: 175–196.

Dollinger, B., Osawa, S. and Schirmer, S. (2021) 'Constructions of Deviance by Japanese and German Youth: A Criminological Comparison as a "Bottom-Up" Project.' *Youth Justice*, 22, 2: 206–221.

Donnelly, E.A. (2015) 'The Disproportionate Minority Contact Mandate: An Examination of its Impacts on Juvenile Justice Processing Outcomes (1997–2011).' *Criminal Justice Policy Review*, 28, 4: 347–369.

Donofrio, B. (1992) *Riding in Cars with Boys: Confessions of a Bad Girl Who Makes Good*. London: Penguin.

Doob, A., Sprott, J. and Webster, C. (2018) 'Learning from Our Success in Reducing Youth Imprisonment.' *Policy Options*, 10 May. Available at: https://policyoptions.irpp.org/magazines/may-2018/learning-from-our-success-in-reducing-youth-imprisonment/

Downes, D. (1988) *Contrasts in Tolerance: Post-war Penal Policy in the Netherlands and England and Wales*. Oxford: Clarendon Press.

Drakeford, M. (2010) 'Children First, Offenders Second: Youth Justice in a Devolved Wales.' *Criminal Justice Matters*, 78, 1: 8–9.

Drew, V., Wilson, M.L. and McCarter, S.A. (2022) 'The Overcriminalisation of Black Girls: Using an Intersectional Lens to Examine the School-to-Prison Pipeline.' *Critical and Radical Social Work*, 10, 2: 242–259.

Duke, S., Balzer, B. and Steinbeck, K. (2014) 'Testosterone and Its Effects on Human Male Aadolescent mood and Behavior: a Systematic Review.' *Journal of Adolesecent Health*, 55, 3: 315–322.

Dwyer, C. (2007) 'Risk Politics and the "Scientification" of Political Judgment: Prison Release and Conflict Transformation in Northern Ireland.' *British Journal of Criminology*, 47, 5: 779–797.

Edwards, A. and Hughes, G. (2009) 'The Preventive Turn and the Promotion of Safer Communities in England and Wales: Political Inventiveness and Governmental Instabilities.' In A Crawford (Ed.), *Crime Prevention Policies in Comparative Perspective*. London: Willan (pp. 62–85).

Ellem, K. and Richards, K. (2018) 'Police Contact with Young People with Cognitive Disabilities: Perceptions of Procedural (In)justice.' *Youth Justice*, 18, 3: 230–247.

Elliott, D. and Ageton, S. (1980) 'Reconciling Race and Class Differences in Self-Reported and Official Estimates of Delinquency.' *American Sociological Review*, 45, 1: 95–110.

Epstein, R., Blake, J. and González, T. (2017) 'Girlhood Interrupted: The Erasure of Black Girls' Childhood.' Available at SSRN: http://dx.doi.org/10.2139/ssrn.3000695

Erickson, M. (1929) 'A Study of the Relationship Between Intelligence and Crime.' *Journal of Criminal Law and Criminology*, 19, 4: 592–634.

Erikson, E. (1978) *Childhood & Society* (Second Edition). New York: Norton.

Eriksson, A. (2009) *Justice in Transition: Community Restorative Justice in Northern Ireland*. Cullompton: Willan.

Evans, J., Jones, R. and Musgrove, N. (2022) '"Dragonisation" Revisited: A Progressive Criminal Justice Policy in Wales?' *Criminology & Criminal Justice*, 22, 4: 636–653.

Evans, J., Kennedy, D., Skuse, T. and Matthew, J. (2020) 'Trauma-informed Practice and Desistance Theories: Competing or Complementary Approaches to Working with Children in Conflict with the Law?' *Salus Journal*, 8, 2: 55–76.

Eysenck, H. (1964) 'Principles and Methods of Personality Description, Classification and Diagnosis.' *British Journal of Psychology*, 55, 3: 284–294

Fair, H. and Walmsley, R. (2021) *World Prison Population List*. London: World Prison Brief.

Farag, D. (2013) *The Knife Crime Prevention Programme Process Evaluation*. London: Youth Justice Board.

Farrington, D. (1995) 'The challenge of teenage antisocial behavior. In M. Rutter (Ed.), *Psychosocial Disturbances in Young People: Challenges for Prevention*. Cambridge: Cambridge University Press (pp. 83–130).

Farrington, D. (2001) 'What Has Been Learned from Self-Reports about Criminal Careers and the Causes of Offending?' Available at: www.crim.cam.ac.uk/sites/www.crim.cam.ac.uk/files/srdrep.pdf

Farrington, D. and Welsh, B. (2007) Saving Children from a Life of Crime: Early Risk Factors and Effective Interventions. Oxford: Oxford University Press.

Feeley, M. and Simon, J. (1992) 'The New Penology: Notes on the Emerging Strategy of Corrections and its Implications.' *Criminology*, 30, 4: 449–474.

Feld, B.C. (2017) *The Evolution of the Juvenile Court: Race, Politics, and the Criminalizing of Juvenile Justice*. New York: New York University Press.

Felitti, V.J., Anda, R.F., Nordenberg, D., Williamson, D.F., Spitz, A.M., Edwards, V., Koss, M.P. and Marks, J.S. (1998) 'Relationship of Childhood Abuse and Household Dysfunction to Many of the Leading Causes of Death in Adults: The Adverse

Childhood Experiences (ACE) Study.' *American Journal of Preventive Medicine*, 14, 4: 245–258.

Felson, R., Teasdale, B. and Burchfield, K. (2008) 'The Influence of Being under the Influence.' *Journal of Research in Crime and Delinquency*, 45, 2: 119–141.

Field, S. (2007) 'Practice Cultures and the "New" Youth Justice in (England and) Wales.' *British Journal of Criminology*, 47, 2: 311–330.

Field, S. (2011) 'Finding or Imposing Coherence? Comparing National Cultures of Youth Justice.' *Journal of Comparative Law*, 5, 2: 216–231.

Field, S. and Nelken, D. (2007) 'Early Intervention and the Cultures of Youth Justice: A Comparison of Italy and Wales.' In V. Gessner and D. Nelken (Eds.), *European Ways of Law.* Oxford: Hart (pp. 349–373).

Field, S. and Nelken, D. (2010) 'Reading and Writing Youth Justice in Italy and (England and) Wales.' *Punishment & Society*, 12, 3: 287–308.

Fitz-Gibbon, K. (2016) 'Protections for Children before the Law: An Empirical Analysis of the Age of Criminal Responsibility, the Abolition of Doli Incapax and the Merits of a Developmental Immaturity Defence in England and Wales.' *Criminology & Criminal Justice*, 16, 4: 391–409.

Fitzpatrick, C., Hunter, K., Shaw, J. and Staines, J. (2022) *Disrupting the Routes between Care and Custody for Girls and Women.* Policy Briefing. London: Nuffield Foundation.

Fleming, J., Hine, J. and Smith, R. (2014) *Use your Situation to Change your Destination.* London: Howard League.

Flood-Page, C., Campbell, S., Harrington, V. and Miller, J. (2000) *Youth Crime: Findings from the 1998/99 Youth Lifestyles Survey*. London: Home Office.

Franko, K. (2017) 'Criminology, Punishment, and the State in a Globalized Society.' In A. Liebling, S. Maruna and L. McAra (Eds.), *The Oxford Handbook of Criminology* (Sixth Edition). Oxford: Oxford University Press (pp. 353–372).

Fraser, A. (2013) 'Street habitus: gangs, territorialism and social change in Glasgow. *Journal of Youth Studies*, 16, 8: 970–985.

Freng, A. and Esbensen, F-A. (2007) 'Race and Gang Affiliation: An Examination of Multiple Marginality.' *Justice Quarterly*, 24, 4: 600–628.

Friedrichs, D.O. (2011) 'Comparative Criminology and Global Criminology as Complementary Projects.' In D. Nelken (Ed.), *Comparative Criminal Justice and Globalization.* Farnham: Ashgate (pp. 163–181).

Garland, D. (1985) *Punishment and Welfare: A History of Penal Strategies.* Aldershot: Gower.

Garland, D. (2001) *The Culture of Control.* Chicago, University of Chicago Press.

Garland, D. (2013) 'Penality and the Penal State.' *Criminology*, 51, 3: 475–517.

Garry, J., O'Leary, B., McNicholl, K. and Pow, J. (2020) 'The Future of Northern Ireland: Border Anxieties and Support for Irish Reunification under Varieties of UKexit.' *Regional Studies*, DOI: 10.1080/00343404.2020.1759796

Gelsthorpe, L. and Morris, A. (1994) 'Juvenile Justice 1945–1992.' In M. Maguire, R. Morgan and R. Reiner (Eds.), *The Oxford Handbook of Criminology*. Oxford: Oxford University Press (pp. 949–993).

Gelsthorpe, L. and Worrall, A. (2009) 'Looking for Trouble: A Recent History of Girls, Young Women and Youth Justice.' *Youth Justice*, 9, 3: 209–223.

Gesch, B. (2013) 'Adolescence: Does good nutrition = good behaviour?' *Nutritional Health*, 22, 1: 55–65.

Gibson, M. and Rafter, N. (2006) 'Editors' Introduction.' In C. Lombroso [1876] *Criminal Man* (trans M. Gibson and N. Rafter), Durham, NC: Duke University Press (pp. 1–39).

Glass, N. (1999) 'Sure Start: The Development of an Early Intervention Programme for Young Children in the United Kingdom.' *Children & Society*, 13, 4: 257–264.

Glendinning, F., Rodriguez, G.R., Newbury, A. and Wilmot, R. (2021)' Adverse Childhood Experience (ACE) and Trauma-informed Approaches in Youth Justice Services in Wales: An Evaluation of the Implementation of the Enhanced Case Management (ECM) Project.' Wales: Bangor University.

Glueck, S. and Glueck, E. (1934). *Five Hundred Delinquent Women*. New York, Knopf.

Glueck, S. and Glueck, E. (1950) *Unravelling Juvenile Delinquency*. New York: Commonwealth Fund.

Glueck, S. and Glueck, E. (1962) *Family Environment and Delinquency*. New York: Routledge.

Goddard, T. and Myers, R. (2017) Against Evidence-based Oppression: Marginalized Youth and the Politics of Risk-based Assessment and Intervention. *Theoretical Criminology*, 2, 2: 151–167.

Goemann, M. (2018) *New Zealand's Youth Justice Transformation: Lessons for the United States*. Washington, DC: National Juvenile Justice Network.

Gold, M. and Reimer, D. (1975) 'Changing Patterns of Delinquent Behaviour among Americans 13 Through 16 Years Old: 1967–72.' *Crime and Delinquency Literature*, 7: 483–517.

Goldberg, L. (1990) 'An Alternative "Description of Personality": The Big-Five Factor Structure.' *Journal of Personality and Social Psychology*, 59, 6: 1216–1229.

Goldson, B. (2006) 'Damage, Harm and Death in Child Prisons in England and Wales. Questions of Abuse and Accountability.' *The Howard Journal*, 45, 5: 449–467.

Goldson, B. (2009) 'Child Incarceration: Institutional Abuse, the Violent State and the Politics of Impunity.' In P. Scraton and J. McCulloch (Eds.), *The Violence of Incarceration*. London: Routledge (pp. 86–106).

Goldson, B. (2013) '"Unsafe, Unjust and Harmful to Wider Society": Grounds for Raising the Minimum Age of Criminal Responsibility.' *Youth Justice*, 13, 2: 111–130.

Goldson, B. (2020) 'Excavating Youth Justice Reform: Historical Mapping and Speculative Prospects.' *The Howard Journal of Criminal Justice*, 59, 3: 317–334.

Goldson, B. and Briggs, D. (2021) *Making Youth Justice. Local Penal Cultures and Differential Outcomes: Lessons and Prospects for Policy and Practice*. London: Howard League for Penal Reform.

Goldson, B. and Jamieson, J. (2002) 'Youth Crime, the "Parenting Deficit" and State Intervention: A Contextual Critique.' *Youth Justice*, 2, 2: 82–99.

Goldson, B. and Kilkelly, U. (2013) 'International Human Rights Standards and Child Imprisonment: Potentialities and Limitations.' *The International Journal of Children's Rights*, 21, 2: 345–371.

Goldson, B. and Muncie, J. (2015) 'Juvenile Justice: International Law and Children's Rights.' *International Encyclopedia of the Social and Behavioural Sciences* (Second Edition). Oxford: Elsevier (pp. 956–962).

Goldson, B., Cunneen, C., Russell, S., Brown, D., Baldry, E., Schwartz, M and Briggs, D. (2021) *Youth Justice and Penality in Comparative Context*. London: Routledge.

Goldstein, P. (1985) 'The Drugs/Violence Nexus: A Tripartite Conceptual Framework.' *Journal of Drug Issues*, 15, 4: 493–506

Gottfredson, M.R. and Hirschi, T. (1990) *A General Theory of Crime*. Palo Alto, CA: Stanford University Press.

Gould, M. (1999) 'Race and Theory: Culture, Poverty, and Adaptation to Discrimination in Wilson and Ogbu.' *Sociological Theory*, 17, 2: 171–200.

GOV.UK (2022) *Children Looked After in England Including Adoptions. Reporting Year 2021*. Available at: https://explore-education-statistics.service.gov.uk/find-statistics/children-looked-after-in-england-including-adoptions/2022

Graham, J. and Bowling, B. (1995) *Young People and Crime*. London: Home Office.

Graham, I. and Liddicoat, J. (2020) *Youth Engagement Statistics for Northern Ireland April 2019 to March 2020*. Belfast: NISRA and Department of Justice.

Gray, P. (2011) 'Youth Custody, Resettlement and the Right to Social Justice.' *Youth Justice*, 11, 3: 235–249.

Green, D. (2008) *When Children Kill Children: Penal Populism and Political Culture*. Oxford: Oxford University Press.

Greer, A. (2018) 'Brexit and Devolution.' *Political Quarterly*, 89, 1: 134–138.

Grimshaw, R. (Ed.) (2011) *My Story: Young People Talk about the Trauma and Violence in their Lives*. London: Centre for Crime and Justice Studies.

Gyateng, T., Moretti, A., May, T. and Turnbull, P.J. (2013) *Young People and the Secure Estate: Needs and Interventions*. London: Youth Justice Board.

Haines, K. (2010) 'The Dragonization of Youth Justice.' In W. Taylor, R. Earle and R. Hester (Eds.), *Youth Justice Handbook: Theory, Policy and Practice*. London: Routledge (pp. 231–242).

Haines, K. and Case, S. (2008) 'The Rhetoric and Reality of the 'Risk Factor Prevention Paradigm' Approach to Preventing and Reducing Youth Offending.' *Youth Justice*, 8(1), 5–20.

Haines, K. and Case, S. (2015) *Positive Youth Justice*. Bristol: Policy Press.

Haines, K. and Case, S. (2018) 'The Future of Youth Justice.' *Youth Justice*, 18, 2: 131–148.

Haines, K., Case, S., Davies, K. and Charles, A. (2013) 'The Swansea Bureau: A Model of Diversion from the Youth Justice System.' *International Journal of Law, Crime and Justice*, 41: 167–187.

Hall, G. (1904) *Adolescence*. New York: D. Appleton and Co.

Hamilton, C. (2014) 'Reconceptualizing Penality: Towards a Multidimensional Measure of Punitiveness.' *British Journal of Criminology*, 54, 2: 321–343.

Hamilton, C. and Harvey, R. (2004) 'The Role of Public Opinion in the Implementation of International Juvenile Justice Standards.' *The International Journal of Children's Rights*, 11, 4: 369–390.

Hamilton, C., Fitzgibbon, W. and Carr, N. (2016) 'Punishment, Youth Justice and Cultural Contingency: Towards a Balanced Approach.' *Youth Justice*, 16, 3: 226–245.

Harris, M. and Fallott, R.D. (2001) 'Envisioning a Trauma-informed Service System: A Vital Paradigm Shift.' *New Directions for Mental Health Services*, 89: 3–22.

Harris, N. and Maruna, S. (2006) 'Shame, Shaming and Restorative Justice. A Critical Appraisal.' In: D. Sullivan and L. Tifft (Eds.) *Handbook of Restorative Justice*. London: Taylor and Francis (pp. 452–462).

Hart, D. and Thompson, C. (2009) *Young People's Participation in the Youth Justice System*. London: National Children's Bureau.

Haydon, D. and McAlister, S. (2015) 'Young People, Crime and Justice in Northern Ireland.' In A. McAlinden and C. Dwyer (Eds.), *Criminal Justice in Transition: The Northern Ireland Context.* Oxford: Hart Publishing.

Haydon, D. and Scraton, P. (2000) '"Condemn a Little More, Understand a Little Less": The Political Context and Rights Implications of the Domestic and European Rulings in the Venables-Thompson Case.' *Journal of Law and Society*, 27, 3: 416–448.

Hayes, D. (2020) 'MultifunC, Scandinavia: International Focus.' *Children & Young People Now*, 28 January.

Hazel, N. (2006) 'Young Offenders' Perceptions of their Experiences under Police Arrest.' Conference paper, British Society of Criminology, Glasgow, 5 July.

Hazel, N. (2008) *Cross-national Comparison of Youth Justice.* London: Youth Justice Board.

Hazel, N. and Bateman, T. (2020) 'Supporting Children's Resettlement ("Reentry") After Custody: Beyond the Risk Paradigm.' *Youth Justice*, 21, 1: 71–89.

Hendrick, H. (1994) *Child Welfare: England 1872–1989.* London: Routledge.

Hendrick, H. (1997) 'Constructions and Reconstructions of British Childhood: an Interpretative Survey, 1800 to the Present.' In A. James and A. Prout (Eds.) *Constructing and Reconstructing Childhood,* London: Routledge Falmer, (pp. 34–62).

Hendrick, H. (2006) 'Histories of Youth Crime and Justice.' In B. Goldson and J. Muncie (Eds.) *Youth Crime and Justice*, . London: Sage (pp. 3–16).

Henriksen, A. and Prieur, A. (2019) '"So, Why Am I Here?" Ambiguous Practices of Protection, Treatment and Punishment in Danish Secure Institutions.' *British Journal of Criminology,* 59, 5: 1161–1177, doi:10.1093/bjc/azz018

Herrnstein, R. and Murray, C. (1994) *The Bell Curve.* New York: Free Press.

Hertsmere Young Researchers (2011) *Unbalanced Negative Media Portrayal of Youth.* Borehamwood, Hertsmere Borough Council.

Herzog, J. and Schmahl, C. (2018) 'Adverse Childhood Experiences and the Consequences on Neurobiological, Psychosocial, and Somatic Conditions Across the Lifespan.' *Frontiers of Psychiatry*, 9: 420.

Heywood, C. (2001) *A History of Childhood. Children and Childhood in the West from Medieval to Modern Times*. Cambridge: Polity Press.

Hirschfield, A., Christmann, K., Wilcox, A., Rogerson, M. and Sharratt, K. (2012) *Process Evaluation of Preventing Violent Extremism Programmes for Young People*. London: Youth Justice Board.

Hirschi, T. and Hindelang, M. (1977) 'Intelligence and Delinquency: A Revisionist Review.' *American Sociological Review*, 42, 4: 571–587.

Hitchcock, J. (2001) 'Adolescent Gang Participation: Psychological Perspectives.' *Journal of Police and Criminal Psychology*, 16, 2: 33–47.

HM Government (2018) *Serious Violence Strategy.* London: The Stationery Office.

HM Inspectorate of Prisons (2021) *Children in Custody 2019–20*. London: HM Inspectorate of Prisons.

HM Inspectorate of Prisons (2019) *HM Chief Inspector of Prisons for England and Wales Annual Report 2018–19*. London: The Stationery Office.

HMIP/HMICFRS (2018) *Out of Court Disposal Work in Youth Offending Teams*. London: HMIP/HMICFRS.

Hodgson, P. and Webb, D. (2005) 'Young People, Crime and School Exclusion: A Case of Some Surprises.' *The Howard Journal of Criminal Justice* 44, 1: 12–28.

Hollingsworth, K. (2013) 'Theorising Children's Rights in Youth Justice: The Significance of Autonomy and Foundational Rights.' *Modern Law Review*, 76, 6: 1046–1069.

Home Office (1968) *Children in Trouble*. London: Her Majesty's Stationery Office.

Home Office (2022) Anti-social Behaviour, Crime and Policing Act 2014: Anti-social Behaviour Powers Statutory Guidance for Frontline Professionals. (Revised in June 2022). London: Home Office.

House of Commons Joint Committee on Human Rights (2015) *The UK's Compliance with the UN Convention on the Rights of the Child. Eighth Report of Session 2014–15*. London: The Stationery Office.

Howard, M., Dayton, M., Foster, K., Vaughn, M. and Zelner, J. (2006) 'Psychopathy Assessment and Juvenile Justice Mental Health Evaluations.' In N. Dowd, D. Singer and R. Wilson, (Eds.) *Handbook of Children, Culture and Violence*. London: Sage (pp. 395–414).

Howard League for Penal Reform (2016) *Criminal Care: Children's Homes and Criminalising Children*. London: Howard League for Penal Reform.

Howard League for Penal Reform (2018) *Ending the Criminalisation of Children in Residential Care. "This is Our Story": Children and Young People on Criminalisation in Residential Care*. London: Howard League for Penal Reform.

Hughes, T., Raines, T. and Malone, C. (2020) 'School Pathways to the Juvenile Justice System.' *Policy Insights from the Behavioral and Brain Sciences*, 7, 1: 72–79.

Hunter, G., Ely, C., Robin-D'Cruz, C. and Whitehead, S. (2020) *Time to Get It Right: Enhancing Problem-solving Practice in the Youth Court*. London: Institute for Crime and Justice Policy Research.

Indig, D., Vecchatio, C., Haysom, L., Beilby, R., Carter, J., Champion, U., Gaskin, C., Heller, E., Kumar, S., Mamone, N., Muir, P., van den Dolder, P. and Whitton, G. (2011) *2009 NSW Young People in Custody Health Survey: Full Report*. Sydney, NSW: Justice Health and Juvenile Justice.

Jacobson, J. and Kirby, A. (2012) *Public Attitudes to Youth Crime. Report on Focus Group Research*. London: Home Office.

Jans, M. (2004) 'Children as Citizens: Towards a Contemporary Notion of Child Participation.' *Childhood*, 11, 1: 27–44.

Jennings, W., Farrall, S., Gray, E. and Hay, C. (2020) 'Moral Panics and Punctuated Equilibrium in Public Policy: An Analysis of the Criminal Justice Policy Agenda in Britain.' *Policy Studies Journal*, 48, 1: 207–234.

Jones, O. (2012) *Chavs*. London: Verso.

Jones, R. (2020) 'Criminology and Criminal Justice in Post-devolution Wales.' *European Journal of Criminology*, DOI: 10.1177/1477370820916447

Joseph, J. (2001) 'Is Crime in the Genes? A Critical Review of Twin and Adoption Studies of Criminality and Antisocial Behavior.' *Journal of Mind and Behavior*, 22, 2: 179–218.

Junger-Tas, J. and Marshall, I. (1999) 'The Self-Report Methodology in Crime Research.' *Crime and Justice*, 25: 291–367.

Kelly-Irving, M. and Delpierre, C. (2019) 'A Critique of the Adverse Childhood Experiences Framework in Epidemiology and Public Health: Uses and Misuses.' *Social Policy and Society*, 18, 3: 445–456.

Kelly, L.C. and Armitage, V. (2015) 'Diverse Diversions: Youth Justice Reform, Localized Practices, and a "New Interventionist Diversion"? '*Youth Justice*, 15, 2: 117–133.

Kempf-Leonard, K. (2007) 'Minority Youths and Juvenile Justice: Disproportionate Minority Contact after Nearly 20 Years of Reform Efforts.' *Youth Violence and Juvenile Justice*, 5, 1: 71–87.

Kendler, K., Lönn, S., Morris, N., Sundquist, J., Långström, N. and Sundquist, K. (2014) 'A Swedish National Adoption Study of Criminality.' *Psychological Medicine*, 44, 9: 1913–1925.

Kendler, K., Maes, H., Lönn, S. and Morris, N. (2015) 'A Swedish National Twin Study of Criminal Behavior and its Violent, White-collar and Property Subtypes.' *Psychological Medicine*, 45, 11: 1–10.

Kerig, P.K. (2018) 'Polyvictimization and Girls' Involvement in the Juvenile Justice System: Investigating Gender-Differentiated Patterns of Risk, Recidivism, and Resilience.' *Journal of Interpersonal Violence*, 33, 5: 789–809.

Kilkelly, U. (2001) 'The Best of Both Worlds for Children's Rights? Interpreting the European Convention on Human Rights in the Light of the UN Convention on the Rights of the Child.' *Human Rights Quarterly*, 23, 2: 308–326.

Kilkelly, U. (2008) 'Youth Justice and Children's Rights: Measuring Compliance with International Standards.' *Youth Justice*, 8, 3: 187–192.

Kirby, A. (2021) *Neurodiversity – A Whole-Child Approach for Youth Justice*. Manchester: HMIP.

Kohlberg, L. (1971) 'Stages of Moral Development as a Basis for Moral Education.' In C. Beck, B. Crittenden and E. Sullivan (Eds.), *Moral Education: Interdisciplinary Approaches*. Toronto: Toronto University Press (pp. 23–92).

Kokkalera, S.S. and Singer, S.I. (2019) 'Discretionary Release Practices for Juveniles Facing Life.' In C. Spohn and P.K. Brennan (Eds.), *Handbook on Sentencing Policies and Practices in the 21st Century*. New York: Routledge.

Kruttschnitt, C. and Dirkzwager, A. (2011) 'Are There Still Contrasts in Tolerance? Imprisonment in the Netherlands and England 20 Years Later.' *Punishment & Society*, 13, 3: 283–306.

Kupchik, A., Green, D.A. and Mowen, T. (2015) 'School Punishment in the US and England: Divergent Frames and Responses.' *Youth Justice*, 15, 1: 3–22.

Lacey, R.E. and Minnis, H. (2019) 'Practitioners Review: Twenty Years of Research with Adverse Childhood Experiences Scores – Advantages, Disadvantages and Applications to Practice.' *Journal of Psychiatry*, 61, 12: 116–130.

Laming, A. (2016) *In Care, Out of Trouble: How the Life Chances of Children in Care Can Be Transformed by Protecting Them from Unnecessary Involvement in the Criminal Justice System*. London: Prison Reform Trust.

Lammy, D. (2017) *The Lammy Review*. Available at: www.gov.uk/government/publications/lammy-review-final-report

Lappi-Seppälä, T. (2006) 'Finland: A Model of Tolerance?' In J. Muncie and B. Goldson (Eds.), *Comparative Youth Justice: Critical Debates*. London: Sage.

Lappi-Seppälä, T. (2012) 'Criminology, Crime and Criminal Justice in Finland.' *European Journal of Criminology*, 9, 2: 206–222.

Lappi-Seppälä, T. (2019) 'Youth Justice and Youth Sanctions in Four Nordic States: Denmark, Finland, Norway and Sweden.' In B. Goldosn (Ed.), *Juvenile Justice in Europe*. London: Routledge (pp. 104–127).

Larsson, I., Staland-Nyman, C., Svedberg, P., Nygren, J. and Carlsson, I-M. (2018) 'Children and Young People's Participation in Developing Interventions in Health and Well-being: A Scoping Review.' *BMC Health Services Research*, 18, 507: 1–20.

Laub, J. and Sampson, R. (1988) 'Unraveling Families and Delinquency: A Reanalysis of the *Gluecks'* Data.' *Criminology*, 26, 3: 355–380.

Lemert, E. (1951) *Social Pathology: A Systematic Approach to the Theory of Sociopathic Behavior*. New York, McGraw-Hill.

Lemert, E. (1967) *Human Deviance, Social Problems and Social Control*. Englewood Cliffs, NJ: Prentice-Hall.

Lester, B., Andreozzi, A. and Appiah, L. (2004) 'Substance Use During Pregnancy: Time for Policy to Catch Up with Research.' *Harm Reduction Journal*, 1, 5: 1–44.

Liefaard, T. (2016) 'Child-Friendly Justice: Protection and Participation of Children in the Justice System.' *Temple Law Review*, 88, 4: 905–927.

Lightowler, C., Orr, D. and Vaswani, N. (2014) *Youth Justice in Scotland: Fixed in the Past or Fit for the Future?* Glasgow: Centre for Youth and Criminal Justice.

Loeber, R., Menting, B., Lynam, D. and Moffitt, T. (2012) 'Findings From the Pittsburgh Youth Study: Cognitive Impulsivity and Intelligence as Predictors of the Age-Crime Curve.' *Journal of the American Academy of Child and Adolescent Psychiatry*, 51, 11: 1136–1149.

Löfholm, C., Olsson, T. and Sundell, K. (2020) 'Effectiveness and Costs of a Therapeutic Residential Care Program for Adolescents with a Serious Behavior Problem (MultifunC). Short-Term Results of a Non-Randomized Controlled Trial.' *Residential Treatment for Children & Youth*, 37, 3: 226–243.

Lundy, L., Kilkelly, U. and Byrne, B. (2013) 'Incorporation of the United Nations Convention on the Rights of the Child in Law: A Comparative Review.' *International Journal of Children's Rights*, 21, 3: 442–463.

Lynch, N. (2012) 'Playing Catch-up? Recent Reform of New Zealand's Youth Justice System.' *Criminology & Criminal Justice*, 12, 5: 507–526.

Lynch, N. (2018) 'Human Rights for "Hard Cases": Alternatives to Imprisonment for Serious Offending by Children and Youth.' In E. Stanley (Ed.), *Human Rights and Incarceration: Critical Explorations*. Basingstoke: Palgrave Macmillan (pp. 153–179).

Lynch, N. and Liefaard, T. (2020) 'What is Left in the "Too Hard Basket"? Developments and Challenges for the Rights of Children in Conflict with the Law.' *The International Journal of Children's Rights*, 28, 1: 89–110.

Lyon, J. and Wilson, A. (2000) *'Tell Them So They Listen': Messages from Young People in Custody*. London: Home Office.

MacDonald, Z. (2002) 'Official Crime Statistics: Their Use and Interpretation.' *Economic Journal*, 112, 477: F85–F106.

MacDonald, R. and King, H. (2021) 'Looking South: What Can Youth Studies in the Global North Learn from Research on Youth and Policy in the Middle East and North African Countries?' *Mediterranean Politics*, 26, 3: 285–307.

Macpherson, W. (1999) *The Stephen Lawrence Inquiry*, Cm 4262-1. London: The Stationery Office.

Maguire, K. and Pastore, A. (1999) *Sourcebook of Criminal Justice Statistics 1998*. Washington, DC: U.S. Bureau of Justice Statistics.

Mallett, C.A. (2018) 'Disproportionate Minority Contact in Juvenile Justice: Today's, and Yesterday's Problems.' *Criminal Justice Studies*, 31, 3: 230–248.

Malvaso, C.G. and Delfabbro, P. (2015) 'Offending Behaviour among Young People with Complex Needs in the Australian Out-of-Home Care System.' *Journal of Child and Family Studies*, 24, 12: 3561–3569.

Marder, I. (2020) 'Developing Restorative Youth Justice in Europe.' Available at: https://rm.coe.int/presentation-ian-marder/16809e4d2b

Marsh, B. and Maruna, S. (2016) 'Desistance and Restorative Justice: Learning from Success Stories of Northern Ireland's Youth Justice Agency.' *Restorative Justice*, 4, 3: 368–387.

Martin, M. and Mbugua, S. (2016) 'An Investigation of Public Perceptions of Youth Crime and Juvenile Delinquency in Embakasi Sub-county in Nairobi County, Kenya.' *Research on Humanities and Social Sciences*, 6, 14: 71–76.

Maslow, A.H. (1943) 'A Theory of Human Motivation.' *Psychological Review*, 50, 4: 370–96.

Maslow, A.H. (1954) *Motivation and Personality*. New York: Harper and Row.

Matthews, R. (2005) 'The Myth of Punitiveness.' *Theoretical Criminology*, 9, 2: 175–201.

Matza, D. (1964) *Delinquency and Drift*. New York: John Wiley and Sons.

Matza, D. (1969) *Becoming Deviant*. Hoboken, NJ: Prentice Hall.

May, M. (1973) 'Innocence and Experience: The Evolution of the Concept of Juvenile Delinquency in the Mid-Nineteenth Century.' *Victorian Studies*, 17, 1: 7–29.

May, T., Gyateng, T. and Hough, M. (2010) *Differential Treatment in the Youth Justice System*. London: Equality and Human Rights Commission.

Mayor of London (2020) *Action Plan - Transparency, Accountability and Trust in Policing*. Available at: www.london.gov.uk/mopac-publications/action-plan-transparency-accountability-and-trust-policing

Maxwell, G. and Morris, A. (2002) 'The Role of Shame, Guilt and Remorse in Restorative Justice Processes for Young People.' In E. Weitekamp and H.J. Kerner (Eds.), *Restorative Justice: Theoretical Foundations*. Cullompton: Willan (pp. 267–284).

McAlinden, A. and Dwyer, C. (2015) *Criminal Justice in Transition: The Northern Ireland Context*. Oxford: Hart Publishing.

McAlister, S. and Carr, N. (2014) 'Experiences of Youth Justice: Youth Justice Discourses and their Multiple Effects.' *Youth Justice*, 14, 3: 241–254.

McAlister, S., Neill, G., Carr, N. and Dwyer, C. (2021) 'Gender, Violence and Cultures of Silence: Young Women and Paramilitary Violence.' *Journal of Youth Studies*, 25, 8: 1148–1163.

McAra, L. (2010) 'Models of Youth Justice.' In D. Smith (Ed.), *A New Response to Youth Crime*. Cullompton: Willan (pp. 287–317).

McAra, L. (2017a) 'Youth Justice.' In A. Liebling, S. Maruna and L. McAra (Eds.), *The Oxford Handbook of Criminology* (Sixth Edition). Oxford: Oxford University Press (pp. 938–966).

McAra, L. (2017b) 'Can Criminologists Change the World? Critical Reflections on the Politics, Performance and Effects of Criminal Justice.' *British Journal of Criminology*, 57, 4: 767–788.

McAra, L. and McVie, S. (2005) 'The Usual Suspects? Street-life, Young People and the Police.' *Criminal Justice*, 5, 1: 5–36.

McAra, L. and McVie, S. (2007) 'Youth Justice? The Impact of System Contact on Patterns of Desistance from Offending.' *European Journal of Criminology*, 4, 3: 315–345.

McAra, L. and McVie, S. (2010a) 'Youth Crime and Justice: Key Messages from the Edinburgh Study of Youth Transitions and Crime.' *Criminology and Criminal Justice*, 10, 2: 179–209.

McAra, L. and McVie, S. (2010b) 'Youth Crime and Justice in Scotland.' In H. Croall, G. Mooney and M. Munro (Eds.), *Criminal Justice in Scotland.* Abingdon: Willan Publishing (pp. 69–89).

McAra, L., and McVie, S. 2012. "Negotiated Order: The Groundwork for a Theory of Offending Pathways." *Criminology and Criminal Justice,* 12 (4): 347–375.

McAra, L. and McVie, S. (2013) 'Delivering Justice for Children and Young People: Key Messages from the Edinburgh Study of Youth Transitions and Crime.' In A. Dockley (Ed.), *Justice for Young People: Papers by Winners of the Research Medal 2013.* London: Howard League for Penal Reform (pp. 3–14).

McAra, L. and McVie, S. (2016) 'Understanding Youth Violence: The Mediating Effects of Gender, Poverty and Vulnerability.' *Journal of Criminal Justice,* 45: 71–77.

McAra, L. and McVie, S. (2019) 'Transformations in Youth Crime and Justice across Europe: Evidencing the Case for Diversion.' In B. Goldson (Ed.), *Juvenile Justice in Europe: Past, Present and Future.* London: Routledge (pp. 74–103).

McEvoy, K. and Mika, H. (2001) 'Punishment, Policing and Praxis: Restorative Justice and Non-violent Alternatives to Paramilitary Punishments in Northern Ireland.' *Policing and Society,* 11, 3–4: 359–382.

McGhee, J. and Waterhouse, L. (1998) 'Justice and Welfare: Has the Children (Scotland) Act 1995 Shifted the Balance?' *Journal of Social Welfare and Family Law,* 20, 1: 49–63.

McGloin, J. and Thomas, K. (2019) 'Peer Influence and Delinquency.' *Annual Review of Criminology,* 2: 241–264.

McKittrick, D. and McVea, D. (2012) *Making Sense of the Troubles: A History of the Northern Ireland Conflict.* London: Penguin Books.

McNeill, F. and Weaver, B. (2010) *Changing Lives? Desistance Research and Offender Management.* Glasgow: The Scottish Centre for Crime and Justice Research.

McVie, S. (2005) 'Patterns of Deviance Underlying the Age Crime Curve: The Long-Term Evidence.' Available at: http://www.britsoccrim.org/volume7/007.pdf

Mendes, P. and Moslehuddin, B. (2006) 'From Dependence to Interdependence: Towards Better Outcomes for Young People Leaving State Care.' *Child Abuse Review,* 15, 2: 110–126.

Mendes, P., Snow, P. and Baidawi, S. (2014) 'Young People Transitioning from Out-of-Home Care in Victoria: Strengthening Support Services for Dual Clients of Child Protection and Youth Justice.' *Australian Social Work,* 67, 1: 6–23.

Mendoza-Denton, N. (2008) *Homegirls.* Malden: MA, Blackwell.

Merlo, A.V. and Benekos, P.J. (2016) 'Is Punitive Juvenile Justice Policy Declining in the United States? A Critique of Emergent Initiatives.' *Youth Justice,* 10, 1: 3–24.

Merton, R. (1957) 'Social Structure and Anomie.' In: R. Merton (Ed.), *Social Theory and Social Structure.* New York: Free Press (pp. 185–214).

Ministry of Justice (2018) 'Referral Order Guidance.' Ministry of Justice. Available at: https://assets.publishing.service.gov.uk/government/uploads/system/uploads/attachment_data/file/746365/referral-order-guidance-9-october-2018.pdf

Ministry of Justice (2020) 'Proven Reoffending Statistics: January to March 2018.' Available at: www.gov.uk/government/statistics/proven-reoffending-statistics-january-to-march-2018

Ministry of Justice and Welsh Government (2019) Youth Justice Blueprint for Wales. Available at: https://gov.wales/sites/default/files/publications/2019-05/youth-justice-blueprint_0.pdf

Moffitt, T. (1993) 'Adolescence-Limited and Life-Course-Persistent Antisocial Behavior: A Developmental Taxonomy.' *Psychological Review*, 100, 4: 674–701.

Mooney, G. and Poole, L. (2004) '"A Land of Milk and Honey"? Social Policy in Scotland after Devolution.' *Critical Social Policy*, 24, 4: 458–483.

Mooney, G., Croall, H., Munro, M. and Scott, G. (2015) 'Scottish Criminal Justice: Devolution, Divergence and Distinctiveness.' *Criminology and Criminal Justice*, 15, 2: 205–224.

Moore, M. (2011) 'Psychological Theories of Crime and Delinquency.' *Journal of Human Behavior in the Social Environment*, 21, 3: 226–239.

Morris, A. (2002) 'Shame, Guilt and Remorse: Experiences from Family Group Conferences in New Zealand.' In I. Weijers and A. Duff (Eds.), *Punishing Juveniles: Principles and Critique*. Oxford: Hart Publishing (pp. 244–265).

Morrow, D. and Byrne, J. (2020) *Countering Paramilitary and Organised Criminal Influence on Youth: A Review*. Belfast: Corrymeela.

Motz, R.T., Barnes, J.C., Caspi, A., Arseneault, L., Cullen, F.T., Wertz, J. and Moffitt, T.E. (2019) 'Does Contact with the Justice System Deter or Promote Future Delinquency? Results from a Longitudinal Study of British Adolescent Twins.' *Criminology*, 58, 2: 307–335.

Muncie, J. (2002) 'A New Deal for Youth? Early Intervention and Correctionalism.' In G. Hughes, E. McLaughlin and J. Muncie (Eds.), *Crime Prevention and Community Safety: New Directions*. London: Sage (pp. 142–162).

Muncie, J. (2006) 'Governing Young People: Coherence and Contradiction in Contemporary Youth Justice.' *Critical Social Policy*, 26, 4: 770–793.

Muncie, J. (2008) 'The "Punitive Turn" in Juvenile Justice: Cultures of Control and Rights Compliance in Western Europe and the USA.' *Youth Justice*, 8, 2: 107–121.

Muncie, J. (2009) *Youth and Crime* (Third Edition). London: Sage.

Muncie, J. (2011) 'Illusions of Difference: Comparative Youth Justice in the Devolved United Kingdom.' *British Journal of Criminology*, 51, 1: 40–57.

Muncie, J. (2015) *Youth & Crime* (Fourth Edition). London: Sage.

Muncie, J. and Goldson, B. (2006) *Comparative Youth Justice: Critical Debates*. London: Sage.

Murray, K. (2015) 'The Proactive Turn: Stop and Search in Scotland (a Study in Elite Power).' PhD thesis, University of Edinburgh.

Murray, K., McGuinness, P., Burman, M. and McVie, S. (2015) *Evaluation of the Whole System Approach to Young People who Offend in Scotland*. Edinburgh: The Scottish Government.

Myers, R. and Goddard, T. (2019) 'Editors' Introduction to the Special Issue: "Neoliberal Youth Carceralism and Alternative Visions of Justice".' *Critical Criminology*, 27: 521–525.

Myers, R., Goddard, T. and Davidtz, J. (2021) 'Reconnecting Youth: Beyond Individualized Programs and Risks.' *Youth Justice*, 21, 1: 55–70.

Nacro Cymru (2009) *Youth Justice and Participation in Wales*. Cardiff: Nacro Cymru.

Narayan, A.J., Rivera, L.M., Bernstein, RE., Harris, W.W., and Lieberman, A.F. (2018) 'Positive Childhood Experiences Predict less Psychopathology and Stress in Pregnant Women with Childhood Adversity: A Pilot Study of the Benevolent Childhood Experiences (BCEs) Scale.' *Child Abuse and Neglect*, 78: 19–30.

National Assembly Policy Unit (2000) *Extending Entitlement: Support for 11 to 25 Year Olds in Wales. Direction and Guidance*. Cardiff: National Assembly for Wales.

Nelken, D. (2006) 'Italian Juvenile Justice: Tolerance, Leniency or Indulgence?' *Youth Justice*, 6, 2: 107–128.

Nelken, D. (2009) 'Comparative Criminal Justice: Beyond Ethnocentrism and Relativism.' *European Journal of Criminology*, 6, 4: 291–311.

Nelken, D. (2015) 'Foil Comparisons or Foiled Comparisons? Learning from Italian Juvenile Justice.' *European Journal of Criminology*, 12, 5: 519–534.

Nelken, D. (2017) 'Rethinking Comparative Criminal Justice.' In A. Liebling, S. Maruna and L. McAra (Eds.), *The Oxford Handbook of Criminology* (Sixth Edition). Oxford: Oxford University Press (pp. 416– 437).

NHS Digital (2019) *Smoking, Drinking and Drug Use among Young People in England 2018*. Available at: https://digital.nhs.uk/data-and-information/publications/statistical/smoking-drinking-and-drug-use-among-young-people-in-england/2018

NIAO (Northern Ireland Audit Office) (2017) *Managing Children Who Offend*. Belfast: Northern Ireland Office.

NIAO (Northern Ireland Audit Office) (2020) *Managing Children who Offend: Follow-up Review*. Belfast: Northern Ireland Office.

Nielsen, M. (1999) 'Navajo Nation Courts, Peacemaking and Restorative Justice Issues.' *Journal of Legal Pluralism and Unofficial Law*, 31, 44: 105–126.

NISRA (2021) *Children's Social Care Statistics for Northern Ireland 2020/21*. Belfast: NISRA.

Nolan, A. and Kilkelly, U. (2016) 'Children's Rights under Regional Human Rights Law: A Tale of Harmonization?' In A. Donald, C.M. Buckley and P. Leach (Eds.), *Towards Convergence in International Human Rights Law: Approaches of Regional and International Systems*. Leiden: Brill.

Northern Ireland Policing Board (NIPB) (2020) *Human Rights Annual Report 2019/20*. Belfast: NIPB. Available at: www.nipolicingboard.org.uk/sites/nipb/files/publications/human-rights-annual-report-2019-2020.pdf

Nowak, M. (2019) *The United Nations Global Study of Children Deprived of their Liberty*. Geneva: United Nations.

NSPCC (2021) *Statistics Briefing: Looked After Children*. Available at: https://learning.nspcc.org.uk/media/1622/statistics-briefing-looked-after-children.pdf

Oberstown Children's Detention Campus (2017) *Annual Report 2016/17*. Dublin: Oberstown Children's Detention Campus.

O'Brien, W. and Fitz-Gibbon, W. (2018) 'Can Human Rights Standards Counter Australia's Punitive Youth Justice Practices?' *The International Journal of Children's Rights*, 26, 2: 197–227.

Oei, J. (2018) 'Adult consequences of prenatal drug exposure.' *Internal Medicine Journal*, 48, 1: 25–31.

Office for National Statistics (2019) *Crime in England and Wales: Year Ending March 2019*. Available at: www.ons.gov.uk/peoplepopulationandcommunity/crimeandjustice/bulletins/crimeinenglandandwales/yearendingmarch2019

Olaghere, A., Wilson, D.B. and Kimbrell, C.S. (2021) 'Trauma-Informed Interventions for At-Risk and Justice-Involved Youth.' *Criminal Justice and Behavior*, 48, 9: 1261–1277.

O'Mahony, P. (2009) 'The Risk Factors Prevention Paradigm and the Causes of Youth Crime: A Deceptively Useful Analysis?' *Youth Justice*, 9, 2: 99–114.

Oudshoorn, J. (2015) *Trauma-Informed Youth Justice in Canada. A New Framework toward a Kinder Future*. Toronto: Canadian Scholars' Press Inc.

Parker, H. (1974) *View from the Boys*. Newton Abbot: David & Charles.

Pearson, G. (1983) *Hooligan: A History of Respectable Fears*. London: Macmillan Press.

Pepper, J. and Dahl, R. (2013) 'Surging Hormones: Brain-Behavior Interactions During Puberty.' *Current Directions in Psychological Science*, 22, 2: 134–139.

Perez, N., Jennings, W. and Baglivio, M. (2018) 'A Path to Serious, Violent, Chronic Delinquency: The Harmful Aftermath of Adverse Childhood Experiences.' *Crime & Delinquency*, 64, 1: 3–25.

Percy-Smith, B. and Thomas, N. (2010) 'Introduction.' In B. Percy-Smith and N. Thomas (Eds.), *A Handbook of Children and Young People's Participation*. Abingdon: Routledge (pp. 1–8).

Petintseva, O. (2016) *Perspectives on 'New' Migrants in Youth Justice: Constitutions, Circularity and Effects of Institutional Discourses on Roma and Caucasian Youth*. Ghent: Ghent University.

Petintseva, O. (2019) '"Entextualisation" Across Institutional Contexts: The Impact of Discourse in School Reports on the Juvenile Justice Trajectories of Roma Youth.' *Youth Justice*, 19, 1: 3–24.

Pettit, B. and Western, B. (2004) 'Mass Imprisonment and the Life Course: Race and Class Inequality in U.S. Incarceration.' *American Sociological Review*, 69, 2: 151–169.

Phillips, C. and Bowling, B. (2017) 'Ethnicities, Racism, Crime, and Criminal Justice.' In A. Liebling, S. Maruna and L. McAra (Eds.) *The Oxford Handbook of Criminology*. Oxford: Oxford University Press.

Phoenix, J. (2016) 'Against Youth Justice and Youth Governance, for Youth Penality.' *British Journal of Criminology*, 56, 1: 123–140.

Phoenix, J. and Kelly, L. (2013) "You Have to Do It for Yourself." Responsibilization in Youth Justice and Young People's Situated Knowledge of Youth Justice Practice ' *British Journal of Criminology*, 53: 419–437.

Piaget, J. (1959). *The Language and Thought of the Child* (Third Edition) (trans M. Gabain & R. Gabain). London: Routledge Kegan Paul.

Pinheiro, P.S. (2006) *World Report on Violence Against Children*. Geneva: United Nations.

Pitts, J. (2008) *Reluctant Gangsters*. London: Routledge.

Piquero, A.R., Schubert, C.A. and Brame, R. (2014) 'Comparing Official and Self-report Records of Offending across Gender and Race/Ethnicity in a Longitudinal Study of Serious Youthful Offenders.' *Journal of Research in Crime and Delinquency*, 51, 4: 526–556.

Platt, A. (2009) *The Child Savers: The Invention of Delinquency*. 40th Anniversary Edition. Newark, NJ: Rutgers University Press.

Pollock, L.A. (1983) *Forgotten Children: Parent-Child Relations from 1500 to 1900*. Cambridge: Cambridge University Press.

Portnoy, J., Chen, F. and Raine, A. (2013) 'Biological Protective Factors for Antisocial and Criminal Behavior.' *Journal of Criminal Justice*, 41, 4: 292–299.

Pratt, J. (2008) 'Scandinavian Exceptionalism in an Era of Penal Excess.' *British Journal of Criminology*, 48, 2: 119–137.

Pratt, J. and Eriksson, A. (2012) 'In defense of Scandinavian exceptionalism.' In T. Ugelvik and J. Dullum (Eds.), *Penal Exceptionalism? Nordic Prison Policy and Practice*. London: Routledge (pp. 235–260).

Pruin, I. and Dünkel, F. (2015) *Better in Europe? European Responses to Young Adult Offending*. Available at: https://t2a.org.uk/wp-content/uploads/2015/02/T2A_Better-in-Europe_Report-_online.pdf

Puzzanchera, C. (2021) *Juvenile Justice Statistics. Juvenile Arrests 2019*. Washington, DC: Department of Justice, Office of Juvenile Justice and Delinquency Prevention.

Quay, H. and Peterson, D. (1960) 'Personality Factors in the Study of Juvenile Delinquency.' *Exceptional Children*, 26, 9: 472–476

Quinsey, V. (2002) 'Evolutionary theory and criminal behaviour.' *Legal and Criminological Psychology*, 7, 1: 1–13.

Rafter, N., Posick, C. and Rocque, M. (2016) *The Criminal Brain* ((Second Edition). New York: New York University Press.

Raine, A. (2002) 'Biosocial Studies of Antisocial and Violent Behavior in Children and Adults: A Review.' *Journal of Abnormal Child Psychology*, 30, 4: 311–326.

Rap, S. (2016) 'A Children's Rights Perspective on the Participation of Juvenile Defendants in the Youth Court.' *International Journal of Children's Rights*, 24: 93–112.

Rebellon, C. (2006) 'Do Adolescents Engage in Delinquency to Attract the Social Attention of Peers? An Extension and Longitudinal Test of the Social Reinforcement Hypothesis.' *Journal of Research in Crime and Delinquency*, 43, 4: 387–411.

Report of The Committee for Investigating the Causes of the Alarming Increase of Juvenile Delinquency in the Metropolis (1816). London: J.F. Dove.

Roberts, J. (2004) 'Public Opinion and Youth Justice.' *Crime and Justice*, 31: 495–542.

Roberts, J.V. and Hough, M. (2005) *Understanding Public Attitudes to Criminal Justice*. Maidenhead: Open University Press.

Roberts, J.V. and Hough, M. (2013) 'Sentencing Riot-Related Offending: Where Do the Public Stand?' *British Journal of Criminology*, 53, 2: 234–256.

Robertson, A.S. (2022) 'Scottish Children's Panels: Where Volunteers Are Essential for Fostering Child Well-Being.' *Journal of Public Child Welfare*, 16, 1: 7–27.

Robertson, L. (2017) 'A Practice-Based Approach to Youth Justice. The Whole System Approach in Scotland.' PhD thesis, University of Glasgow.

Rocca, G., Verde, A. and Gatti, U. (2019) 'Impact of Alcohol and Cannabis Use on Juvenile Delinquency: Results from an International Multi-City Study (ISRD3).' *European Journal on Criminal Policy and Research*, 25: 259–271.

Rocque, M. and Snellings, Q. (2018) 'The New Disciplinology: Research, Theory, and Remaining Puzzles on the School-to-Prison Pipeline.' *Journal of Criminal Justice*, 59: 3–11.

Rocque, M., Welsh B. and Raine A. (2012) 'Biosocial Criminology and Modern Crime Prevention.' *Journal of Criminal Justice*, 40: 306–312.

Ross, A., Duckworth, K., Smith, D., Wyness, G. and Schoon, I. (2011) *Prevention and Reduction: A Review of Strategies for Intervening Early to Prevent or Reduce Youth Crime and Anti-social Behaviour*. DFE-RR 111, Department for Education, https://assets.publishing.service.gov.uk/government/uploads/system/uploads/attachment_data/file/182548/DFE-RR111.pdf

Rowe, R., Maughan B., Worthman C., Costello E. and Angold, A. (2004) 'Testosterone, Conduct Disorder and Social Dominance in Boys: Pubertal Development and Biosocial Interaction.' *Biological Psychiatry*, 55: 546–552.

Rutter, M. (2000) 'Resilience Reconsidered: Conceptual Considerations, Empirical Findings, and Policy Implications.' In J.P. Shonkoff and S.J. Meisels (Eds.), *Handbook of Early Childhood Intervention*. Cambridge: Cambridge University Press (pp. 651–682).

Sampson, R. and Laub, J.H. (1993) *Crime in the Making: Pathways and Turning Points through Life*. Cambridge, MA and London: Harvard University Press.

Sanders, J., Liebenberg, L. and Munford, R. (2020) 'The Impact of School Exclusion on Later Justice System Involvement: Investigating the Experiences of Male and Female Students.' *Educational Review*, 72, 3: 386–403.

Sandøy, T. (2020) 'Alternative (to) Punishment: Assessing Punishment Experiences in Youth Diversion Programmes.' *British Journal of Criminology*, 60, 4: 911–929.

Schiraldi, V. (2020) 'Can We Eliminate The Youth Prison? (And What Should We Replace it With?)'. Available at: https://scholar.google.com/scholar_url?url=https://academiccommons.columbia.edu/doi/10.7916/d8-621e2e75/download&hl=en&sa=X&ei=uVeOY43dDeeR6rQPjbiEmAY&scisig=AAGBfm2TE0C_mhuW06ra9WKi-o23KbC9vg&oi=scholarr

Schissel, B. (2016) 'Justice Undone: Public Panic and the Condemnation of Children and Youth.' In C. Krinsky (Ed.) *Moral Panics over Contemporary Children and Youth*. Abingdon: Routledge (pp. 15–30).

Schnittker, J. and John, A. (2007) 'Enduring Stigma: The Long-Term Effects of Incarceration on Health.' *Journal of Health and Social Behavior*, 48, 2: 115–130.

Scior, K., Addai-Davis, J., Kenyon, M. and Sheridan, A.C. (2013) 'Stigma, Public Awareness about Intellectual Disability and Attitudes to Inclusion among Different Ethnic Groups.' *Journal of Intellectual Disability Research*, 58: 1014–1026.

Scottish Government (2017) *Public Attitudes to Young People in Scotland*. Edinburgh: Scottish Government.

Shammas, V. and Sandberg, S. (2016) 'Habitus, Capital, and Conflict: Bringing Bourdieusian Field Theory to Criminology.' *Criminology & Criminal Justice*, 16, 2: 195–213.

Sharpe, G. (2009) 'The Trouble with Girls Today: Professional Perspectives on Young Women's Offending.' *Youth Justice*, 9, 3: 254–269.

Sharpe, G. (2013) *Offending Girls: Young Women and Youth Justice*. London: Routledge.

Sharpe, G. (2016) 'Re-imagining Justice for Girls: A New Agenda for Research.' *Youth Justice*, 16, 1:3–17.

Shaw, C.R.R. (1966) *The Jack-Roller: A Delinquent Boy's Own Story*. Chicago: University of Chicago Press.

Shenton, F. and Smith, R. (2021) 'Behaviour Management or Institutionalised Repression? Children's Experiences of Physical Restraint in Custody.' *Children & Society*, 35, 1: 159–175.

Sherif, M., Harvey, O., White, B., Hood, W., and Sherif, C. (1961). *Inter-group Co-operation and Competition: The Robber's Cave experiment*. Norman, OK, University of Oklahoma Press.

Shore, H. (1999) *Artful Dodgers: Youth and Crime in Early Nineteenth-Century Ireland*. Woodbridge: The Royal Historical Society/The Boydell Press.

Shore, H. (2003) "Inventing" the Juvenile Delinquent in Nineteenth-Century Europe.' In: B. Godfrey, C. Elmsley and G. Dunstall (Eds.), *Comparative Histories of Youth Crime*. Cullompton: Willan.

Short, J. and Nye, F. (1957) 'Reported Behaviour as a Criterion of Deviant Behaviour.' *Social Problems*, 5: 207–213.

Silvester, N. (2021) 'Developing Trauma-Informed Youth Justice Services.' In P. Willmot and L. Jones (Eds.), *Trauma-Informed Forensic Practice*. Abingdon: Routledge (pp. 333–347).

Simmonds, J. (2016) *Children in Custody 2015–16: An Analysis of 12–18-Year-Olds' Perceptions of their Experiences in Secure Training Centres and Young Offender Institutions*. London: HMIP.

Skiba, R., Reynolds, C., Graham, S., Sheras, P., Conoley, J. and Garcia-Vazquez, E. (2006) *Are Zero Tolerance Policies Effective in Schools? An Evidentiary Review and Recommendations*. Report by the American Psychological Association Zero Tolerance Task Force. Washington, DC: American Psychological Association.

Smith, R. (2004) *A Few Kind Words and a Loaded Gun*. London: Penguin.

Smith, R. (2005) 'Welfare Versus Justice – Again!' *Youth Justice*, 5, 1: 3–16.

Smith, R. (2006) 'Actuarialism and Early Intervention in Contemporary Youth Justice.' In B. Goldson and J. Muncie (Eds.), *Youth Crime and Justice*. London: Sage (pp. 92–109).

Smith, R. (2010) 'Children's Rights and Youth Justice: 20 Years of No Progress.' *Child Care in Practice*, 16, 1: 3–17.

Smith, R. (2011) *Doing Justice to Young People*. Cullompton: Willan.

Smith, R. (2018) *Diversion in Youth Justice: What Can We Learn from Historical and Contemporary Practices?* London: Routledge.

Smith, R. and Gray, P. (2019) 'The Changing Shape of Youth Justice: Models of Practice.' *Criminology & Criminal Justice*, 19, 5: 554–571.

Smithson, H. and Gray, P. (2021) *Supporting Children's Meaningful Participation in the Youth Justice System*. Manchester: Her Majesty's Inspectorate of Probation.

Smithson, H., Gray, P. and Jones, A. (2020) '"They Really Should Start Listening to You": The Benefits and Challenges of Co-Producing a Participatory Framework of Youth Justice Practice.' *Youth Justice*, 21, 3: 321–337.

Souhami, A. (2015) 'Creating the Youth Justice Board: Policy and Policy Making in English and Welsh Youth Justice.' *Criminology and Criminal Justice*, 15, 2: 152–168.

Spier, P. and Wilkinson, R. (2016) *Reoffending Patterns for Participants of Youth Justice Family Group Conferences Held in 2011 and 2012*. Wellington, NZ: Ministry of Social Development.

Spratt, T. (2012) 'Why Multiples Matter: Reconceptualisng the Population Referred to Child and Family Social Workers.' *The British Journal of Social Work*, 42, 8: 1574–1591.

Spratt, T., Frederick, J. and Devaney, J. (2022) 'New Understandings in Childhood Research and their Implications for Child and Family Services.' *Journal of Social Work*, 22, 5: 1137–1152.

Staines, J., Aghtaie, N. and Roy, J. (2021) 'Gendered Justice: Inequalities in the Minimum Age of Criminal Responsibility in Iran.' Available at: https://doi.org/10.1177/14732254211022854

Sutherland, A., Disley, E., Cattell, J. and Bauchowitz, S. (2017) *An Analysis of Trends in First Time Entrants in the Youth Justice System*. Ministry of Justice Analytical Series. Available at: https://assets.publishing.service.gov.uk/government/uploads/system/uploads/attachment_data/file/653182/trends-in-fte-to-the-youth-justice-system.pdf

Sutherland, D. (1939) *Principles of Criminology* (Third Edition). Philadelphia, PA: Lippincott.

Suzuki, M. and Otani, A (2017) 'Myths of Restorative Features in the Japanese Justice System and Society: The Role of Apology, Compensation and Confession, and Application of Reintegrative Shaming.' *Restorative Justice*, 5, 2: 158–177.

Sykes, M. and Matza, D. (1957) 'Techniques of Neutralization: A Theory of Delinquency.' *American Sociological Review*, 22, 6: 664–670.

Tait, M. and Inch, A. (2016) 'Putting Localism in Place: Conservative Images of the Good Community and the Contradictions of Planning Reform in England.' *Planning Practice & Research*, 31, 2: 174–194.

Taylor, C. (2016) *Review of the Youth Justice System in England and Wales*. London: Ministry of Justice.

Taylor, M. (2017) 'USA.' In S.H. Decker and N. Marteache (Eds.), *International Handbook of Juvenile Justice*. Switzerland: Springer International Publishing (pp. 135–152).

Terrio, S.J. (2008) 'New Barbarians at the Gates of Paris? Prosecuting Undocumented Minors in the Juvenile Court – the Problem of the "Petits Roumains".' *Anthropological Quarterly*, 81, 4: 873–901.

Thomas, N. (2011) 'The Role and Impact of Independent Children's Rights Institutions in the UK and in Europe.' *Journal of Social Welfare and Family Law*, 33, 3: 279–288.

Thomas, P. (1997) *Down These Mean Streets*. New York: Vintage Books.

Thornberry, T. (1987) 'Towards and Interactional Theory of Delinquency.' *Criminology*, 25, 4: 863–892.

Thornberry, T., Lizotte, A., Krohn, M., Smith, C. and Porter, P. (2003) 'Causes and Consequences of Delinquency.' In T. Thornberry and M. Krohn (Eds.) *Taking Stock of Delinquency. Longitudinal Research in the Social and Behavioral Sciences: An Interdisciplinary Series*. Boston: Springer (pp. 11–46).

Tilley, J., Evans, G. and Mitchell, C. (2008) 'Consociationalism and the Evolution of Political Cleavages in Northern Ireland, 1989–2004.' *British Journal of Political Science*, 38, 4: 699–717.

Timpson, J. (2019) *Timpson Review of School Exclusion*. London: Department of Education.

Torjesen, I. (2016) 'Austerity Cuts Are Eroding Benefits of Sure Start Children's Centres.' *British Medical Journal*, 352: i335.

Turner, A., Belcher, L. and Pona, I. (2019) 'Counting Lives: Responding to Children Who Are Criminally Exploited.' The Children's Society. Available at: www.childrenssociety.org.uk/sites/default/fles/counting-livesreport.pdf

UK Children's Commissioners (2015) *Report of the UK Children's Commissioners UN Committee on the Rights of the Child Examination of the Fifth Periodic Report of the United Kingdom of Great Britain and Northern Ireland*. Available at: www.cypcs.org.uk/ufiles/UKreport.pdf

UK Government (2014) *Fifth Periodic Reports of States Parties due in 2014 United Kingdom*. Committee on the Rights of the Child/CRC/C/GBR/5. Available at: https://documents-dds-ny.un.org/doc/UNDOC/GEN/G15/044/91/PDF/G1504491.pdf?OpenElement

UN Committee on the Rights of the Child (2016) *Concluding Observations on the Fifth Periodic Report of the United Kingdom of Great Britain and Northern Ireland*. Geneva: United Nations. CRC/C/GBR/CO/5.

UN Committee on the Rights of the Child (2019) General Comment No. 24 replacing General Comment 10 on Children's Rights in Juvenile Justice.

UNICEF (2019) 'Lowering the Age of Criminal Responsibility is Against Children's Rights.' Available at: www.unicef.org/philippines/press-releases/lowering-age-criminal-responsibility-against-child-rights-unicef

van Dam, C., Janssens, J. and De Bruyn, E. (2005) 'PEN, Big Five, juvenile delinquency and criminal recidivism.' *Personality and Individual Differences*, 39, 1: 7–19.

Vaswani, N. (2018) *Adverse Childhood Experiences in Children at High Risk of Harm to Others: A Gendered Perspective*. Glasgow: Centre for Youth and Criminal Justice.

Veneziano, C. and Veneziano, L. (1988) 'Correlates of Moral Development in Juvenile Delinquents.' *American Journal of Criminal Justice*, 13: 97–116.

Vizard, P. and Hills, J. (Eds.) (2021) The Conservative Governments' Record on Social Policy from May 2015 to pre-COVID 2020: Policies, Spending and Outcomes. Available at: https://sticerd.lse.ac.uk/dps/case/spdo/SPDO_overview_paper.pdf

Wacquant, L. (2009) *Punishing the Poor*. Durham, NC: Duke University Press.

Walsh, A. and Jorgensen, C. (2018) 'Evolutionary Theory and Criminology.' In R. Hopcroft (Ed.) *The Oxford Handbook of Evolution, Biology, and Society*. Oxford: Oxford University Press (pp. 517–542).

Ward, T. and Brown, M. (2004) 'The Good Lives Model and Conceptual Issues in Offender Rehabilitation.' *Psychology, Crime & Law*, 10, 3: 243–257.

Wastell, D. and White, S. (2017) *Blinded by Science: Social Implications of Neuroscience and Epigenetics*. Bristol: Policy Press.

Webster, C. (2019) '"Race", Ethnicity, Social Class and Juvenile Justice in Europe.' In B. Goldson (Ed.), *Juvenile Justice in Europe: Past, Present and Future*. London: Routledge (pp. 148–161).

Webster, C.M., Sprott, J.B. and Doob, A.N. (2019) 'The Will to Change: Lessons from Canada's Successful Decarceration of Youth.' *Law & Society Review*, 53, 4: 1092–1131.

Welch, K. and Payne, A.A. (2012) 'Exclusionary School Punishment: The Effect of Racial Threat on Expulsion and Suspension.' *Youth Violence and Juvenile Justice*, 10, 2: 155–171.

West, D. (1969) *Present Conduct and Future Delinquency: First Report of the Cambridge Study in Delinquent Development*. London: Heinemann.

West, D. and Farrington, D. (1973) *Who Becomes Delinquent? Second Report of the Cambridge Study in Delinquent Development*. London: Heinemann.

White, S., Edwards, R., Gillies, V. and Wastell, D. (2019) 'All the ACEs: A Chaotic Concept for Family Policy and Decision-Making?' *Social Policy & Society*, 18, 3: 457–466.

Wikstrom, P-O and Svensson, R. (2008) 'Why are English Youths More Violent Than Swedish Youths?: A Comparative Study of the Role of Crime Propensity, Lifestyles and Their Interactions in Two Cities.' *European Journal of Criminology*, 5, 3: 309–330.

Wikstrom, P-O, Mann, R. and Hardie, B. (2018) 'Young People's Differential Vulnerability to Criminogenic Exposure: Bridging the Gap between People- and Place-Oriented Approaches in the Study of Crime Causation.' *European Journal of Criminology*, 15, 1: 10–31.

Williams, J. and Kamaludeen, M. (2017) 'Muslim Girl Culture and Social Control in Southeast Asia: Exploring the Hijabista and Hijabster Phenomena.' *Crime, Media, Culture*, 13, 2: 199–216.

Williams, K., Papadopoulou, V. and Booth, N. (2012) *Prisoners' Childhood and Family Backgrounds. Results from the Surveying Prisoner Crime Reduction (SPCR) Longitudinal Cohort Study of Prisoners*. London: Ministry of Justice.

Willow, C. (2015) *Children Behind Bars*. Bristol: Policy Press.

Winterdyk, J.A. (Ed.) (2014) *Juvenile Justice: International Perspectives, Models and Trends*. Boca Raton, FL: CRC Press.

Winterdyk, J. (2015) 'Introduction: Juvenile Justice in the International Arena.' In J. Winterdyk (Ed.), *Juvenile Justice: International Perspectives, Models, and Trends*. Boca Raton, FL: CRC Press (pp. 1–24).

Winterdyk, J., Antonopoulos, G. and Corrado, R. (2016) 'Reflections on Norway's Juvenile Justice Model: A Comparative Context.' *Crime Prevention and Community Safety*, 18: 105–121.

Wirth, L. (1931) 'Culture Conflict and Delinquency' *Social Forces*, 9, 4: 484–492.

Yates, J. (2006) '"You Just Don't Grass": Youth, Crime and "Grassing" in a Working-Class Community.' *Youth Justice*, 6, 3: 195–210.

Yates, J. (2012) 'What Prospects Youth Justice? Children in Trouble in the Age of Austerity.' *Social Policy & Administration*, 46, 4: 432–447.

Young, S. (1997) 'The Use of Normalization as a Strategy in the Sexual Exploitation of Children by Adult Offenders.' *Canadian Journal of Human Sexuality*, 6, 4: 285–295.

YJRT (Youth Justice Review Team) (2011) *A Review of the Youth Justice System in Northern Ireland*. Belfast: Department of Justice.

Youth Justice Board (2021) *Strategic Plan 2021–2024*. London: Youth Justice Board.

Youth Justice Board/Ministry of Justice (2021) *Youth Justice Statistics 2019/20 England and Wales*. London: Youth Justice Board.

Youth Justice Board (2022) *Youth Justice Statistics 2020-21*. London: Youth Justice Board.

Youth Justice Board and Welsh Government (2014) Children and Young People First, Offenders Second. Available at: www.gov.uk/government/publications/youth-justice-strategy-for-wales-children-and-young-people-first

Zehr, H. (1990) *Changing Lenses: A New Focus for Crime and Justice*. Scottdale, PA: Herald Press.

Zimring, F.E., Langer, M. and Tanehaus, D.S. (Eds.) (2017) *Juvenile Justice in Global Perspective*. New York: New York University Press.

Glossary

Adultification Adultification means that adults regard Black girls as older than they are and therefore as less innocent and as needing less nurturing, protecting and comforting (Drew et al., 2022: 244).

Adverse Childhood Experiences (ACEs) Adverse Childhood Experiences (ACEs) are potentially traumatic experiences that occur in childhood, and which may impact on health and well-being in later life. Research on ACEs has been undertaken in a range of fields, but some of the findings and the application of this research into policy and practice has been contested, with some arguing that the approach risks being too simplistic and over-deterministic.

Appropriate Adult (AA) An Appropriate Adult (AA) is usually a parent or guardian, but can also be a social worker, carer for a child or volunteer. Under the Police and Criminal Evidence (PACE) provisions, which are rules regarding how police should carry out interviews and deal with people in police custody (including children), an AA should be present when a child is interviewed by the police and when they are subject to searches. The PACE provisions apply in England, Wales and Northern Ireland. Similar provisions in different legislation apply in Scotland.

Child Protection Plan (CPP) A Child Protection Plan is made by Social Services when a child is judged to be at risk of significant harm. The Plan will say what the specific risks are and the actions that are needed to keep the child safe. This could include interventions by professionals and requirements for families to engage with services.

Child-friendly justice Refers to justice systems which guarantee the respect and effective implementation of all children's rights at the highest attainable level.

Children's Hearing System This is the system which operates in Scotland and which deals with children who come to the attention of authorities for either welfare reasons or because of their behaviour.

Corporatist A model of intervention which is based on uniform collective action by state agencies to achieve shared goals.

County lines Refers to the transportation of drugs from one area to another, often across police and local authority boundaries, usually by children and vulnerable people. The 'county line' is the mobile phone used to take the orders of drugs.

Criminogenic Refers to something which is said to cause or is likely to cause criminal behaviour.

Desistance Refers to the process of ceasing offending and of moving from an offending to a non-offending identity.

Differential association Is a theory developed by Edwin Sutherland (1939). Its central idea is that it is through interaction (association) with others that individuals learn the values, attitudes, techniques and motivation for criminal behaviour.

Diversion In the context of youth justice, diversion is understood to mean diverting young people from formal processing in the legal system.

Doli incapax This is a Latin phrase which refers to the presumption in law that a child is incapable of forming the intent to commit a criminal offence. *Doli incapax* legal provisions mean that the onus is on prosecuting authorities to prove that a child has the capacity to form intent.

Ethnography An approach to research inquiry which involves living/working or otherwise getting alongside participants to explore and make sense of their understandings and experiences.

Justiciable Refers to something that can be the subject of a legal action in a court of law.

Minimum intervention A principle of intervention which relies on the claim that doing as little as possible is usually in the child/young person's best interests.

Participation In this context, an approach to working with young people which prioritises their voices, wishes and aspirations and seeks to act in response to these.

Political economy This refers to the interrelationship between economic and political (e.g., law and government) institutions.

Polyvictimisation Polyvictimisation refers to exposure to multiple types of violence and victimisation such as child abuse and neglect, domestic violence, school bullying and community violence.

Punitiveness This refers to approaches favouring expressive forms of punishment.

Responsibilisation This refers to the holding of individuals responsible for something that would previously have been the duty of another. So, for example, in youth justice terms, it might refer to young people been held solely responsible for their actions, when there are broader circumstances at play (e.g., a lack of appropriate supports).

School-to-prison pipeline This is a term, largely used in the United States, to describe the 'funnelling' of people with negative school outcomes (such as school exclusions) into the criminal justice system.

Youth conference A restorative justice conference. In Northern Ireland such conferences are included in legislation as one of the primary responses to dealing with youth offending.

Youth Offending Teams Youth Offending Teams are multi-disciplinary teams based in local authorities in England and Wales, which are responsible for working with young people who offend.

Index

Page numbers in *italics* refer to Figures and Tables.

Abdullahi, A. 36
Aboriginal communities 81, 82, 149, 164, 183
Abrams, L.S. 84–85, *84*
abuse, child
  and adult causes of death 172
  and delinquency 30, 143, 169–170, 178
  involvement of child protection and welfare services 59, 171, 187, 200
  see also violence
accountability of children *see* responsibility and accountability of children
ADHD (attention deficit hyperactivity disorder) 27–28, 167
adolescence
  brain development 19–20
  development theories 23–25
  as developmental stage 23, 45
  see also childhood
adoption studies 18
Adshead, G. 28
adulthood, transition to *see* transition to adulthood
adultification of Black girls 183–185
Adverse Childhood Experiences (ACEs) 22, 29–30, 117, 143, 169–174
  trauma-informed practice 174–176
advice and support services 59
advocacy-based approach 59
affiliation, and delinquency 30
affinity, and delinquency 30
Age of Criminal Majority (AGM) 3, 74, 84, *84*
  see also Minimum Age of Criminal Responsibility (MACR)
Age of Criminal Responsibility (Scotland) Act (2019) 128
'age-crime curve' 21
age-graded theory of informal social control 180
Agnew, R. 34
agreeableness personality trait 27
Aizer, A. 152
Albania 146
Albrecht, A. 16
alcohol
  foetal exposure 18
  use 21–22, 38, 167
Anderson, F. 138
Anti-social Behaviour, Crime and Policing Act (2014) 121
Anti-Social Behaviour Orders (ASBOs) 125
Argentina 84, *84*
Ariès, P. 5
Armitage, V. 52–53
assumptions and attitudes towards young people and youth crime
  historical changes 4–7, 82
  present-day attitudes 13–14, 51, 77, 120, 143, 161, 165, 169
'at-risk' children, interventions *see* risk-based intervention approach
attention deficit hyperactivity disorder (ADHD) 27–28, 167
austerity measures, impacts of (UK) 94–95, 123, 188–190
Australia
  approach to criminal justice 69, *69*
  approach to youth justice 81–82, 107, 149, 164, 168
  'care-criminalisation' 191
  disproportionate representation in youth justice system 167, 191
  indigenous communities 81, 82, 149, 164, 183
  school exclusions 183

Austria 158
autism spectrum disorders (ASDs) 19, 167
autobiographies of young/former offenders 201–202
see also self-report studies of young offenders

Baglivio, M. 173
Baldry, E. 167, 168, 177
Barkan, S. 33
Batchelor, S. 143
Bateman, T. 54, 117, 140, 142, 146–147, 148, 150–152, 159
Becker, H. 181
behaviour change interventions 44, 55, 62–63
Beijing Rules (1985) 3, 91, 92–93, 97
Belgium 6, 146, 158, 165, 182
Belize 84, *84*
Belson, W.A. 137
Benekos, P. 61
Berkoff, S. 201, 202
Bevan, M. 206–208
Big Five personality model 27
biological explanations for delinquency 15–22
biosocial influences on delinquency 17–18
Blakemore, S-J. 19–20
Botley, M. 208
Bowling, B. 138
brain development in adolescence 19–20
Braithwaite, J. 130
Brazil 35
Brexit 11, 99, 112, 113, 133
Brunei Darussalam 103
Bulger, James (murder case) 78, 100–101, 108, 120
Bywaters, P. 188–190

Cambridge Study of Delinquency 26, 30, 37, 173
Canada 14, 48, 148, 158, 175
capital punishment 92
care system *see* child protection services; looked after children (LAC)
Carpenter, Mary 6
Carr, N. 153–154, 190–191, 209–210
Carrington, K. 35, 86
Case, S. 57
causation versus correlation 22, 38, 180
causes of delinquency *see* explanations for delinquency, provided by young people; explanatory frameworks for delinquency
Cavadino, M. 51, 68–75, *69*, *71*
Centre for Crime and Justice Studies, 'My Story' 199–201
child abuse *see* abuse, child
Child Protection Plan 187
child protection services 71, 84, 114, 172, 188
see also looked after children (LAC)
child-friendly justice (Council of Europe guidance) 99–100, 101–102
childhood
definitions and conceptualisations 2, 5, 8, 45, 83, 84–85, 90
phases and characteristics (overview) 2
see also adolescence
children (and young people) first approaches 56–58
Children First strategy (Wales) 56–57, 114–118, 175
see also children's rights model of youth justice; welfare model and welfarism
Children (Scotland) Act (1995) 125
Children Act (1908) 45–46
Children Act (1948) 46
Children and Young People (Scotland) Act (2014) 126
Children and Young Persons Act (1969) 46
children in care *see* looked after children (LAC)
Children's Commissioners (UK) 94–95, 104
Children's Hearing System (CHS) (Scotland) 112–113, 123–125, 126, 145
children's rights
and detention 83, 91, 92, 93, 98, 103, 105–106, 107, 108
due process rights 73, 77, 91, 100–101, 132
as framework for comparative research 83
key instruments and guidelines
Beijing Rules (1985) 3, 91, 92–93, 97
child-friendly justice guidance (Council of Europe) 99–100, 101–102
EU legislation 102
Havana Rules (1985) 3, 91, 93
Riyadh Guidelines (1985) 3, 91
UNCRC *see* United Nations: Convention on the Rights of the Child (UNCRC)
limits of rights standards in practice 103, 104–108, 109, 116
see also human rights
children's rights model of youth justice 59
see also children (and young people) first approaches

children's services, collaboration with 57, 126
Cipriani, D. 83
class, and delinquency 32, 137
  see also poverty
cognitive disabilities 27–28, 167, 168, 182
Cohen, A. 181
Cohen, A.C. 32
Cohen, L.E. 181
Coles, E. 126
colonialism, and dominance of Global North paradigm 9, 85–86
Committee for Investigating the Causes of the Alarming Increase of Juvenile Delinquency in the Metropolis (1816 report) 5
Committee for the Prevention of Torture (CPT) 83, 99–100, 106
community resolution (CR) 145
community-based interventions and 'localism' 62, 64, 92, 121
  see also restorative justice
comparative justice
  international comparisons *see* international comparisons of youth justice
  within-jurisdiction practice variations 9–10, 53–55, 56, 61, 78–79, 82, 113, 133–134
compliance, in offender management model 54
compulsory supervision orders (Scotland) 188
concentration effects 162, 163, 170–171, 191
Connell, R. 85–86
contagion (of behaviours), and delinquency 31
conversion, and delinquency 31
Cooper, A. 37
corporal punishment 92
correlation versus causation 22, 38, 180
Council of Europe
  background and role 98–99
  child-friendly justice guidance 99–100, 101–102
  Committee for the Prevention of Torture (CPT) 83, 99–100, 106
'county lines' drug distribution networks 34, 136, 143, 186
court orders *see* supervision orders (and equivalents)
Courtney, M.E. 194
courts
  Argentina 84
  Belgium 182
  due process rights 73, 77, 91, 100–101, 132
  England and Wales 46, 54, 77–78, 95, 100, 140, 146–147, 159, 204, 208–209, 217
  European Court of Human Rights (ECtHR) 77, 96, 99, 100–101
  experiences of (studies) 208
  France 165
  New Zealand 58, 60
  nineteenth century 6
  Northern Ireland 130, 131, 146
  reporting restrictions 95
  Scandinavia 62, 84, 147
  Scotland 123–125
  Spain 217
  US 61, 72–73, 74, 166
  and youth justice models (overview) *71*
  see also 'out of court' decision-making; sentencing; supervision orders (and equivalents)
Cox, A. 85
crime *see* youth crime
Crime and Disorder Act (1998) 77, 114–115
'crime control' approach 35, 50, 51, 60–61
criminal justice
  approaches, and political economies 68–70, *69*
  historical changes in approach 70
  see also youth justice
Criminal Justice Act (1948) 46
Criminal Justice Review (2000) 129
criminal records 93, 95
criminal responsibility, age of *see* Age of Criminal Majority (AGM); Minimum Age of Criminal Responsibility (MACR)
criminological theories 180–182
Croall, H. 124
Cuba 103
cultural theories of delinquency 31–32
custody (prisons/detention centres/secure care)
  adult prisons 68
  children's rights 83, 91, 92, 93, 98, 103, 105–106, 107, 108
  conditions and treatment in 68, 95, 96, 105–106, 148, 154, 174, 202, 210–214
  detention rates 68, 69, 74, 76, 80, 81, 82, 95, 105, 115, 132, 147–148, 158
  educational provision 45, 93, 95, 105, 115, 211, 213
  experiences of (studies) 207, 210–214

Juvenile Justice Centre (JJC) 132
resettlement post-custody 117, 118, 151–152
secure care 76
Secure Children's Homes (SCHs) 210
secure schools 122
Secure Training Centres (STCs) 106, 210
Young Offender Institutions (YOIs) 96, 210, 217
see also penal policies and practices; punishment and punitive models; sentencing
cybercrimes, shift towards 160

Dahl, R. 20
Day, A. 122, 175
decline in justice system 'subjects' 137, 140, 158–161, 170
Defence for Children International 217
definitions and conceptualisations
childhood 2, 5, 8, 45, 83, 84–85, 90
youth justice 7–8, 86
delay, avoidance of 92
Demie, F. 183
Denmark 62, 76, 107, 137, 158
see also Scandinavia (in general)
deprivation *see* poverty
detention *see* custody (prisons/detention centres/secure care)
Detention and Training Order (1998) 151
deterrence principle 43, 46, 73, 150
development theories of childhood and adolescence 23–25
devolution (UK) 111–112, 113–114, 115, 125
Dierkhising, C.B. 171
diet, and behaviour 21
differential association 25, 30
see also peer influence
Dignan, J. 51, 68–75, *69*, *71*
disabilities
autism spectrum disorders (ASDs) 19, 167
cognitive disabilities 27–28, 167, 168, 182
neuro-disabilities/neurodiversity 167–168
discrimination and disproportionate representation in justice systems
children with ACEs 29–30, 117, 143, 172–173
concentration effects 162, 163, 170–171, 191
looked after children (LAC) 82, 132, 171, 190–194
people with cognitive and neuro-disabilities 167–168
people with mental health disorders 82, 167–168, 171
socio-economic status 11, 128, 137, 166
see also gender discrimination and gender-based oppression; racism and racial discrimination
diversionary approaches and initiatives
Australia 82
England 121
minimum intervention model 3, 57, *71*, 73, 80
Northern Ireland 130, 131–132
Norway 153
rationale 92, 103, 160
Scotland 126, 127–128, 160
Wales 57, 116–117
see also 'out of court' decision-making
domestic violence 170, 200
Doob, A. 148
Downes, D. 68
Doyle, J. 152
Drew, V. 183
drugs
'county lines' networks 34, 136, 143, 186
drug testing of young offenders 153
use by young people 21–22, 30, 136, 138
young people's understanding of offences (study) 207
due process rights 73, 77, 91, 100–101, 132

early intervention, as focus of youth justice systems 49–50
Edinburgh Study of Youth Transitions and Crime 127, 128, 138–139, 161–163, 169, 171, 181–182, 187, 191
education system *see* schools and education system
educational interventions
nineteenth century 6–7
psychoeducational interventions 61
secure schools 122
Egypt 103
Ellem, K. 168
England
approach to criminal justice 68, 69, *69*, 70
arrest rates 158
children in care
rates 188, *189*
representation in justice systems 191–193

community resolution (CR) 145
comparative studies
vs Argentina, Belize and Finland 84, *84*
vs Australian states 81–82, 168
vs Italy 80–81
vs Norway 77–78
detention rates 81, 147–148
disproportionate representation in youth justice system 82, 95, 164, 168, 191–193
ethnographic studies 203–206
experiences of youth justice (studies) 207–209
historical approaches to youth justice 6–7, 44, 45–46
influences of change in youth justice 119–123
James Bulger murder case 78, 100–101, 108, 120
Lammy Review (2017) 164
level and nature of crimes
official records and statistics 140–143
self-report studies 137, 138
longitudinal studies
Cambridge Study of Delinquency 26, 30, 37, 173
Edinburgh Study of Youth Transitions and Crime 127, 128, 138–139, 161–163, 169, 171, 181–182, 187, 191
other studies 33
Minimum Age of Criminal Responsibility (MACR) 77, 78, 80, 104
outcomes of youth justice 149–152
participatory approaches in youth justice 215–217
police targets 159
Referral Orders 64, 121
risk assessment for targeted interventions 55–56
school disciplinary approaches and exclusions 183, 185–187
sentencing 68, 77, 95, 100, 108, 121, 146–147
Youth Justice Board *see* Youth Justice Board (YJB) (England and Wales)
youth offending services and teams *see* youth offending services (YOS) and teams (YOT) (England and Wales)
Youth Rehabilitation Orders (YROs) 146–147
see also United Kingdom (in general)
Enhanced Case Management (ECM) approach 175
environmental influences on delinquency *see* social and environmental explanations for delinquency
Erickson, Milton 26
Erikson, E. 23
ethnicity *see* race; racism and racial discrimination
ethnocentricity, risk of 75, 76, 82
ethnographic studies of young people and crime 202–206
eugenics movement 16
European Committee for the Prevention of Torture (CPT) 83, 99–100, 106
European Convention on Human Rights 99
European Court of Human Rights (ECtHR)
adoption of UNCRC principles 96, 99
and James Bulger murder case 77, 100–101
European Union
Brexit 11, 99, 112, 113, 133
children's rights legislation 102
evolutionary explanations of delinquency 20–21
experiences of youth justice (studies) 152–154, 207–214
explanations for delinquency, provided by young people 38–40, 199–206, 209
explanatory frameworks for delinquency
biological 15–22
complexity and integrated analysis 37–38
correlation versus causation 22, 38, 180
criminological theories 180–182
global (non-Western) perspectives 34–37
psychological 22–28
social and environmental *see* social and environmental explanations for delinquency
structural 32–34, 141, 166, 167, 205
extrovert personality trait 26, 27
Eysenck, H. 26–27

family characteristics, and delinquency 28–30, 38, 39
see also parents, and delinquency
family functional therapy 55
Family Group Conferences (New Zealand) 48, 58, 60, 145
Farag, D. 55–56
Farrington, D. 37–38
see also Cambridge Study of Delinquency
Feld, B.C. 166
Felitti, V.J. 171–172

Felson, M. 181
Field, B.C. 80–81, 149
Finland 69, *69*, 70, *76–77*, 84, *84*, 146
  see also Scandinavia (in general)
First Nations peoples, Canada 48
first-hand accounts of young offenders
  see autobiographies of young/former offenders; self-report studies of young offenders
Fitz-Gibbon, W. 107
Fitzpatrick, C. 192–193
foetal exposure to alcohol and nicotine 18
foil comparisons, risk of 75, 82
force against children, use of 96
foster care 55
France 6, *69*, 165
Franko, K. 85
Fraser, A. 40

gangs 23, 32, 37, 39, 40, 202–205
  see also peer influence
Garland, D. 79
Gault, Jerry (case of, USA) 72–73
gender differences
  nature of offences 7, 169
  offending rates 21, 140
  peak age of offending 138
  pubertal hormones and behaviour 20
  reoffending rates 150
  school exclusion rates 182
  see also girls and women
gender discrimination and gender-based oppression 35, 36, 83, 97, 169, 183–185
gender-specific programming (US) 170
general theory of crime 180
genetic influences on delinquency 16–18, 19
Georgia 146
Germany 6, *69*, 73, 137, 158
Getting it Right for Every Child (GIRFEC) framework (Scotland) 126–128
girls and women
  attitudes towards offenders 169
  'care-criminalisation' 192–193
  detention rates 82
  ethnographic study of Latina gangs (US) 202–203
  'hijabistas' and 'hijabsters' 36
  nature of offences (nineteenth century) 7
  pathways into offending 169–170
  peak age of offending 138
  violent crime (Scotland) 143
  see also gender differences; gender discrimination and gender-based oppression
Glendinning, F. 175, 176
global (non-Western) perspectives on delinquency 34–37
Global North dominance, in comparative studies 9, 85–86
Glueck, S. and Glueck, E. 29
Goemann, M. 59–60
Goldson, B. 32–33, 81–82, 164, 166, 167, 168, 170
Good Friday Agreement 113, 129, 131
Gottfredson, M.R. 180
Graham, J. 138
'gravity score' of offences 142
Gray, P. 53–54, 56, 58, 59, 79, 216
Green, D. 77–78
Grimshaw, R. 199–201
Gyateng, T. 210–211

Haines, K. 57, 116–117
Hart, D. 215
Havana Rules (1985) 3, 91, 93
Hazel, N. 47–48, 49–50, 59, 120, 151–152, 208
Healing Circles (Canada) 48
Hendrick, H. 7
Herrnstein, R. 26
Heywood, C. 5
'hijabistas' and 'hijabsters' 36
Hindelang, M. 26
Hirschfield, A. 55
Hirschi, T. 26, 180
historical perspectives
  approaches to criminal justice 70
  approaches to youth justice 6–7, 45–46, 54, 67, 70, 119
  attitudes and assumptions towards young people 4–7, 82
  conceptualisations of childhood 5, 45–46
Hitchcock, J. 23
Hogg, R. 35
holistic approach to youth justice *see* Whole System Approach (WSA)
homelessness 32
  Vagrancy Act (1824) 6
hormonal influences on delinquency 19, 20
Hough, M. 120
Howard, M. 28
Howard League for Penal Reform 191, 216–217
Hughes, T. 60–61
human rights
  European Convention on Human Rights 99

European Court of Human Rights (ECtHR)
adoption of UNCRC principles 96, 99
and James Bulger murder case 77, 100–101
see also children's rights
Human Rights Act (1998) 99
Hungary 51

Iceland 93
India 103
Indonesia 36
Industrial Schools Act (1857) 6
industrial schools (nineteenth century) 6–7
industrialisation, effect on society and youth crime 5–6, 45, 70
intelligence (IQ score), and delinquency 25–26, 38
international comparisons of youth justice
challenges and methodological considerations 9, 47–49, 75–79, 82, 85–86
examples
Argentina, Belize, England and Wales, Finland 84, *84*
England and Wales vs Australian states 81–82, 168
England and Wales vs Italy 80–81
England vs Norway (cases of children killing children) 77–78
frameworks and typologies 47, 49–52, 59–63, 83–84
Global North dominant perspective 9, 85–86
levels of analysis 9–10, 78–79, 85–86, 113
see also individual countries
introvert personality trait 26, 27
Iran 83
Islamic law 83
Italy *69*, 76, 80–81

Jacobson, J. 120
Jamieson, J. 33
Jans, M. 213
Japan 48–49, 51, 52, 69, *69*
Jorgensen, C. 21
Junger-Tas, J. 137–138
'just deserts' principle 43, 51, 73, 74, 120
Just for Kids Law (advice and support service) 59
Justice Act (Northern Ireland) (2002) 129
justice model
key features and institutional arrangements *71*, 73
versus welfare approach 44, 46, 47, 50, 51, 59, 70, *71*, 72
see also punishment and punitive models
Juvenile Justice Centre (JJC) (Northern Ireland) 132
Juvenile Offenders Act (1847) 6

Kamaludeen, M. 36
Kelly, L. 209
Kenya 13
Kilbrandon Report (1964) 123, 124, 126
see also Children's Hearing System (CHS) (Scotland)
King, H. 35
Kirby, A. 120
knife crime 55–56, 95, 142, 143
Knife Crime Prevention Programme 55–56
Kohlberg, L. 23–24
Kupchik, A. 185–186

'labelling' 32, 57, *71*, 139, 162, 181–182
Laming, A. 193
Lammy Review (2017) 164
Lappi-Seppälä, T. 62
Laub, J.H, 29, 180
legal aid 102
Lemert, E. 181
Liefaard, T. 108
'localism' *see* community-based interventions and 'localism'
Löfholm, C. 63
Lombroso, Cesare 16
longitudinal studies
Cambridge Study of Delinquency 26, 30, 37, 173
Edinburgh Study of Youth Transitions and Crime 127, 128, 138–139, 161–163, 169, 171, 181–182, 187, 191
other studies 33, 37, 137, 179, 180, 194
looked after children (LAC) 82, 132, 171, 187–194, *189*
see also child protection services
Lynch, N. 108
Lyon, J. 212–213

Macdonald, R. 35
MACR *see* Minimum Age of Criminal Responsibility (MACR)
magistrates 80, 81
Malaysia 103
Māori people, New Zealand 48, 58, 60
Marsh, B. 131

Marshall, I. 137–138
Maruna, S. 131
Maslow, A.H. 175
Matza, D. 30–31
May, M. 28–29
May, T. 139
Maycock, P.9 190–191
McAlister, S. 153–154, 209–210
McAra, L. 51, 125, 160, 163, 170, 187
    see also Edinburgh Study of Youth Transitions and Crime
McFarlane, K. 191
McGloin, J. 31
McVie, S. 125, 160, 163, 170
    see also Edinburgh Study of Youth Transitions and Crime
media attention on youth crime 77, 78, 95, 100, 108, 120, 165, 169
Mendoza-Denton, N. 37, 202–203
mental health disorders, disproportionate representation in justice systems 82, 167–168, 171
Merlo, A. 61
Minimum Age of Criminal Responsibility (MACR)
    and children's rights 83–84, 91, 97–98, 103–105, 107
    and *Guidelines on Child-Friendly Justice* 102
    other countries 48, 74, 76–78, 83–84, *84*, 103–104, 147
    UK 3, 48, 77, 80, *84*, 95, 104–105, 120, 128, 131
    see also Age of Criminal Majority (AGM)
minimum intervention model 3, 57, *71*, 73, 80
Ministry of Justice (MoJ) for England and Wales 82
Mooney, G. 125–126
Moore, M. 25, 27
moral development in childhood and adolescence 23–25
Mozambique
    approach to youth justice 103
MultifunC programme (Scandinavia) 62–63
multi-systemic therapy 55
Muncie, J. 10, 11, 44, 75, 119
murder 77–78, 100–101, 104, 108, 125, 158
Murray, C. 26

'nature-nurture' divide 17
Navajo people (USA) 63–64
'needs' versus 'responsibilities' of children 3–4
NEET (Not in Education, Employment or Training) 187
neglect and poor supervision, parental 6–7, 28–29, 38, 138, 170, 171, 180, 181, 187
Nelken, D. 9, 75–76, 77, 80–81, 83
neo-correctionalist model *71*, 74
neo-liberalism
    and approach to criminal justice 68–70, *69*
    and approach to youth justice 74
    as criminogenic 69
Netherlands 6, 27, 68, *69*, 137
neurodiversity 167–168
neurological influences on delinquency 19–20
    detention rates 82
neurotic personality trait 26
New Zealand
    approach to criminal justice 69, *69*
    approach to youth justice 48, 58, 59–60, 74, 75, 145
    Māori people 48, 58, 60
    school exclusions and delinquency (study) 179
nicotine, foetal exposure 18
Nigeria 36
non-governmental organisations (NGOs) 59, 94
Northern Ireland
    and Brexit (Northern Ireland Protocol) 133
    children in care (rates) *189*
    collapse of government (2022) 133
    Criminal Justice Review (2000) 129
    detention rates 158
    devolved powers 111–112, 131
    experiences of youth justice (study) 209–210
    Good Friday Agreement 113, 129, 131
    Justice Act (Northern Ireland) (2002) 129
    Juvenile Justice Centre (JJC) 132
    level and nature of crimes 158
    Minimum Age of Criminal Responsibility (MACR) 104
    overall approach to youth justice 74, 128–133
    paramilitary violence 129, 132–133
    sentencing 108
    Youth Engagement Clinics (YECs) 132
    Youth Justice Agency (YJA) 129, 146
    Youth Justice Review 131, 132
    see also United Kingdom (in general)
Norway 62, 77–78, 147, 153
    see also Scandinavia (in general)
Nye, F. 137

O'Brien, W. 107
obstetric (pre-birth) influences on delinquency 18–19
offence resolution 44
Offences Brought to Justice (OBTJ) targets (England and Wales) 159
offender management model 53–54, 57
Office of Juvenile Justice and Delinquency Prevention (OJJDP) (US) 165
online crime, shift towards 160
Oranga Tamariki Act (1989) (New Zealand) 58
'out of court' decision-making
  Children's Hearing System (CHS) (Scotland) 112–113, 123–125, 126, 145
  Family Group Conferences (New Zealand) 48, 58, 60, 145
  Healing Circles (Canada) 48
  see also diversionary approaches and initiatives
outcomes of youth justice 149–152, 175–176
over-representation by certain groups *see* discrimination and disproportionate representation in justice systems

PADS+ (Peterborough Adolescent and Young Adult Development Study) 33
parents, and delinquency
  neglect and poor supervision 6, 7, 28–29, 38, 138, 170, 171, 180, 181, 187
  parent training 55
  parental abuse 200
  parental criminality 29, 200
  parental mental health problems 30
  pre-birth 18–19
  see also family characteristics, and delinquency
Parker, H. 39, 203–205
participatory approaches in youth justice 214–217, 218
Participatory Youth Practice (PYP) (England) 215–216
peak age of offending 138–139, 140–141
peer influence 19–20, 22, 23, 25, 30–31, 38, 138
PEN (Psychoticism, Extraversion and Neuroticism) personality model 26–27
penal institutions *see* custody (prisons/detention centres/secure care); industrial schools (nineteenth century); reformatory schools (nineteenth century)
penal policies and practices
  and political economies 68–70, 74, *79*, 85
  sentencing *see* sentencing
  UN provisions 90–93
  see also punishment and punitive models
penal-welfarism 70, 72
  see also welfare model and welfarism
Pepper, J. 20
Perez, N. 29–30
personality disorders, and delinquency 27–28
personality types, and delinquency 26–27
Peterborough Adolescent and Young Adult Development Study (PADS+) 33
Peterson, D. 26
Petintseva, O. 165, 182
Philippines 107
Phoenix, J. 52, 209
physical restraint, use of 95, 96, 105, 106, 148, 174, 213
Piaget, J. 23
Pitts, J. 39
Pittsburgh Youth Study 37
Poland 158
police
  care provider's recourse to 191, 193
  collaboration with 57, 60–61, 115, 116, 127, 130
  racism and racial discrimination 184–185, 202
  stop and search by 128, 163, 174
  strip searches 184–185
  targets (England and Wales) 159
  training 92, 168
political economies, and penal policies 68–70, 74, *79*, 85
polyvictimisation of girls and young women 169
Portnoy, J. 18–19
Post-traumatic Stress Disorder (PTSD) 171
poverty
  and ACEs 173
  and austerity measures (UK) 94
  as criminogenic 32, 33, 36, 38, 45, 203–206
  interventions 7, 160, 162
  and over-representation in youth justice system 11, 128, 137, 166
  and school exclusions 183
pre-birth (obstetric) influences on delinquency 18–19
prevention, as focus of youth justice 49–50
prisons *see* custody (prisons/detention centres/secure care)
psychoeducational interventions 61

psychological disorders, and delinquency 27–28
psychological explanations for delinquency 22–28
psychopathic personality traits 26, 27
punishment and punitive models
  capital and corporal punishment 92
  conceptual discussion 68
  and deterrence 43, 46, 73, 150
  historical changes in approach 46, 49
  key features and institutional arrangements *71*, 73
  as means of accessing services 80
  and political economies 68–70, *69*
  and reoffending rates 150–151
  rule of law principles 72–73
  versus welfare approach 44, 46, 47, 50, 51, 59, 70, *71*, 72
  see also custody (prisons/detention centres/secure care); justice model; penal policies and practices
Puzzanchera, C. 170

Quay, H. 26

race
  and delinquency 26, 139
  and intelligence (IQ score) 26
  over-simplified categories of 164
racism and racial discrimination
  adultification of Black girls 183–185
  custodial rates 80–81, 82, 123, 149
  over-representation in youth justice system 11, 74, 95, 97, 137, 139, 141, 163–166
  police 184–185, 202
  racial stereotyping 165, 182, 183
  schools 61, 182–183
  and strain theory 33–34
  treatment of children in detention 123, 148, 214
radicalisation, risk assessment 55
Rafter, N. 16–17
Raine, A. 17, 18
rape 104, 108, 125
rational choice theories 181, 205
Rebellon, C. 25
Redergård, Silje Marie (murder case) 78
Referral Orders (England and Wales) 64, 121
reformation (as youth justice objective) 44, 45
reformatory schools (nineteenth century) 6–7
reintegration (as youth justice objective) 44, 62, 64, *71*, 74
reintegrative shaming 130
relativism, risk of 75, 82
reoffending rates 63, 70, 150–152
Republic of Ireland 103–104, 158, 167, 191, 192
resettlement post-custody 117, 118, 151–152
responsibility and accountability of children
  and approach to youth justice 51
  compared with adults 2–3
  development through youth justice 44
  versus needs of children 3–4
  see also Age of Criminal Majority (AGM); Minimum Age of Criminal Responsibility (MACR)
restorative justice
  Canada 48
  England and Wales 57–58, 64, 121, 145, 146–147, 153–154
  experiences of (study) 153–154
  increased use of (trend) 63–64, 65, 121, 145–146
  key features and institutional arrangements *71*, 74
  New Zealand 48, 58, 60, 145
  Northern Ireland 113, 129–131, 146
  Norway 62, 147
  US 60, 61, 63–64
  see also community-based interventions and 'localism'
restraint (physical), use of 95, 96, 105, 106, 148, 174, 213
Richards, K. 168
risk assessment for targeted interventions 55, 162, 173, 174
risk factors for youth crime *see* explanatory frameworks for delinquency
risk-based intervention approach 33, 50, 51, 54–56, 121, 160, 170, 191
  nineteenth century 6–7
  trauma-informed practice 174–176
risk-taking
  as evolutionary adaptation 21
  neurological basis 19–20
  and poor self-control 180
  as response to trauma 174
Riyadh Guidelines (1985) 3, 91
Robbins, T. 19–20
Roberts, J.V. 120
Robertson, L. 127–128
Rocca, G. 21
Rochester Youth Development Study 37
Rocque, M. 16, 33, 185
Roma communities 165, 182, 183
Ross, A. 55

routine activities theory 181
rule of law principles 72–73

Sampson, R. 29, 180
Sanders, J. 179
Sandøy, T. 152–153
Scandinavia (in general) 62, 73, 217
  see also Denmark; Finland; Norway; Sweden
schools and education system
  collaboration with 57, 126, 182, 187
  disciplinary approaches 60–61, 179, 185–186
  educational provision in custody 45, 93, 95, 105, 115, 211, 213
  exclusion from 139, 162, 179–183, 186–187, 199
  intersection with youth justice system 39, 162, 178–187, 199
  see also educational interventions
Scotland
  attitudes towards young people 13
  children in care (rates) 189, *189*
  Children's Hearing System (CHS) 112–113, 123–125, 126, 145
  compulsory supervision orders 188
  detention rates 158
  devolved powers 111–112
  Edinburgh Study of Youth Transitions and Crime 127, 128, 138–139, 161–163, 169, 171, 181–182, 187, 191
  gangs 40
  Getting it Right for Every Child (GIRFEC) framework 126–128
  Minimum Age of Criminal Responsibility (MACR) 3, 103, 104
  overall approach to youth justice 123–128
  participatory approaches in youth justice 216, 217
  sentencing 108
  Whole System Approach (WSA) 126, 127–128, 160
  young women's involvement in crime (study) 143
  see also United Kingdom (in general)
secure care (detention) 76
  see also custody (prisons/detention centres/secure care)
Secure Children's Homes (SCHs) 210
secure schools 122
Secure Training Centres (STCs) 106, 210
self-report studies of young offenders 136–139, 199–201
sentencing
  Argentina 84
  England 68, 146–147
  Finland 84
  Northern Ireland 108
  Norway 147
  Scotland 108
  Wales 68, 108, 146–147
  see also custody (prisons/detention centres/secure care); penal policies and practices
sexual offences 104, 108, 125, 141–142, 200
shaming, and restorative justice 130
Sharpe, G. 169, 170
Shenton, F. 154, 213
Shore, H. 7
Short, J. 137
Silvester, N. 174
Singapore 36, 48
Slovenia 158
Smith, R. 53–54, 56, 58, 59, 79, 154, 201–202, 213
Smithson, H. 216
Snellings, Q. 185
social and environmental explanations for delinquency 28–32, 38, 138, 139, 143, 169–171
  Adverse Childhood Experiences (ACEs) 22, 29–30, 117, 143, 169–174
  biosocial influences 17–18
  care system 82, 132, 171, 190–194
  criminological theories 180–182
  nineteenth century 5–6, 7, 28–29
  parental neglect and poor supervision 6, 7, 28–29, 38, 138, 170, 171, 180, 181, 187
  peer influence 19–20, 22, 23, 25, 30–31, 38, 138
  poverty *see* poverty
  schools and education 39, 162, 178–187, 199
social learning theory 25
social organisation (national), and youth justice 51, 79
social reaction theories 181–182
Social Work (Scotland) Act (1968) 123
social workers 52, 62, 81, 115, 124, 127
socio-economic status *see* class, and delinquency; poverty
South Africa 69, *69*
Spain 158, 217
stigmatisation and shame, in restorative justice 130

strain theory 34, 35
strip searches 184–185
    at Young Offender Institutions 217
structural explanations for delinquency 32–34, 141, 166, 167, 205
    see also racism and racial discrimination
supervision orders (and equivalents) 54, 62, 64, 92, 124, 147, 188, 209
    participatory approaches 215–216
Sure Start initiative (UK) 160
Sutherland, A. 159
Sutherland, D. 30
Swansea Bureau 57, 116–117
Sweden
    approach to criminal justice 69, *69*, 70, 76
    community-based interventions 62
    decline in justice system 'subjects' 158
    longitudinal studies 37
    self-report studies of young offenders 137
    treatment of migrants 76
    twin and adoption studies 18
    see also Scandinavia (in general)
Switzerland 158, 217

targeted intervention model *see* risk-based intervention approach
tasers, use of 96
Taylor Review of Youth Justice (2016) 122, 151, 178–179
Terrio, S.J. 165
terrorism 85, 108
Thailand 48
therapy 55, 61
Thomas, K. 31
Thomas, P. 201–202
Thompson, C. 215
Thornberry, T. 38
Torres Strait Island communities 81, 82, 164, 183
torture, European Committee for the Prevention of Torture (CPT) 83, 99–100, 106
transition to adulthood
    and care systems 192, 194
    and justice systems 8, 102, 108
Trauma Recovery Model (TRM) 175
trauma-informed practice 174–176
trials *see* courts
twin studies 18

UNCRC *see* United Nations: Convention on the Rights of the Child (UNCRC)
United Kingdom (in general)
    Brexit 11, 99, 112, 113, 133
    child protection rates 188–190
    convergence/divergence in youth justice approaches (overview) 125–126, 133–134
    devolution 111–112, 113–114, 115, 125
    self-report studies of young offenders 137, 138, 199–201
    Sure Start initiative 160
    UNCRC compliance reviews 93, 94–96, 104–105, 108, 131
    Young Offender Institutions (YOIs) 96, 210, 217
    see also England; Northern Ireland; Scotland; Wales
United Nations
    Beijing Rules (1985) 3, 91, 92–93, 97
    Committee on the Rights of the Child
        advocacy of 'child justice' term 8
        composition 94
        General Comment on Juvenile Justice 97–98, 104
        MACR standards 83, 97–98, 104
        UNCRC compliance reviews 93–96, 104–105, 108, 131
    Convention on the Rights of the Child (UNCRC)
        definition of childhood 2, 8, 83, 90
        detention 83, 91, 92, 103, 105, 107
        ECtHR adoption of principles 96, 99
        as framework for comparative research 83
        key principles and Articles 90–91, 103, 198
        MACR standards 83, 91, 97, 104, 107
        participatory approaches in youth justice 214, 217
        ratification and compliance 93–96, 97, 107, 116
        responsibility and accountability 3
    Havana Rules (1985) 3, 91, 93
    Riyadh Guidelines (1985) 3, 91
    World Report on Violence Against Children 105
United States of America
    ACEs and outcomes (studies) 29–30, 170–173
    approach to criminal justice 69, *69*
    approaches to youth justice 51, 60–61, 63–64, 72–73, 74, 175
    arrest rates 158
    'care-criminalisation' 194

disproportionate representation in youth justice system 74, 165–166, 170
ethnographic study 202–203
family characteristics and delinquency (study) 29
gangs (studies) 32, 37, 202–203
gender-specific programming 170
intelligence and delinquency (study) 26
Jerry Gault case 72–73
longitudinal studies 37, 180, 194
Navajo people 63–64
Office of Juvenile Justice and Delinquency Prevention (OJJDP) 165
outcomes of youth justice 152
school disciplinary approaches and exclusions 179, 183, 185–186
self-report studies of young offenders 137, 139
sentencing 166
socializing and delinquency (study) 25
UR Boss Project (England and Wales) 216–217

Vagrancy Act (1824) 6
van Dam, C. 27
Vaswani, N. 169–170
Veneziano, C. and Veneziano, L. 24
violence
in broader society 35, 129, 132–133, 202
against children in detention 105, 106, 148, 154, 202, 213
domestic violence 170, 200
in young people
contributory factors 17, 21, 30, 36, 143
gangs 23, 39
gender differences 169
global (non-Western) perspectives 35–36
knife crime 55–56, 95, 142, 143
official figures (England and Wales) 141–143
see also abuse, child
vitamin supplements, and behaviour 21

Wales
All Wales Youth Offending Strategy (AWYOS) (2004) 115, 116
approach to criminal justice 68, 69, *69*, 70
arrest rates 158
Children First strategy 56–57, 114–118, 175
children in care
rates *189*
representation in justice systems 191–193
community resolution (CR) 145
comparative studies
vs Argentina, Belize and Finland 84, *84*
vs Australian states 81–82, 168
vs Italy 80–81
detention rates 81, 147–148
devolved powers 111–112, 113–114, 115
disproportionate representation in youth justice system 82, 95, 164, 168, 191–193
experiences of youth justice (study) 153–154
historical approaches to youth justice 44, 45–46
Lammy Review (2017) 164
level and nature of crimes
official records and statistics 140–143
self-report studies of young offenders 137, 138
Minimum Age of Criminal Responsibility (MACR) 104
outcomes of youth justice 149–152
participatory approaches in youth justice 216–217
police targets 159
Referral Orders 64, 121
risk assessment for targeted interventions 55–56
school exclusions 183
sentencing 68, 95, 108, 146–147
Swansea Bureau 116–117
Youth Justice Blueprint for Wales (2019) 117–118, 175, 176
Youth Justice Board (YJB) *see* Youth Justice Board (YJB) (England and Wales)
youth offending services and teams *see* youth offending services (YOS) and teams (YOT) (England and Wales)
Youth Rehabilitation Orders (YROs) 146–147
see also United Kingdom (in general)
Walsh, A. 21
welfare model and welfarism
child protection services 71, 84, 114, 172, 188
versus justice, as intervention approach 44, 46, 47, 50, 51, 59, 70, *71*, 72
key features and institutional arrangements *71*, 72

nineteenth century 7, 44
penal-welfarism 70, 72
Scandinavian model 62, 70
see also children (and young people) first approaches
Welsh, B. 37–38
West, D. *see* Cambridge Study of Delinquency
White, S. 173
Whole System Approach (WSA)
Scotland 126, 127–128, 160
Wales 57, 116–117
Willcock, H. 137
Williams, J. 36
Williams, K. 194
Wilson, A. 212–213
Winterdyk, J.A. 50–51, 62, 64, 85, 147
women *see* gender differences; gender discrimination and gender-based oppression; girls and women
World Report on Violence Against Children 105

Yates, J. 205–206
Young Offender Institutions (YOIs) (UK) 96, 210, 217
youth conferences (Northern Ireland) 129–132, 146
youth crime
assumptions and attitudes towards *see* assumptions and attitudes towards young people and youth crime
explanatory frameworks *see* explanatory frameworks for delinquency
level and nature of crimes
autobiographies of young/former offenders 201–202
official records and statistics 140–144, 158
reoffending rates 63, 70, 150–152
self-report studies 136–139, 199–201
shift towards online crime 160
peak age of offending 138–139, 140–141
Youth Crime Surveys (England and Wales) 138
Youth Engagement Clinics (YECs) (Northern Ireland) 132
youth justice
aims and objectives 43–44
children's rights *see* children's rights
competing ideas and principles 44–45
concentration effects 162, 163, 170–171, 191
decline in 'subjects' 137, 140, 158–161, 170
definitions and scope 7–8, 86
frameworks and typologies 47, 49–52, 53–58, 174–176
historical changes in approach 6–7, 45–46, 54, 67, 70, 119
international comparisons *see* international comparisons of youth justice
intersection with care system 187–194
intersection with education (schools) 39, 162, 178–187, 199
models and institutional arrangements 71–75, *71*
outcomes 149–152, 175–176
participatory approaches 214–217, 218
policy versus practice 52–53, 103, 104–108, 109
and social organisation 51, 79
within-jurisdiction practice variations 9–10, 53–55, 56, 61, 78–79, 82, 113, 133–134
young people's experiences of 152–154, 207–214
young people's understanding of (studies) 206–208
see also criminal justice
Youth Justice Agency (YJA) (Northern Ireland) 129, 146
Youth Justice and Criminal Evidence Act (1999) 121
Youth Justice Blueprint for Wales (2019) 117–118, 175, 176
Youth Justice Board (YJB) (England and Wales)
and child-first principles 56, 117, 118, 122
Knife Crime Prevention Programme 55–56
Participatory Youth Practice (PYP) 215–216
remit 53, 82, 114–115
resettlement framework 151
risk assessment tools 173, 174
youth crime statistics 142, 158
Youth Crime Surveys 138
Youth Justice Review (Northern Ireland) 131, 132
Youth Lifestyle Survey (UK) 138
youth offending services (YOS) and teams (YOT) (England and Wales)
establishment and remit 114–115
participatory approaches 215–216
providing training for police 168
Swansea Bureau 57, 116–117
training needs 175

variations in approach 53–57, 59, 79, 82
young offender's perceptions of 208, 209
Youth Rehabilitation Orders (YROs) (England and Wales) 146–147
Youthful Offenders Act (1854) 6